™

References for the Rest of Us! ™

BESTSELLING BOOK SERIES

Do you find that traditional reference books are overloaded with technical details and advice you'll never use? Do you postpone important life decisions because you just don't want to deal with them? Then our *...For Dummies®* business and general reference book series is for you.

...For Dummies business and general reference books are written for those frustrated and hard-working souls who know they aren't dumb, but find that the myriad of personal and business issues and the accompanying horror stories make them feel helpless. *...For Dummies* books use a lighthearted approach, a down-to-earth style, and even cartoons and humorous icons to dispel fears and build confidence. Lighthearted but not lightweight, these books are perfect survival guides to solve your everyday personal and business problems.

> *"More than a publishing phenomenon, 'Dummies' is a sign of the times."*
>
> — The New York Times

> *"A world of detailed and authoritative information is packed into them..."*
>
> — U.S. News and World Report

> *"...you won't go wrong buying them."*
>
> — Walter Mossberg, Wall Street Journal, on IDG Books' ...For Dummies books

Already, millions of satisfied readers agree. They have made *...For Dummies* the #1 introductory level computer book series and a best-selling business book series. They have written asking for more. So, if you're looking for the best and easiest way to learn about business and other general reference topics, look to *...For Dummies* to give you a helping hand.

IDG BOOKS WORLDWIDE®

German

FOR

DUMMIES®

German FOR DUMMIES®

by Paulina Christensen and Anne Fox

Berlitz® Series Editor: Juergen Lorenz

IDG Books Worldwide, Inc.
An International Data Group Company

Foster City, CA ◆ Chicago, IL ◆ Indianapolis, IN ◆ New York, NY

German For Dummies®

Published by
IDG Books Worldwide, Inc.
An International Data Group Company
919 E. Hillsdale Blvd.
Suite 400
Foster City, CA 94404
www.idgbooks.com (IDG Books Worldwide Web site)
www.dummies.com (Dummies Press Web site)

Library of Congress Catalog Card No.: 99-69715

ISBN: 0-7645-5195-7

Printed in the United States of America

10 9 8 7 6 5 4 3 2 1

1B/RQ/QU/QQ/IN

Distributed in the United States by IDG Books Worldwide, Inc.

Distributed by CDG Books Canada Inc. for Canada; by Transworld Publishers Limited in the United Kingdom; by IDG Norge Books for Norway; by IDG Sweden Books for Sweden; by IDG Books Australia Publishing Corporation Pty. Ltd. for Australia and New Zealand; by TransQuest Publishers Pte Ltd. for Singapore, Malaysia, Thailand, Indonesia, and Hong Kong; by Gotop Information Inc. for Taiwan; by ICG Muse, Inc. for Japan; by Intersoft for South Africa; by Eyrolles for France; by International Thomson Publishing for Germany, Austria and Switzerland; by Distribuidora Cuspide for Argentina; by LR International for Brazil; by Galileo Libros for Chile; by Ediciones ZETA S.C.R. Ltda. for Peru; by WS Computer Publishing Corporation, Inc., for the Philippines; by Contemporanea de Ediciones for Venezuela; by Express Computer Distributors for the Caribbean and West Indies; by Micronesia Media Distributor, Inc. for Micronesia; by Chips Computadoras S.A. de C.V. for Mexico; by Editorial Norma de Panama S.A. for Panama; by American Bookshops for Finland.

For general information on IDG Books Worldwide's books in the U.S., please call our Consumer Customer Service department at 800-762-2974. For reseller information, including discounts and premium sales, please call our Reseller Customer Service department at 800-434-3422.

For information on where to purchase IDG Books Worldwide's books outside the U.S., please contact our International Sales department at 317-596-5530 or fax 317-572-4002.

For consumer information on foreign language translations, please contact our Customer Service department at 1-800-434-3422, fax 317-572-4002, or e-mail rights@idgbooks.com.

For information on licensing foreign or domestic rights, please phone +1-650-653-7098.

For sales inquiries and special prices for bulk quantities, please contact our Order Services department at 800-434-3422 or write to the address above.

For information on using IDG Books Worldwide's books in the classroom or for ordering examination copies, please contact our Educational Sales department at 800-434-2086 or fax 317-572-4005.

For press review copies, author interviews, or other publicity information, please contact our Public Relations department at 650-653-7000 or fax 650-653-7500.

For authorization to photocopy items for corporate, personal, or educational use, please contact Copyright Clearance Center, 222 Rosewood Drive, Danvers, MA 01923, or fax 978-750-4470.

About the Authors

Paulina Christensen has been working as a writer, editor, and translator for almost ten years. She holds a degree in English and German literature and has developed, written, and edited numerous German-language textbooks and teachers' handbooks for Berlitz International. Her work as a translator ranges from new media art to science fiction (*Starlog* magazine). She occasionally works as a court interpreter and does consulting and interpreting at educational conferences, as well as voice-overs for educational videos and CD-ROMs. Dr. Christensen received her M.A. and Ph.D. from Düsseldorf University, Germany, and has taught at Berlitz Language Schools, New York University, and Fordham University.

Anne Fox has been working as a translator, editor, and writer for the past twelve years. She studied at Interpreters' School, Zurich, Switzerland, and holds a degree in translation. Her various assignments have taken her to outer space, hyperspace, and around the world. She has also taught at Berlitz Language Schools and worked as a legal and technical proofreader in the editorial departments of several law firms. Most recently she has been developing, writing, and editing student textbooks and teacher handbooks for Berlitz.

About Berlitz

The name "Berlitz" has meant excellence in language services for more than 120 years. At more than 400 locations and in 50 countries worldwide, Berlitz offers a full range of language and language related services, including instruction, cross-cultural training, document translation, software localization, and interpretation services. Berlitz also offers a wide array of publishing products, such as self-study language courses, phrase books, travel guides, and dictionaries.

The world-famous Berlitz Method is the core of all Berlitz language instruction. From the time of its introduction in 1878, millions have used this method to learn new languages. For more information about Berlitz classes and products, please consult your local telephone directory for the Language Center nearest you or visit the Berlitz Web site at www.berlitz.com, where you can enroll in classes or shop directly for products online.

ABOUT IDG BOOKS WORLDWIDE

Welcome to the world of IDG Books Worldwide.

IDG Books Worldwide, Inc., is a subsidiary of International Data Group, the world's largest publisher of computer-related information and the leading global provider of information services on information technology. IDG was founded more than 30 years ago by Patrick J. McGovern and now employs more than 9,000 people worldwide. IDG publishes more than 290 computer publications in over 75 countries. More than 90 million people read one or more IDG publications each month.

Launched in 1990, IDG Books Worldwide is today the #1 publisher of best-selling computer books in the United States. We are proud to have received eight awards from the Computer Press Association in recognition of editorial excellence and three from Computer Currents' First Annual Readers' Choice Awards. Our best-selling ...For Dummies® series has more than 50 million copies in print with translations in 31 languages. IDG Books Worldwide, through a joint venture with IDG's Hi-Tech Beijing, became the first U.S. publisher to publish a computer book in the People's Republic of China. In record time, IDG Books Worldwide has become the first choice for millions of readers around the world who want to learn how to better manage their businesses.

Our mission is simple: Every one of our books is designed to bring extra value and skill-building instructions to the reader. Our books are written by experts who understand and care about our readers. The knowledge base of our editorial staff comes from years of experience in publishing, education, and journalism — experience we use to produce books to carry us into the new millennium. In short, we care about books, so we attract the best people. We devote special attention to details such as audience, interior design, use of icons, and illustrations. And because we use an efficient process of authoring, editing, and desktop publishing our books electronically, we can spend more time ensuring superior content and less time on the technicalities of making books.

You can count on our commitment to deliver high-quality books at competitive prices on topics you want to read about. At IDG Books Worldwide, we continue in the IDG tradition of delivering quality for more than 30 years. You'll find no better book on a subject than one from IDG Books Worldwide.

John J. Kilcullen
John Kilcullen
Chairman and CEO
IDG Books Worldwide, Inc.

*Eighth Annual
Computer Press
Awards ≥1992*

*Ninth Annual
Computer Press
Awards ≥1993*

*Tenth Annual
Computer Press
Awards ≥1994*

*Eleventh Annual
Computer Press
Awards ≥1995*

IDG is the world's leading IT media, research and exposition company. Founded in 1964, IDG had 1997 revenues of $2.05 billion and has more than 9,000 employees worldwide. IDG offers the widest range of media options that reach IT buyers in 75 countries representing 95% of worldwide IT spending. IDG's diverse product and services portfolio spans six key areas including print publishing, online publishing, expositions and conferences, market research, education and training, and global marketing services. More than 90 million people read one or more of IDG's 290 magazines and newspapers, including IDG's leading global brands — Computerworld, PC World, Network World, Macworld and the Channel World family of publications. IDG Books Worldwide is one of the fastest-growing computer book publishers in the world, with more than 700 titles in 36 languages. The "...For Dummies®" series alone has more than 50 million copies in print. IDG offers online users the largest network of technology-specific Web sites around the world through IDG.net (http://www.idg.net), which comprises more than 225 targeted Web sites in 55 countries worldwide. International Data Corporation (IDC) is the world's largest provider of information technology data, analysis and consulting, with research centers in over 41 countries and more than 400 research analysts worldwide. IDG World Expo is a leading producer of more than 168 globally branded conferences and expositions in 35 countries including E3 (Electronic Entertainment Expo), Macworld Expo, ComNet, Windows World Expo, ICE (Internet Commerce Expo), Agenda, DEMO, and Spotlight. IDG's training subsidiary, ExecuTrain, is the world's largest computer training company, with more than 230 locations worldwide and 785 training courses. IDG Marketing Services helps industry-leading IT companies build international brand recognition by developing global integrated marketing programs via IDG's print, online and exposition products worldwide. Further information about the company can be found at www.idg.com.   1/26/00

Authors' Acknowledgments

Paulina Christensen: Many thanks to Juergen Lorenz and Sheryl Olinsky Borg at Berlitz Publishing for their coordination, supervision, and invaluable help in developing this book. Special thanks go to my partner in crime Anne Fox for the smooth collaboration and continuous brainstorming, input, tips, and feedback (around the clock and at odd hours). Last, but not least, thanks to all the people at IDG Books for making this book possible.

Anne Fox: Many thanks to a host of helpful people. First and foremost to my crony Paulina Christensen for being my second half and soundboard. Thanks to the Berlitz crew Juergen Lorenz and Sheryl Olinsky Borg for their valuable advice and insight. Thanks to Mary Goodwin at IDG for her tireless efforts. Special thanks to my buddies David and Kirk for their timely assistance, as well as to Phoebe, Trotsky, Frida, Dubseline, and Bonnie for keeping off the keyboard.

Berlitz would like to thank the following:

Paulina Christensen and Anne Fox, an outstanding team of writers, for their tireless dedication to creating this book.

Our NYC audio producer, Paul Ruben, for bringing the written German language to life.

The audio postproduction team at Big Media Productions in NYC, John Cheary, Philip Clark, and Tim Franklin, for endless hours of listening, cutting, and pasting.

Our editors, Juergen Lorenz and Sheryl Olinsky Borg, for their professionalism and commitment to putting this challenging and exciting project together.

And our deep appreciation goes to the staff at IDG Books, especially Holly McGuire, Pam Mourouzis, and Mary Goodwin, who guided *German For Dummies* from start to finish.

Publisher's Acknowledgments

We're proud of this book; please register your comments through our IDG Books Worldwide Online Registration Form located at http://my2cents.dummies.com.

Some of the people who helped bring this book to market include the following:

Acquisitions, Editorial, and Media Development

Project Editor: Mary Goodwin

Acquisitions Editor: Holly McGuire

Acquisitions Coordinator: Karen Young

Media Development Coordinator: Megan Roney

Technical Editor: Wilfried Wilms

General Reviewer: Esther Neuendorf

Editorial Manager: Kristin Cocks

Editorial Assistant: Beth Parlon

Production

Project Coordinator: Regina Snyder

Layout and Graphics: Joe Bucki, Karl Brandt, Tracy K. Oliver, Jill Piscitelli, Janet Seib, Brian Torwelle, Erin Zeltner

Proofreaders: Laura Albert, Corey Bowen, Charles Spencer

Indexer: Liz Cunningham

Special Help
Seta K. Frantz, Sherry Gomoll, Samuel Goodwin

General and Administrative

IDG Books Worldwide, Inc.: John Kilcullen, CEO

IDG Books Technology Publishing Group: Richard Swadley, Senior Vice President and Publisher; Walter Bruce III, Vice President and Associate Publisher; Joseph Wikert, Associate Publisher; Mary Bednarek, Branded Product Development Director; Mary Corder, Editorial Director; Barry Pruett, Publishing Manager; Michelle Baxter, Publishing Manager

IDG Books Consumer Publishing Group: Roland Elgey, Senior Vice President and Publisher; Kathleen A. Welton, Vice President and Publisher; Kevin Thornton, Acquisitions Manager; Kristin A. Cocks, Editorial Director

IDG Books Internet Publishing Group: Brenda McLaughlin, Senior Vice President and Publisher; Diane Graves Steele, Vice President and Associate Publisher; Sofia Marchant, Online Marketing Manager

IDG Books Production for Dummies Press: Debbie Stailey, Associate Director of Production; Cindy L. Phipps, Manager of Project Coordination, Production Proofreading, and Indexing; Tony Augsburger, Manager of Prepress, Reprints, and Systems; Laura Carpenter, Production Control Manager; Shelley Lea, Supervisor of Graphics and Design; Debbie J. Gates, Production Systems Specialist; Robert Springer, Supervisor of Proofreading; Kathie Schutte, Production Supervisor

Dummies Packaging and Book Design: Patty Page, Manager, Promotions Marketing

◆

The publisher would like to give special thanks to Patrick J. McGovern, without whom this book would not have been possible.

◆

Contents at a Glance

Cartoons at a Glance

By Rich Tennant

page 7

page 63

page 185

page 281

page 303

Fax: 978-546-7747
E-mail: richtennant@the5thwave.com
World Wide Web: www.the5thwave.com

Table of Contents

Introduction

• •

As society becomes more and more international in nature, knowing how to say at least a few words in other languages becomes more and more useful. Inexpensive airfares make travel abroad a more realistic option. Global business environments necessitate overseas travel. Or you may just have friends and neighbors who speak other languages, or you may want to get in touch with your heritage by learning a little bit of the language that your ancestors spoke.

Whatever your reason for wanting to learn some German, *German For Dummies* can help. Two experts at helping readers develop knowledge — Berlitz, experts in teaching foreign languages; and IDG Books Worldwide, Inc., publishers of the best-selling *For Dummies* series — have teamed up to produce a book that gives you the skills you need for basic communication in German. We're not promising fluency here, but if you need to greet someone, purchase a ticket, or order off a menu in German, you need look no further than *German For Dummies*.

About This Book

This is not a class that you have to drag yourself to twice a week for a specified period of time. You can use *German For Dummies* however you want to, whether your goal is to learn some words and phrases to help you get around when you visit Germany, or you just want to be able to say "Hello, how are you?" to your German-speaking neighbor. Go through this book at your own pace, reading as much or as little at a time as you like. You don't have to trudge through the chapters in order, either; just read the sections that interest you.

Note: If you've never taken German before, you may want to read the chapters in Part I before you tackle the later chapters. Part I gives you some of the basics that you need to know about the language, such as how to pronounce the various sounds.

Conventions Used in This Book

To make this book easy for you to navigate, we've set up a couple of conventions:

- ✔ German terms are set in **boldface** to make them stand out.

- ✔ Pronunciations set in *italics* follow the German terms.

- ✔ Verb conjugations (lists that show you the forms of a verb) are given in tables in this order: the "I" form, the "you" (singular, informal) form, the "you" (singular, formal) form, the "he/she/it" form, the "we" form, the "you" (plural, informal) form, the "you" (plural, formal) form, and the "they" form. Pronunciations follow in the second column. Here's an example:

Conjugation	*Pronunciation*
ich werde	îH <u>vehr</u>-de
du wirst	dû vîrst
Sie werden	zee <u>vehr</u>-dn
er, sie, es wird	ehr/zee/ês vîrt
wir werden	veer <u>vehr</u>-dn
ihr werdet	eer <u>vehr</u>-det
Sie werden	zee <u>vehr</u>-dn
sie werden	zee <u>vehr</u>-dn

Language learning is a peculiar beast, so this book includes a few elements that other *For Dummies* books do not. Following are the new elements that you'll find:

- ✔ **Talkin' the Talk dialogues:** The best way to learn a language is to see and hear how it's used in conversation, so we include dialogues throughout the book. The dialogues come under the heading "Talkin' the Talk" and show you the German words, their pronunciations, and the English translations.

- ✔ **Words to Know blackboards:** Memorizing key words and phrases is also important in language learning, so we collect the important words in a chapter (or section within a chapter) in a chalkboard, with the heading "Words to Know."

- ✔ **Fun & Games activities:** If you don't have actual German speakers to practice your new language skills on, you can use the Fun & Games activities to reinforce what you learn. These word games are fun ways to gauge your progress.

Also note that, because each language has its own ways of expressing ideas, the English translations that we provide for the German terms may not be exactly literal. We want you to know the gist of what's being said, not just the words that are being said. For example, the phrase **Es geht** *(ēs geht)* can be translated literally as "It goes," but the phrase really means "So, so." This book gives the "So, so" translation.

Foolish Assumptions

To write this book, we had to make some assumptions about who you are and what you want from a book called *German For Dummies*. Here are the assumptions that we've made about you:

- ✔ You know no German — or if you took German back in school, you don't remember a word of it.
- ✔ You're not looking for a book that will make you fluent in German; you just want to know some words, phrases, and sentence constructions so that you can communicate basic information in German.
- ✔ You don't want to have to memorize long lists of vocabulary words or a bunch of boring grammar rules.
- ✔ You want to have fun and learn a little bit of German at the same time.

If these statements apply to you, you've found the right book!

How This Book Is Organized

This book is divided by topic into parts, and then into chapters. The following sections tell you what types of information you can find in each part.

Part I: Getting Started

This part lets you get your feet wet by giving you some German basics: how to pronounce words, how to form sentences, and so on. We even boost your confidence by reintroducing you to some German words that you probably already know. Finally, we outline the basics of German grammar that you may need to know when you work through later chapters in the book.

Part II: German in Action

In this part, you begin learning and using German. Instead of focusing on grammar points as many language textbooks do, this part focuses on everyday situations, such as shopping, dining, and making small talk.

Part III: German on the Go

This part gives you the tools you need to take your German on the road, whether it's to a local German restaurant or to a museum in Germany. This part covers all aspects of travel in Germany, and it even has a chapter on handling emergencies.

Part IV: The Part of Tens

If you're looking for small, easily digestible pieces of information about German, this part is for you. Here, you can find ten ways to learn German quickly, ten useful German expressions to know, ten things never to say in German, and more.

Part V: Appendixes

This part of the book includes important information that you can use for reference. We include verb tables, which show you how to conjugate a regular verb and then how to conjugate those verbs that stubbornly don't fit the pattern. We also provide a listing of the tracks that appear on the audio CD that comes with this book so that you can find out where in the book those dialogues are and follow along. We also include answer keys to some of the Fun & Games puzzles that appear in the book. Finally, we give you a mini-dictionary in both German-to-English and English-to-German formats. If you encounter a German word that you don't understand, or if you need to know a specific word in German, you can look it up here.

Icons Used in This Book

You may be looking for particular information while reading this book. To make certain types of information easier for you to find, we've placed the following icons in the left-hand margins throughout the book:

This icon highlights tips that can make learning German easier.

 This icon points out interesting information that you shouldn't forget.

 Languages are full of quirks that may trip you up if you're not prepared for them. This icon points to discussions of these weird grammar rules.

 If you're looking for information and advice about culture and travel, look for these icons. They draw your attention to interesting tidbits about the countries in which German is spoken.

 The audio CD that comes with this book gives you the opportunity to listen to real German speakers so that you can get a better understanding of what German sounds like. This icon marks the Talkin' the Talk dialogues that you can find on the CD.

Where to Go from Here

Learning a language is all about jumping in and giving it a try (no matter how bad your pronunciation is at first). So make the leap! Start at the beginning, pick a chapter that interests you, or pop the CD into your stereo or computer and listen to a few dialogues. Before long, you'll be able to respond, "Ja!" when people ask, "Sprechen Sie Deutsch?"

Part I
Getting Started

The 5th Wave By Rich Tennant

"What do you say – formal or informal greeting?"

In this part . . .

You have to start somewhere, but we bet that you know a lot more German than you think. Don't think so? Then check out Chapter 1. Chapters 2 and 3 cover some nuts-and-bolts grammar info that, well, you need to absorb. But don't worry — we make it fun.

Chapter 1

You Already Know a Little German

In This Chapter

▶ Recognizing the German you already know

▶ Using popular expressions

▶ Mouthing off: Basic pronunciation

*T*he best way to learn a new language is total immersion — so in this chapter, you jump right into the German language. This chapter shows you the German you already know, introduces you to some popular German expressions, and explains how to pronounce German.

The German You Know

Since both German and English belong to the group of Germanic languages, there are quite a few words that are either identical or similar in both languages. These words are called *cognates*.

Friendly allies (perfect cognates)

The following words are spelled the same way and have the same meaning in German and in English. The only things that are different are the pronunciation and the fact that in German, nouns are always capitalized:

der Arm *(ârm)*

der Bandit *(bân-deet)*

die Bank *(bânk)*

die Basis *(bah-zîs)*

blind *(blînt)*

die Butter *(bû-ter)*

elegant *(êle-gânt)*

die Emotion *(êmoh-tsîohn)*

emotional *(êmoh-tsîoh-nahl)*

der Finger *(finger)*

die Garage *(gâ-rah-je)*

die Hand *(hânt)*

das Hotel *(hoh-têl)*

die Inspiration *(în-spee-râ-tsîohn)*

international *(în-ter-nâtsîo-nahl)*

irrational *(îrâ-tsîoh-nahl)*

der Kitsch *(kîtsh)*

modern *(moh-dêrn)*

der Moment *(moh-mênt)*

das Museum *(mû-zeh-ûm)*

der Name *(nah-me)*

die Nation *(nâts-îohn)*

die Olive *(oh-lee-ve)*

die Orange *(oh-rong-je)*

parallel *(pârâ-lehl)*

das Photo *(foh-toh)*

das Problem *(prô-blehm)*

die Religion *(rêlî-gîohn)*

das Restaurant *(rês-toh-rong)*

die Rose *(roh-ze)*

der Service *(ser-vîs)*

das Signal *(zîg-nahl)*

der Sport *(shpôrt)*

die Statue *(shtah-tooe)*

das System *(zuus-tehm)*

das Taxi *(tâ-xee)*

der Tiger *(tee-ger)*

der Tunnel *(tû-nel)*

wild *(vîlt)*

der Wind *(vînt)*

Kissing cousins (near cognates)

And then there are all those words, like the ones shown in Table 1-1, that are spelled almost the same in German as in English and have the same meaning. Table 1-1 also shows you something about German spelling conventions: for example, that the English "c" is a "k" in most German words.

Table 1-1 Words Similar in Meaning, Slightly Different in Spelling	
German	*English*
die Adresse *(dee ah-<u>drê</u>-sse)*	address
der Aspekt *(dehr âs-pêkt)*	aspect
blond *(blônt)*	blond/blonde
die Bluse *(dee <u>bloo</u>-ze)*	blouse
die Demokratie *(dee dêmô-krah-<u>tee</u>)*	democracy
direkt *(dî-<u>rêkt</u>)*	direct
der Doktor *(dehr <u>dôk</u>-tohr)*	doctor
exzellent *(êxtse-<u>lênt</u>)*	excellent
fantastisch *(fân-<u>tâs</u>-tish)*	fantastic
das Glas *(dâs glahs)*	glass
der Kaffee *(dehr <u>kâ</u>-feh)*	coffee
die Komödie *(dee kô-<u>muo</u>-dee-e)*	comedy
die Kondition *(dee kôn-dî-<u>tsîohn</u>)*	condition
das Konzert *(dâs kôn-tsêrt)*	concert
die Kultur *(dee kûl-<u>toor</u>)*	culture
lang *(lâng)*	long
die Maschine *(dee mâ-<u>shee</u>-ne)*	machine
die Maus *(dee mows)*	mouse
die Methode *(dee mê-<u>toh</u>-de)*	method
die Musik *(dee mû-<u>zeek</u>)*	music
die Nationalität *(dee <u>nâtsîo</u>-nahl-îtait)*	nationality
die Natur *(dee nâ-<u>toor</u>)*	nature

(continued)

Table 1-1 *(continued)*

German	English
der Ozean *(dehr oh-tseh-ahn)*	ocean
das Papier *(dâs pâ-peer)*	paper
perfekt *(pêr-fêkt)*	perfect
potentiell *(pô-tên-tsîel)*	potential (adjective)
das Programm *(dâs proh-grâm)*	program
das Salz *(dâs zâlts)*	salt
der Scheck *(dehr shêk)*	check
der Supermarkt *(dehr zoo-pêr-mârkt)*	supermarket
das Telefon *(dâs têle-fohn)*	telephone
die Theorie *(dee teh-oh-ree)*	theory
die Tragödie *(dee trâ-guo-dee-e)*	tragedy
die Walnuss *(dee vahl-nûs)*	walnut

False friends

As in every language, German contains some false friends — those words that look very similar to English but often have a completely different meaning:

- **After** *(ahf-ter)*: If you want to avoid embarassment, you should remember the meaning of this word. It means "anus" and not "after." The German word for "after" is **nach** *(nahH)* or **nachdem** *(nahH-dehm)*.

- **aktuell** *(âk-too-êl)*: This word means "up-to-date" and "current," not "actually." The German translation for "actually" is **tatsächlich** *(taht-sêH-lîH)*.

- **also** *(âl-zoh)*: This one means "so, therefore" and not "also." The German word for "also" is **auch** *(owH)*.

- **bekommen** *(be-kô-men)*: This verb is an important one to remember. It means "to get" and not "to become." The German word for "to become" is **werden** *(vehr-den)*.

- **Bowle** *(boh-le)*: This is a mixed drink of fruits and alcohol and not a "bowl," which in German, is **Schüssel** *(shuu-sel)* (the one you put food into) or **Kugel** *(koo-gel)* (sports-type ball).

- **brav** *(brahf)*: This word means "well behaved" and not "brave." The German word for "brave" is **tapfer** *(tâp-fer)*.

- **Brief** *(breef)*: This word is a noun and means "letter" and not "brief." The German translation for the adjective "brief" is **kurz** *(kûrts)*, and, for the noun, **Auftrag** *(<u>owf</u>-trahgk)* or **Unterlagen** *(<u>ûn</u>-ter-lah-gen)*.

- **Chef** *(shêf)*: This is the guy you take orders from, your boss or principal, and not the guy who's in charge of the cooking. The German word for "chef" is **Küchenchef** *(kuu-Hên-shêf)* or **Chefkoch** *(shêf-kôH)*.

- **eventuell** *(eh-<u>vên</u>-too-êl)*: This one means "possibly" and not "eventually," which would be **schließlich** *(<u>shlees</u>-līH)* in German.

- **genial** *(gê-nee-ahl)*: This adjective describes an idea or person "of genius" and has nothing to do with "genial." The German word for "genial" is **heiter** *(<u>hy</u>-ter)*.

- **Kind** *(kīnt)*: This is the German word for "child" and has nothing to do with the English "kind," which would be **nett** *(nêt)* or **liebenswürdig** *(<u>lee</u>-bens-vuur-digk)* in German.

- **Komfort** *(kôm-<u>fohr</u>)*: This word means "amenity" — describing something that is comfortable — and not "comfort." The German word for "comfort" is **Trost** *(trohst)*.

- **kurios** *(<u>kûrî</u>-ohs)*: This word means "strange" and not "curious." The German word for "curious" is **neugierig** *(<u>noy</u>-gee-rīgk)*.

- **Most** *(môst)*: This is the German word for a young wine. The German word for the English "most" is **das meiste** *(dâs my-ste)*; for example, you would say **die meisten Leute** *(die <u>my</u>-sten <u>loy</u>-te)* (most people).

- **ordinär** *(ôr-dī-<u>nêr</u>)*: This word means "vulgar" rather than "ordinary." The German word for "ordinary" is **normal** *(nôr-<u>mahl</u>)* or **gewöhnlich** *(ge-<u>vuohn</u>-līH)*.

- **pathetisch** *(pâ-<u>teh</u>-tîsh)*: This one means "overly emotional" and not "pathetic," which, in German, is **jämmerlich** *(<u>yê</u>-mer-līH)* or **armselig** *(<u>ârm</u>-zeh-ligk)*.

- **Provision** *(<u>prô</u>-vî-zîohn)*: The meaning of this word is "commission" and not "provision." The German word for "provision" is **Vorsorge** *(<u>fohr</u>-zôr-ge)* or **Versorgung** *(fêr-<u>zôr</u>-gungk)*.

- **psychisch** *(<u>psuu</u>-Hîsh)*: This word means "psychological" and not "psychic." The German translation for "psychic" is **Medium** *(<u>meh</u>-dî-um)* (if you mean the person) or **telepathisch** *(têle-<u>pah</u>-tîsh)*.

- **See** *(zeh)*: This word means "lake" or "sea." In German, the verb "to see" is **sehen** *(<u>seh</u>-hên)*.

- **sensibel** *(zen-<u>zee</u>-bel)*: The meaning of this word is "sensitive" and not "sensible," which translates into **vernünftig** *(fêr-<u>nuunf</u>-tīgk)*.

- **sympathisch** *(zuum-<u>pah</u>-tîsh)*: This word means "nice" and not "sympathetic." The German word for "sympathetic" is **mitfühlend** *(<u>mît</u>-fuu-lent)*.

Lenders and borrowers

A few German words have been adopted by the English language and have retained their meaning with a different pronunciation, such as **Kindergarten** (_kīn-der-gār-ten_) (**Garten** is the German word for garden), **Zeitgeist** (_tsyt-gyst_), **Leitmotiv** (_lyt-mō-teef_), and **Angst** (_āngst_) — a term that lately has become quite fashionable.

However, the number of these German words is minimal compared to the English words that have made their way into the German language. In fact, language purists constantly complain about the growing number of "anglicisms." Sometimes, the combination of English and German leads to quite remarkable linguistic oddities. For example, you might hear **das ist gerade in/out** (_dâs īst gê-rah-de in/out_) (that's in/out right now) or **check das mal ab** (_check dâs mahl âp_) (check that out).

The following is a list of English words that are commonly used in German:

- **der Boss**
- **das Business**
- **die City**
- **cool**
- **das Design**
- **der Dress Code**
- **das Event**
- **Fashion (used without article)**
- **das Feeling**
- **das Fast Food**
- **Hi**
- **hip**
- **der Hit**
- **das Jet Set**
- **der Job**
- **das Jogging**
- **der Manager**
- **das Marketing**
- **Okay**
- **das Outing**

 ✔ overdressed/underdressed

 ✔ die Party

 ✔ das Ranking (mostly sports)

 ✔ das Shopping

 ✔ die Show/Talkshow

 ✔ das Steak

 ✔ der Thriller

 ✔ das Understatement

 ✔ Wow

And finally, there are a few "fake" English terms that are frequently used in German. They are English words that wouldn't be used in the same context in the English language. For example, the German word for a mobile phone is "Handy," and a "Party Service" is a company that does catering for parties and public events.

Talkin' the Talk

Don't get the wrong impression and think that the following conversation gives you an idea of how the average German talks. However, it's not unlikely that you might overhear this kind of mixed language conversation between "hip" youngsters — it sure would leave language purists ranting and raving. In this scenario, two friends — let's call them Claudia and Heike — meet on the street.

Claudia:	**Hi, wie geht's? Wie ist der neue Job?** *hi, vee gêhts? vee îst dehr noye job* Hi. How are you? How is the new job?
Heike:	**Super! Ich mache Marketing und mein Boss ist total nett.** *super! îH <u>mâ</u>-He marketing ûnt myn boss îst tô-<u>tahl</u> nêt* Super! I'm doing marketing and my boss is totally nice.
Claudia:	**Warst Du in der City?** *vahrst doo în dehr city* Have you been to the city?
Heike:	**Ja, Shopping. Heute ist eine Party bei meiner Firma. Der Dress Code ist da ziemlich hart. Ich hatte Angst, underdressed zu sein.** *yah, shopping. <u>hoy</u>-te îst <u>ay</u>-ne party by <u>my</u>-ner <u>fîr</u>-mah. dehr dress code îst dah <u>tseem</u>-lîH hârt. îH <u>hâ</u>-te ângst, underdressed tsû zyn*

	Yes, shopping. There is a party at my company today. The dress code there is pretty tough. I was afraid to be underdressed.
Claudia:	**Zeig mal . . . wow, cool!** *tsygk mahl . . . wow, cool* Show me . . . wow, cool!
Heike:	**Tja, ich dachte mir, Understatement ist sowieso out.** *tîâ, îH dâHte meer, understatement îst zo-vee-<u>zoh</u> out* Well, I thought understatement is out anyway.

Using Popular Expressions

Just like the English language, German has many *idioms,* expressions typical of a language and culture. If you translate these idioms word for word, they often just sound obscure, and you actually have to memorize each of them and what they really mean in order to use them appropriately. For example, the German idiom **ein Fisch auf dem Trockenen** *(ayn fish owf dehm <u>trôk</u>-nen)* would literally translate into "a fish on the dry," but the expression corresponds to the English "a fish out of water." You would find yourself wondering what a German person is trying to say when he or she declares, "It's raining twine." It's the literal translation of **Es regnet Bindfäden.** *(ês <u>rehgk</u>-nêt <u>bînt</u>-fê-den),* the German equivalent of "It's raining cats and dogs."

Other typical German idioms are

- **Das macht den Braten (den Kohl) nicht fett.** *(dâs mâHt dehn <u>brah</u>-ten [dehn kohl] nîHt fêt)* (That doesn't make the roast (the cabbage) fat, meaning: "that won't make much difference" or "that won't help.")

- **den Braten riechen** *(dehn <u>brah</u>-ten <u>ree</u>-Hen)* (to smell the roast, meaning: "to get wind of something")

Apart from these idioms, there are many handy German expressions that are frequently used and can easily be learned:

- **Prima!** *(<u>pree</u>-mah)* (Great!)

- **Klasse!** *(<u>klâ</u>-se)* (Great!)

- **Toll!** *(tôl)* (Great!)

- **Einverstanden.** *(<u>ayn</u>-fêr-shtân-den)* (Agreed./Okay.)

- **Geht in Ordnung.** *(geht în ôrt-nûngk)* (I'll do it.)

- **Wird gemacht.** *(vîrt ge-<u>mâHt</u>)* (Okay./Will be done.)

- ✔ **Keine Frage.** *(ky-ne frah-ge)* (No question.)
- ✔ **Macht nichts.** *(mâHt nĩHts)* (Never mind/That's okay.)
- ✔ **Nicht der Rede wert.** *(nĩHt dehr reh-de vehrt)* (Don't mention it.)
- ✔ **Schade!** *(shah-de)* (Too bad!)
- ✔ **So ein Pech!** *(zoh ayn pêH)* (Bad luck!)
- ✔ **Viel Glück!** *(feel gluuk)* (Good luck!)
- ✔ **Prost!** *(prohst)* (Cheers!)

Mouthing Off: Basic Pronunciation

The key to pronouncing a foreign language is forgetting your fear of sounding awkward and never getting it right. If you hear a foreign language spoken at normal speed, you might not even be able to identify any reproducible word or sound. To master the language, you need to learn the basic rules of pronunciation and concentrate on small units, which can gradually be expanded — from sounds to words and sentences. The rest is practice, practice, practice.

Dealing with stress in German

This is not about what happens to you at the office or when a BMW is tailgating you at a speed of 110 miles an hour on the Autobahn. This is about stressed syllables in German words. In the pronunciations given throughout this book, the syllables you should stress are underlined.

Learning the German alphabet

The German alphabet has the same number of letters as the English one, 26. However, many of the letters are pronounced differently than their English counterparts. The good news is that German words are pronounced exactly as they are spelled — that's why those spelling contests at school are an English language phenomenon. Words such as "hippopotamus" are favorites in those contests — the "i" is pronounced as an "e"; the "u" sounds closer to an "a" and so on. In German, you don't have these doubts: a "u" is always a "u."

 Track 1 on the CD gives you the sounds in the German alphabet.

Pronouncing vowels

In German, vowels *(a, e, i, o,* and *u)* can have long, drawn out vowel sounds or shorter vowel sounds. Luckily, there are some general rules that apply:

- ✓ A vowel is long when it is followed by an "h," as in **Stahl** *(shtahl)* (steel).

- ✓ A vowel is long when it is followed by a single consonant as in **Tag** *(tahgk)* (day).

- ✓ A vowel is long when it is doubled, as in **Teer** *(tehr)* (tar) or **Aal** *(ahl)* (eel).

- ✓ In general, a vowel is short when it is followed by two or more consonants, as in **Tanne** *(tâ-ne)* (fir tree).

Table 1-2 gives you an idea of how German vowels are pronounced by providing you with examples and a phonetic script — the letter combinations that serve as the English equivalent of the German letter's pronunciation.

In this book's phonetic script, diacritics (the little "hats" on letters) indicate that a vowel sound is short.

Table 1-2	Pronouncing German Vowels		
German Letter	*Symbol*	*As in English*	*German Word*
a (long)	ah	father	**Laden** *(lah-den)* (store)
a (short)	â	dark	**Platz** *(plâts)* (place)
e (long)	eh	bed	**Leben** *(leh-ben)* (life)
e (short/stressed)	ê	let	**Bett** *(bêt)* (bed)
e (short/unstressed)	e	elevator (second e)	**Lachen** *(lâ-Hen)* (laughter)
i (long)	ee	deer	**Ritus** *(ree-tûs)* (rite)
i (short)	î	winter	**Milch** *(mîlH)* (milk)
o (long)	oh	born	**Lob** *(lohp)* (praise)
o (short)	ô	lottery	**Motte** *(mô-te)* (moth)

German Letter	Symbol	As in English	German Word
u (long)	oo	moon	**Tube** *(too-be)*
u (short)	û	look	**Rum** *(rûm)* (rum)

The German vowel "i" (long and short) is pronounced like the English letter "e"!

Pronouncing umlauts

You may have seen those pesky little dots that sometimes appear over vowels in German words. They are called **Umlaute** (<u>ûm</u>-*low-te)* (umlauts). They slightly alter the sound of a vowel, as outlined in Table 1-3.

Table 1-3	Pronouncing Vowels with Umlauts		
German Letter	*Symbol*	*As in English*	*German Word*
ä (long)	ai	hair	**nächste** *(naiH-ste)* (next)
ä (short)	ê	let	**Bäcker** *(bê-ker)* (baker)
ö	uo	learn	**hören** *(huo-ren)* (hear)
ü	uu	lure	**Tür** *(tuur)* (door)

Nouns sometimes acquire an umlaut in their plural form.

Pronouncing diphthongs

Diphthongs are combinations of two vowels in one syllable (as in the Eglish "lie"), and the German language has quite a few of them, as shown in Table 1-4.

Table 1-4	Pronouncing German Dipthongs		
German Diphtongs	*Symbol*	*As in English*	*German word*
ai	y	cry	**Mais** *(mys)* (corn)
au	ow	now	**laut** *(lowt)* (noisy)

(continued)

Table 1-4	Pronouncing German Dipthongs *(continued)*		
German Diphtongs	*Symbol*	*As in English*	*German word*
au	oh	restaurant	**Restaurant** *(rês-toh-rong)* (restaurant)
äu / eu	oy	boy	**Häuser** *(hoy-zer)* (houses) / **Leute** *(loy-te)* (people)
ei	ay / y	cry	**ein** *(ayn)* (a) / **mein** *(myn)* (my)
ie	ee	deer	**Liebe** *(lee-be)* (love)

Pronouncing consonants

You may be relieved to find out that the sounds of German consonants aren't as unfamiliar as those of the vowels. In fact, German consonants are either pronounced like their English equivalents or like other English consonants. Well, there are a couple of oddities and exceptions, which we show you later.

The letters **f, h, k, l, m, n, p, t, x** are pronounced the same as in English.

Although the English "r" is represented as "r" in the phonetic script of this book, it's pronounced differently. In German, you don't roll the "r": position your tongue as if you want to make the "r" sound but instead of rolling the tip of your tongue off your palate, leave the tongue straight and try to produce the sound in the back of your throat!

Table 1-5 tells you how the rest of the German consonants are pronounced by providing you with examples and a phonetic script.

Table 1-5	Pronouncing German Selected Consonants		
German Letter	*Symbol*	*As in English*	*German Word*
b	p	up / Peter	**Abfahrt** *(âp-fahrt)* (departure)
b	b	bright	**Bild** *(bîlt)* (image, picture)
c	k	cat	**Café** *(kâ-feh)* (café)

German Letter	Symbol	As in English	German Word
c	ts	tsar	**Celsius** *(tsêl-zî-ûs)* (Celsius)
c	tsh	cello	**Cello** *(tshê-loh)*
d	t	"t" as in moot	**blind** *(blînt)* (blind)
d	d	do	**durstig** *(dûrstigk)* (thirsty)
g	gg	o	**geben** *(geh-ben)* (give)
g	gk	lag	**Tag** *(tahgk)* (day)
j	y	es	**ja** *(yah)* (yes)
qu	kv	quick	**Quatsch** *(kvâtsh)* (nonsense)
s (beginning of a word)	z	zoo	**sieben** *(zee-ben)* (seven)
s (middle / end of a word)	s	sit	**Haus** *(hows)* (house)
v	f	"f" as in fire	**Vogel** *(foh-gel)* (bird)
v	v	velvet	**Vase** *(vah-ze)* (vase)
w	v	vice	**Wald** *(vâlt)* (forest)
y	y	yes	**Yoga** *(yoh-gâ)* (yoga)
y	uu	syllable	**System** *(zuus-tehm)* (system)
z	ts	"ts" as in tsar	**Zahl** *(tsahl)* (number)

Learning a new letter: ß

In written German, you come across a letter, **ß** *(ês-tsêt)*, which is a combination of the letters **s** *(ês)* and **z** *(tsêt)* and is pronounced as a sharp "s." It's considered a single consonant but isn't an additional letter of the alphabet.

There used to be quite a few German words that were spelled either with "ss" or "ß" (the sound is identical) and it was tricky to get the spelling right. The German language has recently undergone a spelling reform which solved this problem. Here's the scoop:

- ✔ After a long vowel, the sharp "s" is spelled "ß" — for example in **Fuß** *(foos)* (foot).

- ✔ After a short vowel, the sharp "s" is spelled "ss" — for example in **Fass** *(fâs)* (barrel).

Please note that in Switzerland, the ß is not used at all. Instead, they always spell words with the double "ss."

Pronouncing combinations of consonants

The German language has a few combinations of consonants that don't occur in the English language. Most of them are easy to pronounce, with the exception of "ch," which is unfamiliar to the English tongue.

Pronouncing "ch"

The letter combination **ch** is the trickiest one in the German language and the most difficult one to learn for English speakers. There is absolutely no equivalent for it in English (that's why it's represented by a capital "H" in the phonetic script in this book), and you actually have to learn a new sound — a kind of gargling hiss — in order to say it.

Try to approximate this sound by starting with the way you pronounce the letter "h" in the beginning of the word human and then drawing out and emphasizing the "h." The "ch" sound is produced at the same place in the back of your throat as the "k" sound. But instead of rolling your tongue in the back of your mouth — as you do when you pronounce a "k" — you have to lower it and bring it forward to your front teeth. If you practice it a little, you shouldn't have problems pronouncing the words **ich** *(îH)* (I) and **vielleicht** *(fee-lyHt)* (perhaps).

The good news is that there are a couple of words where "ch" is simply pronounced as a "k," for example in **Wachs** *(vâks)* (wax) or **Lachs** *(lâks)* (salmon).

Pronouncing ck, sch, sp, and st

Table 1-6 shows you how to pronounce some other common consonant combinations.

Table 1-6	Pronouncing ck, sch, sp, and st		
German Letter	*Symbol*	*As in English*	*German Word*
ck	k	check	**Dreck** *(drêk)* (dirt)
sch	sh	shut	**Tisch** *(tîsh)* (table)
sp	shp	"sh" as in shut and "p" as in people	**spät** *(shpait)* (late)
st (beginning of a word)	sht	"sh" as in shut and "t" as in table	**Stadt** *(shtât)* (city)
st (middle / end of a word)	st	stable	**Last** *(lâst)* (burden)
tsch	tsh	switch	**Deutsch** *(doytsh)* (German)

There is no English "th" sound in the German language. The "h" is either silent, as in the words **Theorie** *(teh-oh-ree)* (theory) or **Theologie** *(teh-oh-lô-gee)* (theology). Or, the letters "t" and "h" are pronounced separately, because they actually belong to different components of a compound noun, as in the words **Rasthaus** *(râst-hows)* (inn) or **Basthut** *(bâst-hoot)* (straw hat).

Chapter 2

The Nitty Gritty: Basic German Grammar

*W*hen thinking about grammar, you might imagine a great big dresser with lots of drawers. But instead of being filled with plenty of clothing, the dresser drawers contain different parts of speech (nouns, verbs, adjectives, and adverbs), a separate drawer for each part of speech. Now imagine it's early morning and you are about to utter your first German sentence of the day. To begin with, you reach into the drawer marked nouns and pull out the word **Socken** (*zô-kn*) (socks). Next, you need to describe your socks, so you reach into the drawer marked adjectives and pull out the word **grün** (*gruun*) (green). So what to do with your green socks? Well you put them on, of course. So you fish through the verb drawer and pull out the verb **anziehen** (*ân-tseen*) (to put on). You're doing great so far, but then you look up at the clock and see that are you are running late. What to do? You dive straight into the adverb drawer and grab the word **schnell** (*shnêl*) (quickly). Before you know it, you have pulled a complete sentence out of the dresser: **Ich ziehe schnell die grünen Socken an.** (*îH tsee-he shnêl dee gruu-nen zô-kn ân*) (I quickly put my green socks on.)

This chapter makes using grammar as easy as getting dressed in the morning. At first, you might be full of indecision, but once you get the hang of some basic rules, you'll be using grammar without thinking — just like the natives. Go with the flow, keep your cool, and you'll be alright.

Throughout this book you encounter dialogs that use basic grammar in sentences that you will also be able to hear on the accompanying CD. Important grammar points are explained in short sections marked with a Grammatically Speaking icon. And then before you know it, you will be out the door and speaking German.

Types of Words

To construct a simple sentence, you need a certain number of building elements: nouns, adjectives, verbs, and adverbs are the most important types of words.

Nouns

All German nouns have genders. They can be masculine, feminine, or neuter. And most of them can be singular or plural.

Nouns usually appear in the company of articles like "the" or "a." The best way to familiarize yourself with the gender of a German noun is to remember the word together with its definite article, which indicates the word's gender. The English definite article "the" is transformed into the German **der** *(dehr)* (masculine), **die** *(dee)* (feminine), or **das** *(dâs)* (neuter) depending on the gender of the noun.

When meeting new nouns, remember the word together with its definite article. For example, memorize **der Garten** *(dehr gârtn)* (the garden) rather than just **Garten** *(gârtn)* (garden), **die Tür** *(dee tuur)* (the door) rather than **Tür** *(tuur)* (door), and **das Haus** *(dâs hows)* (the house) rather than **Haus** *(hows)* (house).

In the plural, things are comparatively easy. The definite article for all plural words is **die** *(dee)*. And, as in English, the indefinite article "a" just vanishes in the plural: "a garden" becomes "gardens."

In the various cases, on the other hand, the three definite articles **der, die,** and **das** go through all kinds of permutations. Read the section "Putting the Language in the Proper Case" later in this chapter to encounter their different incarnations.

Adjectives

Adjectives describe nouns. In German, adjectives have different endings depending on the gender, case (more about that later in this chapter), and number (singular or plural) of the noun they accompany, and depending on whether the adjective is accompanied by a definite article, indefinite article, or no article at all.

These are the endings for adjectives accompanied by a definite article: We use the adjectives **schön** (*shuon*) (beautiful), **weiß** (*vys*) (white), **groß** (*grohs*) (large), and **klein** (*klyn*) (small) as examples. The adjective endings appear in italics:

- **der schön*e* Garten** (*dehr shuo-ne gâr-tn*) (the beautiful garden)
- **die weiß*e* Tür** (*dee vy-sse tuur*) (the white door)
- **das klein*e* Haus** (*dâss kly-ne hows*) (the small house)
- **die groß*en* Häuser** (*dee groh-ssn hoi-zer*) (the large houses)

These are the endings for adjectives accompanied by an indefinite article:

- **ein schön*er* Garten** (*ayn shuo-ner gâr-tn*) (a beautiful garden)
- **eine weiß*e* Tür** (*ay-ne vy-sse tuur*) (a white door)
- **ein klein*es* Haus** (*ayn kly-nes hows*) (a small house)
- **groß*e* Häuser** (*groh-sse hoi-zer*) (large houses)

These are the endings for adjectives when used alone:

- **schön*er* Garten** (*shuo-ner gâr-tn*) (beautiful garden)
- **weiß*e* Tür** (*vy-sse tuur*) (white door)
- **klein*es* Haus** (*kly-nes hows*) (small house)
- **groß*e* Häuser** (*groh-sse hoi-zer*) (large houses)

These are the adjective endings in the subject case (or nominative case). The endings for the other cases follow a little later.

If the adjective is not preceded by a definite article, the adjective takes the ending of the definite article.

Verbs

Verbs express actions or states. The person doing the action is its subject, and the verb always adjusts its ending to the subject. For example, the door opens, but the doors open, and so on.

The verb form that has no marking to indicate its subject or a tense (past, present, or future) is called the *infinitive*. German infinitives usually have the ending **–en,** as in **lachen** (*lâ-Hen*) (to laugh). Some verbs end in **-n, -rn,** or **-ln.** In English the infinitive is usually preceded by "to."

Regular verbs don't change their stem, and their endings are always the same.

Here are the endings of the verb **sagen** *(sah-ghen)* (to say), tagged on to its stem **sag-** :

ich sag-e (I say)

du sag-st (you [informal] say)

Sie sag-en (you [formal] say)

er, sie, es sag-t (he/she/it says)

wir sag-en (we say)

ihr sag-t (you [informal, plural] say)

Sie sag-en (you [formal, plural] say)

sie sag-en (they say)

Seems easy, doesn't it? But there are — as usual — some exceptions to the rule: When the stem of the verb ends in **-m**, **-n**, **-d**, or **-t**, you have to insert an **-e** before the ending in the **du**, **er/sie/es**, and **ihr** constructions:

du atm-e-st (you [informal] breathe)

er arbeit-e-t (he works)

ihr bad-e-t (you [informal, plural] bathe)

Why do they do that? Try to pronounce "atmst," and you'll figure out why.

Adverbs

Adverbs accompany verbs or adjectives and describe them. In English, most adverbs end with -ly (as in: I quickly put my green socks on.) In German, adverbs are most often adjectives with unmodified endings.

Simple Sentence Construction

Nouns, verbs, adjectives, and adverbs are usually not thrown together haphazardly; words are arranged into sentences according to certain rules.

Arranging words in the right order

"Normal" word order in German is much like English word order. The subject comes first, followed by the verb, followed by the rest of the sentence. Unless there is a reason not to use it, this is the word order to follow.

Subject	Verb	Object
Meine Freundin	**hat**	**einen VW-Bus.**
_my_-ne _froyn_-dīn	hât	_ay_-nen fow-_veh_ būs
My girlfriend	has	a VW van

Putting the verb in second place

One of the most important things to remember is the place of the verb in a German sentence. In independent clauses, like the one in the preceding section, and in the following sentence, the verb is always in second place, no matter what.

> **Meine Freundin fährt nach Dänemark.** (_my_-ne _froyn_-dīn fehrt nâH _deh_-ne-mârk) (My girlfriend drives to Denmark.)

How about adding some more information?

> **Meine Freundin fährt morgen nach Dänemark.** (_my_-ne _froyn_-dīn fehrt môrgn nâH _deh_-ne-mârk) (My girlfriend is drives to Denmark tomorrow.)

Again, the verb is in second place.

What happens if the sentence starts with **morgen** (_môrgn_) (tomorrow)?

> **Morgen fährt meine Freundin nach Dänemark.**

Morgen is in first place, and the verb has to be in second place, so the subject follows the verb. Technically, this is called _inversion of the verb_. All it means is that verb and subject switch places. This happens whenever there is anything other than the subject in the first place of a sentence.

Having said that, what about the very first statement in this section? Can you give that one a twirl and change the word order? Absolutely, as long as the verb stays in second place. **Meine Freundin hat einen VW-Bus** becomes **Einen VW-Bus hat meine Freundin.** No problem. But why would you want to do that? Generally, to shift emphasis. For example, you might want to say

Hat deine Schwester einen VW-Bus? Nein, meine Schwester hat einen BMW. Einen VW-Bus hat meine Freundin Heike. *(hât dy-ne shvês-ter ay-nen fow-veh bûs? nyn, my-ne shvês-ter hât ay-nen beh-em-veh. ay-nen fow-veh bûs hât my-ne froyn-dîn hy-ke)* (Does your sister have a VW van? No, my sister has a BMW. It's my girlfriend Heike who has a VW van.)

Fährt deine Freundin heute nach Dänemark? Nein, morgen fährt sie nach Dänemark. *(fehrt dy-ne froyn-dîn hoy-te nâH dehne-mârk? nyn, môrgn fehrt zee nâH dehne-mârk)* (Is your girlfriend driving to Denmark today? No, tomorrow she drives to Denmark.)

Don't German speakers get all confused playing around with word order like that? That's where the famous German case system comes into play. The adjectives and articles that accompany nouns, and in some cases, the nouns themselves, assume different endings depending on their function in a sentence. So no matter where a noun appears in a sentence, you know what its role is by checking the ending of the article (and/or adjective) accompanying it. See "Putting the Language in the Right Case" later in this chapter for the details.

Pushing the verb to the end

The examples used so far in this section have all been independent, stand-alone sentences, but sometimes several statements combine to form a more complex structure:

> **Meine Freundin sagt, dass sie nach Dänemark fährt.** *(my-ne froyn-dîn zahgt, dâs zee nâH dehne-mârk fehrt)* (My girlfriend says that she drives to Denmark.)

The main verb **sagt** *(zahgt)* (says) is in second place where you would expect it, but the verb in the second clause introduced by **dass** *(dâs)* (that) goes all the way to the end. That happens in all dependent clauses.

Dependent clauses typically start with (subordinating) conjunctions (words that link sentences) like **dass, weil, damit** *(dâs, vyl, dâ-mît)* (that, because, so that), and they always end with the verb.

Forming questions

The German word order for asking questions corresponds nicely to the English word order for questions. You begin with a verb and the subject follows.

> **Fährt deine Freundin nach Dänemark?** *(fehrt dy-ne froyn-dîn nâH dehne-mârk)* (Is your girlfriend driving to Denmark?)

Hat deine Freundin einen VW-Bus? *(hât <u>dy</u>-ne <u>froyn</u>-dîn <u>ay</u>-nen fow-<u>veh</u>-bûs)* (Does your girlfriend have a VW van?)

Note that you don't have to worry about the verb "do" in German when forming questions.

Another way to elicit information is to form a question using a question word like **wer?** *(vehr)* (who?), **was?** *(vâs)* (what?), **wo?** *(voh)* (where?), **wann?** *(vân)* (when?), **wie?** *(vee)* (how?), or **warum?** *(vah-<u>rûm</u>)* (why?). You can also form a question with words and phrases like **was für ein(e/en) . . .?** *(vâs fuur ayn/e/en)* (what kind of . . .?) or **welche/r/s . . .?** *(vêl-He/r/s?)* (which?). When forming questions with these words, the verb goes in its usual place — second:

- ✔ **Wer fährt nach Dänemark?** *(vehr fehrt nâH <u>dehne</u>-mârk)* (Who drives to Denmark?)

- ✔ **Was für ein Auto hat deine Freundin?** *(vâs fuur ayn <u>ow</u>-tô hât <u>dy</u>-ne <u>froyn</u>-dîn)* (What kind of car does your girlfriend have?)

- ✔ **Wann fährt sie nach Dänemark?** *(vân fehrt zee nâH <u>dehne</u>-mârk)* (When does she drive to Denmark?)

- ✔ **Wie kommt deine Freundin nach Dänemark?** *(vee kômt <u>dy</u>-ne <u>froyn</u>-dîn nâH <u>dehne</u>-mârk)* (How does your girlfriend get to Denmark?)

The Tenses: Past, Present, and Future

"Tense" is the grammarians' preferred word for "time". Depending when the action that you're talking about is taking place, you pick a tense. The ways to look at the concept of time differ slightly from one culture and language to the next, so the way tenses are used sometimes differs, too.

Looking at the present

The present tense is a very useful tense in German. You can get a long way with just this one tense. The German present tense corresponds to three forms in English. For example, **ich denke** *(îH <u>dên</u>-ke)* can be used as the equivalent of "I think," "I do think," or "I am thinking" in English. And depending on the context, German present tense may even be rendered with another tense, future or past, in English.

The present tense is used to describe what's happening now:

- ✔ **Was machst du gerade?** *(vâs mâHst dû ge-<u>rah</u>-de)* (What are you doing right now?)

✔ **Ich lese die Zeitung.** *(īH leh-ze dee tsy-tûng)* (I am reading the newspaper.)

The present tense can also describe what happens sometimes, usually, or always:

> **Freitags gehe ich oft ins Kino.** *(fry-tahgks geh-e īH ôft īns kee-nô)* (On Fridays, I often go to the movies.)

The present tense can also describe what's going to happen:

✔ **Morgen fährt meine Freundin nach Dänemark.** *(môrgn fehrt my-ne froyn-dīn nâH dehne-mârk)* (Tomorrow my girlfriend will drive to Denmark.)

✔ **Nächste Woche fahre ich nach Bremen.** *(naiH-ste vô-He fah-re īH nâH breh-men)* (Next week I am going to drive to Bremen.)

This is a very common way of talking about future events in German, particularly if there's a time expression in the sentence which anchors the action clearly in the future — for example, **nächste Woche** *(naiH-ste vô-He)* (next week) or **morgen** *(môrgn)* (tomorrow).

And finally, the present tense can also describe what's been happening up to now:

> **Ich bin seit drei Tagen in Hamburg.** *(īH bīn zyt dry tah-gn īn hâm-bûrg)* (I have been in Hamburg for three days.)

Note that English uses present perfect tense to say the same type of thing.

Talking about the past: using the perfect tense

Perfect tense is the main past tense used in spoken German. It is very versatile: You can use it to talk about most actions and situations in the past. Contrast this with the English perfect tense (I have gone, I have read, and so on), which can only be used in certain specific contexts. For example, "I have seen Anna last week" would be incorrect English, but **Ich habe Anna letzte Woche gesehen** *(īH hah-be ânâ lêts-te vô-He ge-zehn)* is a correct German statement.

Most verbs form the perfect tense with the verb **haben** *(hah-ben)* (have):

✔ **David hat mir geholfen.** *(dah-veed hât meer ge-hôlfn)* (David has helped me /has been helping me / helped me.)

✔ **Gestern haben wir ein Auto gekauft.** *(gês-tern hah-bn veer ayn ow-tô ge-kowft)* (Yesterday we bought a car.)

✔ **Anna hat die Zeitung gelesen.** *(ânâ hât dee <u>tsy</u>-tûng ge-<u>lehzn</u>)* (Anna has read the newspaper / read the newspaper.)

✔ **Ich habe den Film gesehen.** *(îH <u>hah</u>-be dehn film ge-<u>zehn</u>)* (I have seen the film. / I saw the film.)

Certain verbs require **sein** *(zyn)* (to be) instead of **haben** *(<u>hah</u>-ben)* (to have) to form the perfect tense. These verbs often describe some form of movement or a state. Here are a few examples:

✔ **Ich bin ins Kino gegangen.** *(îH bîn îns <u>kee</u>-nô ge-<u>gân</u>-gen)* (I have gone to the movies / went to the movies.)

✔ **Meine Freundin ist nach Dänemark gefahren.** *(<u>my</u>-ne <u>froyn</u>-dîn îst nâH <u>dehne</u>-mârk ge-<u>fah</u>-ren)* (My girlfriend has gone to Denmark / went to Denmark.)

✔ **Ich bin in Hamburg gewesen.** *(îH bîn în <u>hâm</u>-bûrg ge-<u>vehzn</u>)* (I have been to Hamburg. / I was in Hamburg.)

✔ **Du bist mit dem Auto gekommen.** *(dû bîst mît dehm <u>ow</u>-tô ge-<u>kô</u>-men)* (You came by car. / You have come by car.)

✔ **Sie ist mit dem Zug gefahren.** *(zee îst mît dehm tsoogk ge-<u>fah</u>-ren)* (She has gone by train. / She went by train.)

✔ **Wir sind letzte Woche ins Kino gegangen.** *(veer zînt <u>lêts</u>-te <u>wô</u>-He îns <u>kee</u>-nô ge-<u>gân</u>-gen)* (We went to the movies last week.)

✔ **Seid ihr durch den Park gelaufen?** *(zyt eer dûrH dehn pârk ge-<u>low</u>-fen)* (Have you run through the park? / Did you run through the park?)

✔ **Sie sind gestern im Theater gewesen.** *(zee zînt <u>gês</u>-tern îm teh-<u>ah</u>-ter ge-<u>veh</u>-zen)* (They were at the theater yesterday.)

German verbs fall into two categories: weak and strong verbs. Regular verbs, known as weak verbs, form the largest group of German verbs.

Forming the past participle of a weak verb

Here is the formula for forming the past participle of a weak verb:

> **ge + verb stem (the infinitive minus -en) + (e)t = past participle**

For example, for the verb **fragen** *(<u>frah</u>-gen)* (to ask), here's how the formula would play out:

> **ge + frag + t = gefragt**

Forming the past participle of a strong verb

Here is the formula for forming the past participle of a strong verb:

> **ge + verb stem (the infinitive minus -en) + en = past participle**

For the verb **kommen** (*kô-men*) (to come), the past participle would be:

ge + komm + en = gekommen

See Chapter 7 for more information on the perfect tense.

Writing about the past: using simple past tense

Simple past tense is used all the time in newspapers, books, and so on, but it is less common in speech. For this reason, you don't come across it much in this book. One exception is the simple past tense of **sein** (*zyn*) (to be). This is often used in preference to perfect tense in both speech and writing. Table 2-1 shows you the various forms of the simple past tense of sein.

Table 2-1	Simple Past Tense Forms of sein	
Conjugation	*Pronunciation*	*Translation*
ich war	(*îH vahr*)	I was
du warst	(*dû vahrst*)	you were (informal)
Sie waren	(*zee vah-ren*)	you were (formal)
er / sie / es war	(*ehr / zee / ês vahr*)	he / she / it was
wir waren	(*veer vah-ren*)	we were
ihr wart	(*eer vahrt*)	you were (informal)
Sie waren	(*zee vah-ren*)	you were (formal)
sie waren	(*zee vah-ren*)	they were

Talking about the future

In German, the future tense is not used as consistently as it is in English. In many situations, you can use the present tense instead (see "Looking at the present" in this chapter). When talking about things that are going to take place in the future, you can, of course, use future tense. The way to form future tense in German is pretty similar to English. You take the verb **werden** (*vehr-den*) (to become) and add an infinitive.

Table 2-2 shows you the forms of **werden** in the present tense.

Table 2-2	Present Tense Forms of werden	
Conjugation	*Pronunciation*	*Translation*
ich werde	*(îH vehr-de)*	I will
du wirst	*(dû vîrst)*	you will (informal)
Sie werden	*(zee vehr-dn)*	you will (formal)
er / sie / es wird	*(ehr / zee / ês vîrt)*	he / she / it will
wir werden	*(veer vehr-dn)*	we will
ihr werdet	*(eer vehr-det)*	you will (informal)
Sie werden	*(zee vehr-dn)*	you will (formal)
sie werden	*(zee vehr-dn)*	they will

And this is how you incorporate future tense into sentences:

> ✔ **Ich werde anrufen.** *(îH vehr-de ân-roo-fen)* (I am going to call.)
>
> ✔ **Wir werden morgen kommen.** *(veer vehr-dn môr-gn kô-men)* (We will come tomorrow.)
>
> ✔ **Es wird regnen.** *(ês vîrt rehg-nen)* (It will rain. / It's going to rain.)

Putting the Language in the Right Case

All languages have ways of showing what role each noun is playing in a particular sentence; for example, who (or what) is doing what to whom. In English, you show a noun's role mainly by its position in a sentence. German speakers, on the other hand, indicate the function of a noun in a sentence mainly by adding endings to any articles or adjectives accompanying that noun (and sometimes to the noun itself).

When they are used in a sentence, nouns appear in one of four cases, depending on their role in the sentence: nominative for the subject, accusative for the direct object, dative for the indirect object, and genitive for the genitive object (possessive). In this book you mainly encounter the nominative, accusative, and dative cases. The genitive case is used less frequently; we only mention it here for the sake of completeness.

Nominative case

The subject of a sentence is always in the nominative case. As a rule of thumb, the subject is the person or thing performing the action of the verb. For example, in the sentence **Der Junge nimmt den Kuchen** *(dehr yûn-ge nîmt dehn koo-Hn)* (The boy takes the cake.), the boy is the one taking the cake: He is the subject of the sentence.

Accusative case

The direct object of the sentence is always in the accusative case. The direct object is the person or thing directly affected by the action of the verb. So in the sentence **Der Junge nimmt den Kuchen** *(dehr yûn-ge nîmt dehn koo-Hn)* (The boy takes the cake.), the cake is the direct object — it is the thing that's being taken.

Dative case

The indirect object of the sentence is always in the dative case. Think of the indirect object as the person or thing indirectly affected by the action of the verb. For example, in the sentence **Der Junge gibt dem Hund den Kuchen** *(dehr yûn-ge gîpt dehm hûnt dehn koo-Hn)* (The boy gives the dog the cake.), the dog is the indirect object, the one to whom the boy gives the cake. (The cake is the direct object, the thing which is given.)

If there are two objects in a sentence, one of them is probably an indirect object. If in doubt, try translating the sentence into English: If you can put "to" before any of the nouns, that is the indirect object in the German sentence.

Genitive case

The genitive case is used to indicate possession. The person or thing that possesses is in the genitive case. For example, in the phrase **der Hund des Jungen** *(dehr hûnt dês yûn-gen)* (the boy's dog), it's the boy who possesses the dog, so it's the boy who is in the genitive case.

Why all these cases matter

You may be asking why we're making such a big deal about this case business. Unfortunately, learning about the various cases is a complicated, but necessary, step when learning German. You see, the different cases make pronouns change form. And the cases also make the endings of articles and adjectives change. Read on for the nitty gritty.

How pronouns change

Pronouns are useful little words that can replace nouns. Pronouns are used instead of nouns as a way to avoid clumsy repetition.

Pronouns change form depending on how they are used in a sentence.

Table 2-3 shows you the pronouns in the subject case. And Table 2-4 shows you how the pronouns change according to case.

Table 2-3	Personal Pronouns in the Subject Case
German	*English*
ich	I
du	you (informal address)
German	*English*
Sie	you (formal address)
er / sie / es	he / she / it
wir	we
ihr	you (informal address)
Sie	you (formal address)
sie	they

Table 2-4		Personal Pronouns by Case	
Nominative	*Dative*	*Accusative*	*English*
ich	mir	mich	I, to me, me
du	dir	dich	you, to you, you (informal address)
Sie	Ihnen	Sie	you, to you, you (formal address)
er	ihm	ihn	he, to him, him
sie	ihr	sie	she, to her, her

(continued)

Table 2-4 (continued)

Nominative	Dative	Accusative	English
es	ihm	es	it, to it, it
wir	uns	uns	we, to us, us
ihr	euch	euch	you, to you, you (informal address)
Sie	Ihnen	Sie	you, to you, you (formal address)
sie	ihnen	sie	they, to them, them

Here is an example of the second person singular pronoun **du** appearing in the nominative, dative, and accusative cases depending on its function in a sentence.

- ✔ **Du** bist müde. *(dû bîst muu-de)* (You are tired.) du = nominative

- ✔ Ich gebe **dir** das Buch. *(îH geh-be deer dâs booH)* (I'm giving you the book.) dir = dative

- ✔ Ich frage **dich**. *(îH frah-ge dîH)* (I'm asking you.) dich = accusative

How indefinite articles change

The German indefinite article **ein** *(ayn)* (a) can assume different endings. Which ending it takes depends on whether it accompanies the subject of a sentence (nominative), a genitive object, the direct object (accusative), or the indirect object (dative).

Table 2-5 shows you the indefinite article **ein** being put through the paces of the various cases.

Table 2-5 — Endings of ein by Case

Gender	Nominative	Genitive	Dative	Accusative
Masculine	ein	eines	einem	einen
Feminine	eine	einer	einer	eine
Neuter	ein	eines	einem	ein

The following examples show the indefinite article **ein** with its appropriate masculine endings in the four different cases.

- ✔ **Ein** Wagen steht auf der Straße. *(ayn vah-gen shteht owf dehr shtrah-se)* (A car is standing on the road.) ein = nominative

✔ Du liest das Buch **eines** Freundes. *(dū leest dâs booH ay-nes froyn-des)* (You are reading a friend's book.) eines = genitive

✔ Ich leihe **einem** Freund mein Auto. *(īH ly-he ay-nem froynt myn ow-tô)* (I'm lending my car to a friend.) einem = dative

✔ Ich habe **einen** Hund. *(īH hah-be ay-nen hûnt)* (I have a dog.) einen = accusative

How definite articles change

The definite articles also morph depending on which case they are used in, as shown in Table 2-6.

Gender	Nominative	Genitive	Dative	Accusative
Masculine	der	des	dem	den
Feminine	die	der	der	die
Neuter	das	des	dem	das
Plural	die	der	den	die

Table 2-6 — Definite Articles by Case

The following examples show the masculine definite article **der** with its appropriate endings in the four different cases.

✔ **Der** Wagen steht auf der Straße. *(dehr vah-gen shteht owf dehr shtrah-se)* (The car is standing on the road.) der = nominative

✔ Du liest das Buch **des** Freundes. *(dū leest dâs booH dês froyn-dês)* (You are reading the friend's book.) des = genitive

✔ Ich leihe **dem** Freund mein Auto. *(īH ly-he dehm froynt myn ow-tô)* (I'm lending my car to the friend.) dem = dative

✔ Ich habe **den** Hund. *(īH hah-be dehn hûnt)* (I have the dog.) den = accusative

How possessives change

Possessive pronouns establish ownership. They mark the difference between what belongs to you ("your book") and what belongs to me ("my book"), and so on. Here is a run-through of the forms for the different persons:

✔ **mein** *(myn)* (my)

✔ **dein** *(dyn)* (your) (informal address)

✔ **Ihr** *(eer)* (your) (formal address)

- **sein / ihr / sein** *(zyn / eer / zyn)* (his / her / its)
- **unser** *(ûn-zer)* (our)
- **euer** *(oy-er)* (your) (informal address)
- **Ihr** *(eer)* (your) (formal address)
- **ihr** *(eer)* (their)

Table 2-7 presents all the forms in the singular of a sample possessive, **mein** *(myn)*. The other possessives take the same endings. These endings may look familiar; they are the same as those for the indefinite article **ein**.

Table 2-7	Possessive Endings by Case			
Gender	**Nominative**	**Genitive**	**Dative**	**Accusative**
Masculine	mein	meines	meinem	meinen
Feminine	meine	meiner	meiner	meine
Neuter	mein	meines	meinem	mein

How adjective endings change

As mentioned in the beginning of this chapter, adjectives and articles accompanying nouns change their endings depending on the role of the noun in the sentence, as shown in Table 2-8.

Table 2-8	Endings for Adjectives Preceded by the Definite and Indefinite Articles			
Gender	**Nominative**	**Genitive**	**Dative**	**Accusative**
Masculine	e/er	en/en	en/en	en/en
Feminine	e/e	en/en	en/en	e/e
Neuter	e/es	en/en	en/en	e/es

To illustrate the endings shown in Table 2-8, we provide examples of nouns accompanied by an adjective and the definite or indefinite article, repectively in Table 2-9 and Table 2-10.

Table 2-9	Examples of Adjective Endings Preceded by Indefinite Articles			
Gender	**Nominative**	**Genitive**	**Dative**	**Accusative**
Masculine	ein schöner Garten	eines schönen Gartens	einem schönen Garten	einen schönen Garten
Feminine	eine weiße	einer weißen Tür	einer weißen Tür	eine weiße Tür
Neuter	ein kleines Haus	eines kleinen Hauses	einem kleinen Haus	ein kleines Haus

Table 2-10	Examples of Adjective Endings Preceded by Definite Articles			
Gender	**Nominative**	**Genitive**	**Dative**	**Accusative**
Masculine	der schöne Garten	des schönen Gartens	dem schönen Garten	den schönen Garten
Feminine	die weiße Tür	der weißen Tür	der weißen Tür	die weiße Tür
Neuter	das kleine Haus	des kleinen Hauses	dem kleinen Haus	das kleine Haus

Numbers

Chances are that you won't need to worry about numbers much beyond using them to tell time (which we talk about in Chapter 7) or exchange money (see Chapter 11). Knowing the following numbers should make it easy to do any counting you may need to do.

0 null (*nûl*)

1 eins (*ayns*)

2 zwei (*tsvy*)

3 drei (*dry*)

4 vier (*veer*)

5 fünf (*fuunf*)

6 sechs (*zêks*)

7 sieben (*zeebn*)

8 acht *(āHt)*	**23 dreiundzwanzig** *(dry-ūnt-tsvân-tsîgk)*
9 neun *(noyn)*	**24 vierundzwanzig** *(feer-ūnt-tsvân-tsîgk)*
10 zehn *(tsehn)*	**25 fünfundzwanzig** *(fuunf-ūnt-tsvân-tsîgk)*
11 elf *(êlf)*	**30 dreissig** *(dry-sîgk)*
12 zwölf *(tsvuolf)*	**40 vierzig** *(fīr-tsîgk)*
13 dreizehn *(dry-tsehn)*	**50 fünfzig** *(fuunf-tsîgk)*
14 vierzehn *(feer-tsehn)*	**60 sechzig** *(sêH-tsîgk)*
15 fünfzehn *(fuunf-tsehn)*	**70 siebzig** *(zeep-tsîgk)*
16 sechzehn *(zêH-tsehn)*	**80 achtzig** *(āH-tsîgk)*
17 siebzehn *(zeeb-tsehn)*	**90 neunzig** *(noyn-tsîgk)*
18 achtzehn *(āH-tsehn)*	**100 hundert** *(hūn-dert)*
19 neunzehn *(noyn-tsehn)*	**200 zweihundert** *(tsvy-hūn-dert)*
20 zwanzig *(tsvân-tsîgk)*	**300 dreihundert** *(dry-hūn-dert)*
21 einundzwanzig *(ayn-ūnt-tsvân-tsîgk)*	**400 vierhundert** *(feer-hūn-dert)*
22 zweiundzwanzig *(tsvy-ūnt-tzvân-tsîgk)*	**500 fünfhundert** *(fuunf-hūn-dert)*
	1000 tausend *(tow-zent)*

Many of the numbers between 20 and 100 may appear a bit backwards at first. Just look at 21, **einundzwanzig** *(ayn-ūnt-tsvân-tsîgk)* in German. What you actually say is "one and twenty." Just remember to stick to this pattern for all the double-digit numbers.

Chapter 3

Guten Tag! Hallo! Greetings and Introductions

. . . .

In This Chapter

▶ Addressing people formally or informally

▶ Saying hello

▶ Introducing yourself and your friends

▶ Asking about cities, countries, and nationalities

▶ Saying good-bye

. . . .

Greetings and introductions are the first steps in establishing contact with other people and making an important first impression. Handled correctly, this first contact can open doors for you and help you meet people. If you botch your greetings and introductions, you may at best encounter a quizzical look — in the worst case scenario, you could actually offend the person you are addressing! Read on for specifics.

Getting Formal or Informal

Germans tend to have a reputation for being formal, an impression that might, at least to some extent, be created by the distinction they make between different ways of saying "you." In German, you use either the formal **Sie** *(zee)* or the informal **du** *(dū)* — depending on who you are addressing.

Observing the distinction between the two forms of "you" is quite important: People will consider you fresh and impolite if you use the informal way of addressing them in a situation that asks for more formality.

In general, you use the formal **Sie** when addressing somebody you have never met, an official, a superior, or someone who is older than you. As you get to know somebody better, you may switch to **du.** There even is a verb for using the informal "you" — **duzen** *(dū-tsen).* **Wir duzen uns.** *(veer dū-tsen ūnts)* means "We are using the informal you."

However, there are no fixed rules and a lot of exceptions when it comes to using **du** or **Sie.** For example, say that you're traveling in Germany and one of your German friends takes you to a party. Even though you haven't met any of the people there, they may just address you with **du,** which is particularly true if they are younger, and they will probably expect you to address them with **du.** Basically, it all depends on the environment you find yourself in. In some offices, co-workers address each other with **du,** and in others, everybody sticks to the formal **Sie.**

If you are the least bit unsure of whether to use **du** or **Sie,** use **Sie** until the person you are addressing asks you to use **du** or addresses you with **du.**

Discovering Common Greetings and Salutations

The first part of your greeting is a basic hello. How you say hello depends upon what time of day it is. The most commonly used hellos include the following:

- ✔ **Guten Morgen!** *(gûtn môr-gn)* (Good morning!) This is the greeting you use in the morning (until about noon).
- ✔ **Guten Tag!** *(gûtn tahgk)* (Good day!) This is the most common greeting you use, except early in the morning and late in the day.
- ✔ **Guten Abend!** *(gûtn ah-bnt)* (Good evening!) Obviously, this is the greeting of choice in the evening.
- ✔ **Gute Nacht!** *(gû-te nâHt)* (Good night!) This is the greeting you use when you say goodbye late at night.
- ✔ **Hallo!** *(hâ-lo)* (Hello!) You should be pretty familiar with this greeting since it's basically the same in English.

Asking "How are you?"

The question "How are you?" is an important part of meeting and greeting in German. This question usually comes right after your initial hello. When you ask, you either use the formal or the informal version of the question, depending on who you are talking to, which makes things slightly more complicated. But don't worry, it's easier than you might think.

Before you find out more about meeting and greeting, it's important for you to know that the words **ich** *(îH)* (I), **du** *(dû)* (you, informal), and **Sie** *(zee)* (you, formal) can change form depending on how they are used in a sentence. In German, asking "How are you?" and saying "I'm fine" requires a

Mr., Mrs., and the forbidden Miss

Herr *(hair)* is the German word for "Mr.," and **Frau** *(frow),* which literally means "woman" and also is the German word for "wife," corresponds to "Mrs." and "Ms." German also has the word **Fräulein** *(froy-lyn),* which used to be the German version of "Miss", but you definitely shouldn't try it on anyone — unless you want to get whopped over the head.

Fräulein doesn't simply correspond to the English "Miss" — the syllable "lein" is a diminutive form and "Fräulein" literally means "little woman." Many modern German women find this reference offensive, and it is rarely used, so you should always address a woman as **Frau,** regardless of her age or marital status.

different form of the personal pronouns **ich, du,** or **Sie** — the form taken in the dative case. (See Chapter 2 for more information on the dative case.)

Table 3-1 shows you how it works.

Table 3-1	Personal Pronouns, Dative Case	
Pronoun	*Nominative Case*	*Dative Case*
I	ich	mir
you (informal)	du	dir
you (formal)	Sie	Ihnen

The formal version of "How are you?" is

> **Wie geht es Ihnen?** *(vee geht êss <u>ee</u>-nen)* (How are you?)

The literal translation of the German expression is actually closer to the English "How is it going?" and is combined with the formal "Ihnen," so it would translate into "How is it going with you?"

More informally, you say

> **Wie geht es dir?** *(vee geht êss deer)* (How are you?)

Which means the same thing but uses the informal **dir.**

Meeting and greeting go hand in hand

Greetings and introductions are often accompanied by some form of body contact. In Germany, Austria, and Switzerland, hand-shaking is the most common form of body contact during greetings and introductions. Female friends often kiss each other on one cheek (kissing each other on both cheeks is less common) or give each other a hug. Men usually don't kiss and seldom hug each other, though they may greet a woman friend with a hug (and a kiss). In Germany, this type of contact is reserved only for very good friends. However, you may notice that people in Germany may stand closer to you than you are used to — for example, in stores, on the bus or subway, or while they are talking to you.

And if you really know someone well, you can go for the most casual version of the question:

> **Wie geht's?** *(vee gehts)* (How's it going?)

Replying to "How are you?"

In English, the question "How are you?" is often just a way of saying hello, and no one expects you to answer. In German, however, you are usually expected to reply. The following are acceptable answers to the question "How are you?":

- ✔ **Danke, gut.** *(dâng-ke, gût)* / **Gut, danke.** *(gût, dâng-ke)* (Thanks, I'm fine. / Fine, thanks.) The literal translation would be "Thanks, good" / "Good, thanks."
- ✔ **Sehr gut.** *(zehr gût)* (Very good.)
- ✔ **Ganz gut.** *(gânts gût)* (Pretty good.)
- ✔ **Es geht.** *(êss geht)* (So, so.) The German expression actually means "it goes" and implies that it's not going too well.
- ✔ **Nicht so gut.** *(nîHt zoh gût)* (Not so good.)

As in English, the reply would usually be accompanied by the question "And (how are) you?" which is an easy one. First the formal version:

> **Und Ihnen?** *(ûnt ee-nen)* (And you?)

And here's how you pose the question informally:

> **Und dir?** *(ûnt deer)* (And you?)

Talkin' the Talk

 In the following dialogue, you'll find some phrases that are commonly used for greetings in a more formal setting.

Herr Schulte: **Guten Tag, Frau Berger!**
gûtn tahgk, frow <u>bêr</u>-ger
Good day, Ms. Berger!

Frau Berger: **Herr Schulte, guten Tag! Wie geht es Ihnen?**
hêr <u>shûl</u>-tê, gûtn tahgk! vee geht êss <u>ee</u>-nen
Mr. Schulte, good day! How are you?

Herr Schulte: **Danke, gut! Und Ihnen?**
<u>dâng</u>-ke, gût! ûnt <u>ee</u>-nen
Thanks, I'm fine! And how are you?

Frau Berger: **Danke, auch gut.**
<u>dâng</u>-ke, owH gût.
Thanks, I'm fine, too.

Talkin' the Talk

 Now check out this dialog between Mike and Sylvia, two old friends who run into each other on the street.

Mike: **Hallo Sylvia!**
<u>hâ</u>-lo sylvia
Hello Sylvia!

Sylvia: **Michael, hallo! Wie geht's?**
mî-<u>Hâ</u>-êl <u>hâ</u>-lo! vee gehts
Michael, hello! How's it going?

Mike: **Danke, mir geht's gut! Und selbst?**
<u>dâng</u>-ke, meer gehts gût! oont zêlpst
Thanks, I'm fine! And yourself?

Sylvia: **Auch gut.**
owH gût
I'm fine, too.

Introducing Yourself and Your Friends

Meeting and greeting often requires introductions. You might be accompanied by friends when you meet somebody, or you might have to introduce your wife or husband to your boss at a formal dinner party. On some occasions, there won't be anyone to introduce you to the person you want to meet, and you have to do it yourself.

Introducing your friends

Commonplace, everyday introductions are easy to make. All you need are the words

> **Das ist . . .** *(dâs îsst)* (This is . . .)

Then you simply add the name of the person. To indicate that it is a friend of yours, you say

> **Das ist meine Freundin** (f) / **mein Freund** (m) . . . *(dâs îsst my-ne froyn-dîn / myn froynt)* (This is my friend . . .)

If you are introduced to somebody, you might want to say "Nice to meet you." In German, there's no very casual way of saying this, and if the introductions have been informal, you might just want to reply with a "Hallo" or "Guten Tag."

If the introductions have been slightly more formal, you express "Nice to meet you" by saying

> **Freut mich.** *(froyt mîH)* (I'm pleased.)

The person you have been introduced to might then reply

> **Mich auch.** *(mîH owH)* (Me, too.)

Talkin' the Talk

In the following dialog, Frau Berger, Herr Schulte, and Frau Lempert meet for the first time and are therefore using formal introductions.

Frau Berger: **Herr Schulte, das ist Frau Lempert.**
hêr shûl-tê, dâs îsst frow lêm-pert
Mr. Schulte, this is Ms. Lempert.

Herr Schulte: **Freut mich.**
froyt mîH
I'm pleased.

Frau
Lempert:
Mich auch.
mîH owH
Me, too.

More informally, the introduction would sound like this.

Karin:
Michael, das ist meine Freundin Ute.
mî-Hâ-êl, dâs îsst my-ne froyn-dîn oo-te
Michael, this is my friend Ute.

Michael:
Hallo Ute.
hâ-lo oo-te
Hello, Ute.

Introductions for special occasions

You might find yourself in a situation which calls for a very high level of formal introduction. Here are some of the phrases you would use then:

- **Darf ich Ihnen . . . vorstellen?** *(dârf îH ee-nen . . . fohr-shtêln)* (May I introduce you to . . .?)

- **Freut mich, Sie kennenzulernen.** *(froyt mîH, zee kên-nen-tsû-lêr-nen)* (I'm pleased to meet you.)

- **Meinerseits.** *(my-ner-zyts)* / **Ganz meinerseits.** *(gânts my-ner-zyts)* (Likewise.)

Though you would probably use the English expression "likewise," it is not the literal translation of the German expression used here. **Meinerseits** just means "mine" and **Ganz meinerseits** would be "all mine," which, in this case, is a short form of "the pleasure is all mine."

Talkin' the Talk

The following is a dialogue between the directors of two companies, Herr Kramer and Herr Huber. They meet at an official function, and Herr Huber introduces his wife.

Herr Kramer: **Guten Abend, Herr Huber!**
gûtn ah-bnt, hêr hoo-ber
Good evening, Mr. Huber!

Herr Huber: **Guten Abend! Herr Kramer. Darf ich Ihnen meine Frau vorstellen?**
gûtn ah-bnt! hêr krah-mer. dârf îH ee-nen my-nê frow fohr-shtêln
Good evening! Mr. Kramer. May I introduce you to my wife?

Herr Kramer: **Guten Abend, Frau Huber! Freut mich sehr, Sie kennenzulernen.**
gûtn ah-bnt frow hoo-bêr! froit mîH zehr zee kên-nen-tsû-lêr-nen
Good evening, Mrs. Huber! Very nice to meet you.

Frau Huber: **Ganz meinerseits, Herr Kramer.**
gânts my-ner-zyts, hêr krah-mer
Likewise, Mr. Kramer.

Words to Know

auch	owH	also
ganz	gânts	entirely, all
gut	gût	good
sehr	zehr	very
freuen	froyn	to be glad / delighted
gehen	gehn	to go
kennenlernen	kên-nen-lêr-nen	to become acquainted with / to get to know
vorstellen	fohr-shtêln	to introduce
der Freund (m)	der froynt	friend
die Freundin (f)	dee froyn-dîn	friend

Introducing yourself

There might be situations where you can't rely on somebody else to introduce you and have to do the job yourself. It's an easy thing to do, since
people often introduce themselves by just stating their name, even in a more
formal setting.

In German, there are two ways of telling people your name. One of them is

Mein Name ist . . . *(myn nah-me îsst)* (My name is . . .)

There also is a verb that expresses the same idea, **heißen** *(hy-ssen),* which
means "to be called":

Ich heiße . . . *(îH hy-sse)* (My name is . . .)

Talkin' the Talk

In the following conversation, Herr Hauser arrives at a meeting
with several people he hasn't been introduced to yet and is looking
for a seat at the conference table.

Herr Hauser: **Guten Tag! Ist der Platz noch frei?**
gûtn tahgk, îsst dehr plâts nôH fry
Good day! Is this seat still free?

Frau Berger: **Ja, bitte.**
yah, bî-te
Yes, please.

Herr Hauser: **Vielen Dank. Mein Name ist Max Hauser.**
fee-lên dângk. myn nah-me îsst mâx how-ser
Thank you very much. My name is Max Hauser.

Frau Berger: **Freut mich. Karin Berger.**
froyt mîH. kah-rîn bêr-ger
I'm pleased. Karin Berger.

The previous conversation would sound entirely different if it took
place among younger people who meet in an informal setting, like
a party. They would forego any formalities and would probably
introduce each other like this:

Martin:	**Hallo, wie heißt Du?**
	hâ-lo, vee hysst dû
	Hello, what's your name?
Susanne:	**Ich heiße Susanne. Und Du?**
	îH hy-ssê zoo-zâ-ne. ûnt dû
	My name is Susanne. And you?
Martin:	**Martin. Und wer ist das?**
	mâr-tîn. ûnt vear îsst dâss
	Martin. And who is that?
Susanne:	**Das ist meine Freundin Anne.**
	dâss îsst my-ne froyn-dîn ân-ne
	This is my friend Anne.

Talking about Cities, Countries, and Nationalities

Introducing yourself is a good start, but it still doesn't make a conversation, which is the only way to get to know somebody. As you've seen, quite a lot of people around the world speak German, and quite a lot of people like to visit places where German is spoken. In this section, you learn how to tell people what city or country you are from and to ask them where they come from and what languages they speak.

Telling people where you come from

It's basically easy to say where you're from in German — the magic words are

> **Ich komme aus . . .** *(îH kô-me ows)* (I come from . . .)

> **Ich bin aus . . .** *(îH bîn ows)* (I am from . . .)

These few words go a long way. They work for countries, states, and cities. For example:

- ✔ **Ich komme aus Amerika.** *(îH kôm-me ows â-meh-ree-kâ)* (I come from America.)
- ✔ **Ich bin aus Pennsylvania.** *(îH bîn ows Pennsylvania)* (I am from Pennsylvania.)

✔ **Ich komme aus Zürich.** *(îH kô-me ows tsuu-rîH)* (I come from Zurich.)

✔ **Ich bin aus Wien.** *(îH bîn ows veen)* (I am from Vienna.)

Sounds easy right? However, German likes to be a bit challenging at times. Some countries' and regions' names are used with the feminine definite article, **die** *(dee)* (the). The United States (USA) is one such country. In German, it is referred to as **die USA** *(dee oo-êss-ah)* or **die Vereinigten Staaten** *(dee fer-y-nîk-ten stah-ten)*. To avoid grammatical quagmires, an American might say **Ich bin aus Amerika.** *(îH bîn ows â-meh-ree-kâ)* (I am from America.), but if you want to be a little more specific, you say **Ich bin aus den USA.** *(îH bîn ows dehn oo-êss-ah)* (I am from the US.). Or you might venture the tongue twister **Ich bin aus den Vereinigten Staaten.** *(îH bîn ows dehn fer-y-nîk-ten stah-ten)* (I am from the United States.).

The names of some countries are considered female. Switzerland, for example, is **die Schweiz** *(dee shvyts)* in German. Ms. Egli, who you can meet later in this chapter, is Swiss. So to say where Ms. Egli is from, you say **Frau Egli ist aus der Schweiz.** *(frow eh-glee îsst ows dehr shvyts)* (Ms. Egli is from Switzerland.).

Sein: the being verb

One of the fundamental verbs in any language is "to be" or, in German, **sein** *(zyn)*. You use this verb in the expressions **das ist** *(dâs îsst)* (this is) and **ich bin** *(îH bîn)* (I am). **Sein** is one of the most common verbs in the German language. As in English, it is used to describe everything from states of being (sick, sad, happy, and so on) to physical characteristics (being tall, dark-haired, and so on) and of course, it's an irregular verb, just as in English. Sorry, no easy way out! The only way to figure this one out is to memorize the different forms.

Conjugation	*Pronunciation*
ich bin	îH bîn
du bist (informal)	dû bîsst
Sie sind (formal)	zee zînt
er, sie, es ist	ehr, zee, êss îsst
wir sind	veer zînt
ihr seid (informal)	eer site
Sie sind (formal)	zee zînt
sie sind	zee zînt

Asking people where they come from

To ask somebody where they're from, you only need to decide if you're addressing somebody formally with **Sie** or informally with **du** (one person), or **ihr** (several people). Then you choose one of these three questions to ask "Where are you from?":

- ✔ **Wo kommen Sie her?** *(voh kô-men zee hehr)*
- ✔ **Wo kommst du her?** *(voh kômst dû hehr)*
- ✔ **Wo kommt ihr her?** *(voh kômt eer hehr)*

Talkin' the Talk

Frau Egli and Frau Myers are on a train. After looking out the window for a while, they strike up a conversation. They have just introduced themselves and are curious to learn a little more about each other.

Frau Egli: **Und wo kommen Sie her, Frau Myers?**
ûnt voh kô-men zee hehr, frow Myers
And where do you come from, Ms. Myers?

Frau Myers: **Ich komme aus den USA, aus Pennsylvania.**
ÎH kô-me ows dehn oo-êss-ah, ows Pennsylvania
I come from the US, from Pennsylvania.

Frau Egli: **Aus den USA, wie interessant. Kommen Sie aus einer großen Stadt?**
ows dehn oo-êss-ah, vee în-te-re-ssânt. kô-men zee ows ay-ner groh-ssn shtât
From the US, how interesting. Do you come from a large city?

Frau Myers: **Nein, ich komme aus Doylestown. Das ist eine kleine Stadt, aber sie ist sehr schön. Und Sie Frau Egli, wo kommen Sie her?**
nyn, îH kô-me ows Doylestown. Dâss îsst ay-ne kly-ne shtat, ah-ber zee îsst zehr shuon. ûnt zee frow eh-glee, voh kô-mên zee hehr
No, I come from Doylestown. It's a small town, but it's very pretty. And you Ms. Egli, where do you come from?

Frau Egli: **Ich bin aus der Schweiz, aus Zürich.**
îH bîn ows dehr shvyts, ows tsuu-rîH
I am from Switzerland, from Zurich.

In the next compartment, Claire and Michelle, two backpacking high-school students, are getting to know Mark, another back-packer. Easygoing youngsters that they are, they have used the informal address **du** and **ihr** right from the start.

Claire:	**Bist du aus Deutschland?** *Bîsst dû ows doytsh-lânt* Are you from Germany?
Mark:	**Nein, ich bin aus Österreich, aus Wien. Und ihr, wo kommt ihr her?** *nyn, îH bîn ows uo-sste-ryH, ows veen. ûnt eer, voh kômt eer hehr* No, I am from Austria, from Vienna. And you, where do you come from?
Michelle:	**Wir sind aus Frankreich. Meine Freundin Claire kommt aus Lyon, und ich komme aus Avignon.** *veer zînt ows frângk-ryH. my-ne froyn-dîn clair kômt ows lee-ôn, ûnt îH kô-me ows ah-vee-nyon* We are from France. My friend Claire comes from Lyons, and I come from Avignon.

Kommen: to come

The verb **kommen** *(kô-men)* (to come), is a verb that you will hear often when speaking German. This is a regular verb and quite easy to remember; it even looks a little like its English cousin.

Conjugation	*Pronunciation*
ich komme	îH kô-me
du kommst (informal)	dû kômst
Sie kommen (formal)	zee kô-men
er, sie, es kommt	ehr, zee, êss kô-mt
wir kommen	veer kô-men
ihr kommt (informal)	eer kô-mt
Sie kommen (formal)	zee kô-men
sie kommen	zee kô-men

Learning about nationalities

Unlike English, where the adjective of a country's name is used to indicate nationality ("She is French"), German speakers like to indicate nationality with a noun. And as you already know, genders are important in German, and these nationality-nouns have genders, too. An American therefore is either **Amerikaner** (*â-meh-ree-kah-ner*) if he is a man or a boy, or **Amerikanerin** (*â-meh-ree-kah-ne-rîn*) if she is a woman or a girl.

Table 3-2 lists the names of some selected countries, plus the corresponding noun and adjective.

Table 3-2	Country Names, Nouns, and Adjectives		
English	*German*	*Noun*	*Adjective*
Belgium	**Belgien** (*bêl-gee-ên*)	**Belgier(in)** (*bêl-gee-êr[în]*)	belgisch (*bêl-gîsh*)
Germany	**Deutschland** (*doytsh-lânt*)	**Deutsche(r)** (*doy-tshe[r]*)	deutsch (*doytsh*)
England	**England** (*êng-lânt*)	**Engländer(in)** (*êng-lain-der[în]*)	englisch (*êng-lish*)
France	**Frankreich** (*frânk-ryH*)	**Franzose/Französin** (*frân-tsoh-ze/frân-tsuo-zîn*)	französisch (*frân-tsuo-zîsh*)
Italy	**Italien** (*î-tah-lee-ên*)	**Italiener(in)** (*î-tah-ljeh-ner[în]*)	italienisch (*î-tah-ljeh-nish*)
Austria	**Österreich** (*uo-ste-ryH*)	**Österreicher(in)** (*uo-ste-ry-Her[în]*)	österreichisch (*uo-ste-ry-Hîsh*)
Switzerland	**die Schweiz** (*dee shvyts*)	**Schweizer(in)** (*shvy-tser[în]*)	schweizerisch (*shvy-tse-rîsh*)
USA	**die USA** (*dee oo-êss-ah*)	**Amerikaner(in)** (*â-meh-ree-kah-ner[în]*)	amerikanisch

Here are a few examples of how these words may be used in sentences:

✔ **Frau Myers ist Amerikanerin.** (*frow myers îsst â-meh-ree-kah-ne-rîn*) (Ms. Myers is American.)

✔ **Michelle ist Französin.** (*mee-shêl îsst frân-tsuo-zîn*) (Michelle is French.)

✔ **Ich bin Schweizerin.** (*îH bîn shvy-tse-rîn*) (I am Swiss.)

✔ **Ich bin Österreicher.** (*îH bîn uo-ste-ry-Her*) (I am Austrian.)

What languages do you speak?

To tell people what language you speak, you use the verb **sprechen** (*shprê-Hen*) (to speak) and combine it with the language's name (see Table 3-2 for a list of some common language names). But watch out: although the adjective and the language for a country or nationality are identical, the adjective is capitalized when it is used on its own to describe the language, so you would say:

> **Ich spreche Deutsch.** (*îH shprê-He doytsh*) (I speak German.)

If you want to ask somebody if he or she speaks English, the question is (informally):

> **Sprichst du Englisch?** (*shprîHst dû êng-lîsh*) (Do you speak English?)

Or (formally)

> **Sprechen Sie Englisch?** (*shprê-Hen zee êng-lîsh*) (Do you speak English?)

Here is the conjugation of the verb sprechen:

Conjugation	*Pronunciation*
ich spreche	îH shprê-He
du sprichst (informal	dû shprîHst
Sie sprechen (formal)	zee shprê-Hen
er, sie, es spricht	ehr, zee, êss shprîHt
wir sprechen	veer shprê-Hen
ihr sprecht (informal)	eer shprêHt
Sie sprechen (formal)	zee shprê-Hen
sie sprechen	zee shprê-Hen

Talkin' the Talk

Claire, Michelle, and Mark are talking about languages they speak.

Claire: **Sprichst du Französisch?**
shprîHst dû frân-tsuo-zîsh
Do you speak French?

Mark:	**Nein, gar nicht. Aber ich spreche Englisch. Ihr auch?** *nyn, gâr nîHt. ah-ber îH shprê-He êng-lîsh. eer owH* No, not at all, but I speak English. How about you?
Michelle:	**Ich spreche ein bisschen Englisch, und ich spreche auch Spanisch.** *îH shprê-He ayn bîss-Hen êng-lish ûnt îH shprê-He owH shpah-nîsh* I speak a little English, and I speak Spanish, too.
Claire:	**Spanisch spreche ich nicht, aber ich spreche auch Englisch. Englisch ist einfach.** *shpah-nîsh shprê-He îH nîHt, ah-ber îH shprê-He owH êng-lish. êng-lish îsst ayn-fâH* I don't speak Spanish, but I do speak English. English is easy.
Mark:	**Deutsch auch.** *doytsh owH* German, too.
Claire:	**Ich weiß nicht recht.** *îH vyss nîHt rêHt* I'm not so sure.

Saying Good-Bye

When it's time to take your leave, you can say (formally):

Auf Wiedersehen! *(owf vee-der-zehn)* (Good-bye!)

or (informally)

Tschüs! *(tshuuss)* (Bye!)

And if you want to say "It was nice meeting you," the expression you use is

War nett, Sie kennenzulernen. *(vahr nêt, zee kên-nen-tsû-lêr-nen)*

Words to Know

einfach	ayn-fâH	easy / simple
groß	grohss	large / big
interessant	în-te-re-ssânt	interesting
klein	klyn	small
schön	shuon	pretty
aber	ah-ber	but
ein bisschen	ayn bîss-Hen	a little
gar nicht	gâr nîHt	not at all
nie	nee	never
sein	zyn	to be
sprechen	shprê-Hen	to speak
ich weiß nicht	îH wyss nîHt	I don't know

Talkin' the Talk

The train is just entering a station, and Frau Egli is getting ready to get off.

Frau Egli: **Das ist meine Station. War nett, Sie kennenzulernen, Frau Myers.**
dâs îsst my-ne shtâts-yohn. vahr nêt, zee kên-nen-tsû-lêr-nen, frow myers
This is my stop. It was nice to meet you, Ms. Myers.

Frau Myers: **Ganz meinerseits. Auf Wiedersehen, Frau Egli.**
gânts my-ner-zyts. owf vee-der-zehn, frow eh-gle
Likewise. Good bye, Ms. Egli.

Frau Egli: **Auf Wiedersehen.**
owf vee-der-zehn
Good bye.

Michelle and Claire are getting off as well.

Michelle und Claire:	**Tschüs Mark.**
	tshuuss mark
	Bye, Mark.

Mark:	**Tschüs Claire, tschüs Michelle. Schöne Ferien!**
	tshuuss clair, tshuuss mee-<u>shêl</u>, <u>shuo</u>-ne <u>feh</u>-rî-ên
	Bye Claire, bye Michelle. Have a nice vacation!

CULTURAL WISDOM

You say "hallo" and I say "Grüezi"

You will be understood perfectly in the German-speaking part of Switzerland and in Austria if you simply say **hallo** in more casual situations, or if you wish people **Guten Morgen / Guten Tag / Guten Abend** (depending on the time of day). However, people in those countries also use some other greetings.

In Switzerland, you hear **Grüezi** *(gruu-e-tzee)* most often. It means quite literally "I greet you." Among people who know each other well, the greeting **salü** *(sâ-luu)* is quite common.

And in Southern Germany and Austria, you wish someone **Grüß Gott** *(gruuss gôt)* or approach people with the more casual **servus** *(ser-vûss)*, which means "your servant."

In Switzerland, you say "Auf Wiedersehen," but you can also try to get your tongue around the same expression in the vernacular, **Uff wiederluege** *(ûf vee-der-lu-ê-ge)*. Though **ade** *(â-deh)*, which is quite common and a little less formal, might prove to be considerably more manageable.

 *Fun & Games*

• •

Here is a list of words that got loose. See if you can find a place for them in the text below.

bin   spricht   Österreicher   aus   ich   ist   Freundin

Hallo, ich _____ Claire Latour. _____ komme aus Lyon. Das _____ in Frankreich. Meine _____ Michelle ist aus Avignon. Michelle _____ Spanisch und ein bisschen Englisch. Mark ist _____ . Er kommt _____ Wien.

And here is a dialogue between Frau Lempert and the Hubers:

Ihnen   gut   geht   freut   ist   auch

Herr Huber: Guten Tag, Frau Lempert. Wie _____ es Ihnen?

Frau Lempert: Danke, gut. Und _____?

Herr Huber: Danke, auch _____ . Frau Lempert, das _____ meine Frau.

Frau Lempert: Guten Tag, Frau Huber! _____ mich sehr, Sie kennenzulernen.

Frau Huber: Mich _____.

Answer key: bin ich ist Freundin spricht Österreicher aus. geht Ihnen gut ist freut auch

• •

Part II

German in Action

The 5th Wave   By Rich Tennant

"Wait! Wait! I want to find out what gender 'eggplant' is so I know how to pick it up."

In this part . . .

We present German in the context of daily life. We show you how to keep up casual conversations, how to order food in a German restaurant, how to shop, how to communicate with coworkers, and much, much more. And we throw in some helpful grammar lessons to boot.

Chapter 4

Getting to Know You: Making Small Talk

*I*f you really want to get to know somebody, you have to engage in conversation. Small talk is an easy way to develop contacts and improve your German. It can be considered a social skill in itself, but luckily, it's not too difficult to start up a light and casual conversation. No matter if you're meeting somebody at a party, or if you want to talk to the person sitting next to you on the train, plane, or bus, there are three topics that always work as an opener: yourself, your family, and, of course, the weather.

Talking about Yourself

What kind of job do you do? Are you studying? Where do you live? What's your address and phone number? These are the key questions to ask and answer when you talk about yourself.

Describing your work

A couple of simple words and expressions help you to describe your job and company.

In most cases, you can describe what kind of work you do by connecting **Ich bin** *(îH bîn)* (I am) with the name of your profession, without any article. The names of most professions and jobs exist in a female and male version. The male version ends with *–er,* and the female version ends with *–in.* For example:

- ✔ **Ich bin Buchhalter** (m) / **Buchhalterin** (f). *(îH bîn booH-hâl-ter / booH-hâl-terîn)* (I am an accountant.)

- ✔ **Ich bin Student** (m) / **Studentin** (f). *(îH bîn shtû-dênt / shtû-dên-tîn)* (I am a student.)

If you are a student, you may want to communicate what you're studying. You do this with the phrase **Ich studiere** *(îH shtû-dee-re)* (I am studying). At the end of the sentence you supply the name of your field (without any article), which could include:

- ✔ **Architektur** *(âr-Hî-têk-toor)* (architecture)

- ✔ **Betriebswirtschaft** *(be-treeps-vîrt-shâft)* (business)

- ✔ **Jura** *(yoo-rah)* (law)

- ✔ **Kunst** *(kûnst)* (art)

- ✔ **Literaturwissenschaft** *(lî-te-rah-toor-vîsn-shâft)* (literature)

- ✔ **Medizin** *(mê-dî-tseen)* (medicine)

In other cases, you describe your work by the phrase **Ich bin** *(îH bîn)* (I am), ending with an appropriate adjective. For example:

- ✔ **Ich bin pensioniert.** *(îH bîn pâng-zyô-neert)* (I am retired.)

- ✔ **Ich bin angestellt.** *(îH bîn ân-ge-shtêlt)* (I am employed.)

- ✔ **Ich bin geschäftlich unterwegs.** *(îH bîn ge-shêft-lîH ûn-ter-vehgks)* (I am travelling on business.)

- ✔ **Ich bin selbständig.** *(îH bîn zelpst-shtan-digk)* (I am self-employed.)

The location of your work is almost as important as the work you do. The phrase **Ich arbeite bei** *(îH âr-by-te by)* (I work at) tells someone, in a nutshell, where you spend most of your time. In some cases, you may need to substitute another preposition for *bei.* For example:

- ✔ **Ich arbeite bei der Firma . . .** *(îH âr-by-te by der fîr-mâ)* (I work at the company . . .) After the word **Firma,** you simply insert the name of the company you work for.

- ✔ **Ich arbeite im Büro Steiner.** *(îH âr-by-te îm buu-roh shty-ner)* (I work at the office Steiner.)

The word **Büro** is used in connection with the name of the company you're working for and is reserved for smaller companies. If you don't expect people to know what field your company is working in, you use a compound noun (with the indefinite article) to describe what kind of office it is, for example:

> **Ich arbeite in einem Ingenieurbüro / Architekturbüro.** *(īH âr-by-te în ay-nem în-jeh-nîuor-buu-roh / âr-Hî-têk-toor-buu-roh)* (I work at an engineering office / architecture office.)

Before you introduce the subject in conversation, someone may ask you what you do for a living. You may be asked one of the following questions:

- ✔ **Bei welcher Firma arbeiten Sie?** *(by vêl-Her fîr-mâ âr-by-tn zee)* (At what company are you working?)

- ✔ **Was machen Sie beruflich?** *(vâss mâ-Hen zee be-roof-lîH?)* (What kind of work do you do?)

- ✔ **Sind Sie berufstätig?** *(zînt zee be-roofs-teh-tîgk?)* (Are you employed?)

Giving somebody your address and phone number

Telling people where you live and how you can be reached may well be the key to continuing your social contacts. Some of the German words you will use are pretty similar to their English cousins — but watch out: in German, **Adresse** (ah-drê-sse) is spelled with only one "d"!

Telling where you live

When someone asks you **Wo wohnen Sie?** *(voh voh-nen zee)* (Where do you live?) You can respond with any of the following:

- ✔ **Ich wohne in Berlin.** *(īH voh-ne în bêr-leen)* (I live in Berlin.) Just insert the name of the city you live in.

- ✔ **Ich wohne in der Stadt / auf dem Land.** *(īH voh-ne în dehr shtât / owf dehm lânt)* (I live in the city / in the country.)

- ✔ **Ich habe ein Haus / eine Wohnung.** *(īH hah-be ayn hows / ay-ne voh-nûng)* (I have a house / an apartment.)

Depending upon the circumstances, someone may ask you **Wie ist Ihre Adresse?** *(vee îst ee-re â-drê-se)* (What is your address?). When it gets down to specifics on where you live, you need to know the following words:

CULTURAL WISDOM

Spelling numbers

Germans "spell" their phone numbers in pairs of numbers. If your number is 23 86 57, for example, you say **dreiundzwanzig sechsundachtzig siebenundfünfzig** *(dry-ûnt-tsvân-tsîgk zêks-ûnt-âH-tsigk zeebn-ûnt-fuunf-tsîgk).* If the numbers are read one by one, you might hear the number 2, or **zwei** *(tsvy),* pronounced as **zwo** *(tsvoh),* making 23 86 57 sound like **zwo drei acht sechs fünf sieben** *(tsvoh dry âHt zeks fuunf zeebn).* (See Chapter 2 for more information on saying numbers in German.)

> ✔ **die Adresse** *(dee â-drê-sse)* (address)
>
> ✔ **die Straße** *(dee shtrah-se)* (street)
>
> ✔ **die Hausnummer** *(dee hows-nû-mer)* (house number)
>
> ✔ **die Postleitzahl** *(dee pôst-lyt-tsahl)* (zip code)

When the time comes, you can substitute the appropriate word into the following sentence: **Die Adresse / Straße / Hausnummer / Postleitzahl ist . . .** *(dee â-drê-se / shtrah-se / hows-nû-mer/ pôst-lyt-tsahl îst . . .)* (The address / street / house number / zip code is . . .).

Giving your phone number

Whether you're talking casually with a new acquaintance or making a business deal, the time will come when you need to tell someone your phone number. Knowing the following words make this an easy transaction:

> ✔ **die Telefonnummer** *(dee tê-le-fohn-nû-mer)* (phone number)
>
> ✔ **die Vorwahl** *(dee fohr-vahl)* (area code)

Using these words in a sentence is as easy as **Die Telefonnummer / die Vorwahl ist . . .** *(dee tê-le-fohn-nû-mer / fohr-vahl îst . . .)* (The telephone number / area code is . . .).

Giving out your business card

Sometimes one business card can say 1,000 words. If you're lucky enough to have your business card with you, you can save yourself quite a bit of talking by presenting it with the following words: **Hier ist meine Karte.** *(heer îst my-ne- kâr-te)* (Here is my business card.).

Nouns and their articles

In English, you have only one form of the word *the* (the definite article). In German, all nouns have one of three genders:

- **Masculine: der** *(dehr)*
- **Feminine: die** *(dee)*
- **Neuter: das** *(dãs)*

The plural form of nouns uses the form **die** *(dee)*.

Unfortunately, the meaning of a noun isn't usually much help in predicting its gender. Sorry, no easy way out: You must memorize the gender that belongs with each noun. However, there are at least some rules of thumb:

- Nouns for male persons are usually masculine.
- Nouns for female persons are usually feminine.

In English, you use the indefinite article *a* or *an* when you want to specify one of a particular thing. Since you are dealing with three different genders in German, you also have to use three different indefinite articles. Luckily, the indefinite article for masculine and neuter nouns is the same:

- **For masculine nouns:** You use just **ein** *(ayn)*. For example, **ein Name** *(ayn nah-me* (a name), **ein Beruf** *(ayn be-roof)* (a profession), and **ein Architekt** *(ayn âr-Hee-tekt)* (a male architect).

- **For neuter nouns:** You also use **ein: ein Büro** *(ayn buu-roh)* (an office), **ein Haus** *(ayn hows)* (a house), **ein Geschäft** *(ayn ge-shêft)* (a store).

- **For feminine nouns:** You add an *e* to **ein,** making **eine** *(ay-ne)*. For example, **eine Firma** *(ay-ne fîr-mah)* (a company), **eine Adresse** *(ay-ne ah-drê-sse)* (an address), and **eine Architektin** *(ay-ne âr-Hee-tek-tîn)* (a female architect).

Not too difficult, right? But things can get a little more complicated. You already know that the gender of a noun determines the articles that are used with it. But the endings of the articles also change depending on whether the noun they're attached to is in the *nominative, genitive, dative,* or *accusative* case. The endings specified in the preceding bulleted list are those of the nominative case.

Don't worry — we don't expect you to memorize all the endings of the articles in all the different cases. We tell you exactly which form of the articles to use in specific sentences and phrases throughout the book. To understand how these cases work and how they affect the endings used on articles, you can refer to the section on articles in Chapter 2.

Compound nouns

German is famous, or rather infamous, for its long nouns. But they are not as incomprehensible as they seem. Most long nouns are just shorter words that have been joined together. If you recognize the components that make up a long noun, you can guess the meaning of many of these compounds without looking them up. A good example is the word **Postleitzahl** *(pôst-lyt-tsahl)*. It consists of the components **Post** *(pôst)* (post), **leit** *(lyt)* (guide), and **Zahl** *(tsahl)* (number), combining to mean a "post guiding number" — a zip code.

Talkin' the Talk

Kurt Hanser is on the plane from München to Frankfurt. He sits next to Frau Schneider, a businesswoman. After the two have introduced themselves, they talk about their jobs.

Herr Hanser:	**Was machen Sie beruflich, wenn ich fragen darf?**
	vâss mâ-Hen zee be-roof-lîH, vên îH frah-gen dârf
	What kind of work do you do, if I may ask?
Frau Schneider:	**Ich arbeite als Architektin bei der Firma Listex.**
	îH âr-by-te âls âr-Hee-tek-tîn by dehr fîr-mah Listex
	I work as an architect at a company called Listex.
Herr Hanser:	**Das ist ja interessant. Haben Sie eine Karte?**
	dâs îst yah în-te-re-sânt. hah-bn zee ay-ne kârte
	That's interesting. Do you have a business card?
Frau Schneider:	**Ja, hier bitte. Was machen Sie beruflich?**
	yah, heer bî-te. vâss mâ-Hen zee be-roof-lîH
	Yes, here it is. What kind of work do you do?
Herr Hanser:	**Ich arbeite in einem Ingenieurbüro. Ich habe leider meine Karte nicht dabei.**
	îH âr-by-te în ay-nem în-jen-nîuor-buu-roh. îH hah-be ly-der my-ne kâr-te nîHt dâ-by
	I work at an engineering office. I unfortunately don't have my card with me.
Frau Schneider:	**Ist Ihre Firma in Frankfurt?**
	ist ee-re fîr-ma în Frânkfûrt
	Is your company in Frankfurt?

Herr Hanser:	**Ja, in der Bockenheimer Straße 27.**
	jah, în dehr <u>bô</u>-ken-hy-mer <u>shtrah</u>-se <u>zeebn</u>-ûnt-tsvân-tsîgk
	Yes, it's at Bockenheimer Street 27.

Words to Know

fragen	<u>frah</u>-gen	to ask
geben	geh-ben	to give
dabei haben	d<u>â</u>-by <u>hah</u>-ben	to have on/with oneself
leider	ly-der	unfortunately

Possessive pronouns

Let's go back for a moment and take a look at the German version of "my" and "your," which we used in the previous dialogue — **mein** *(myn)* and **Ihr** *(eer)*. These possessive pronouns are used to show that a noun belongs to somebody or something. What ending they take depends on the gender, case, and number of the thing possessed. For example, "This is my card" would be

> **Das ist meine Karte.** *(dâs îsst <u>my</u>-ne <u>kâr</u>-te)*

Karte *(<u>kâr</u>-te)* is feminine, and the feminine possessive pronoun in the first person singular is "meine."

The basic forms of the possessives (masculine and neuter) in the nominative case are:

- ✔ **mein** *(myn)* (my)
- ✔ **dein** *(dyn)* (your; informal)
- ✔ **Ihr** *(eer)* (your; formal)
- ✔ **sein, ihr, sein** *(zyn, eer, zyn)* (his, her, its)
- ✔ **unser** *(<u>ûn</u>-zer)* (our)

✔ **euer** *(oyr)* (your; plural, informal)

✔ **Ihr** *(eer)* (your; plural, formal)

✔ **ihr** *(eer)* (their)

Table 4-1 shows all the forms of **mein** *(myn)* for all genders and all the different cases (the other possessives take the same endings):

Table 4-1	Forms of mein by Case			
Gender	*Nominative*	*Genitive*	*Dative*	*Accusative*
Masculine	mein	meines	meinem	meinen
Feminine	meine	meiner	meiner	meine
Neuter	mein	meines	meinem	mein

Talking about Your Family

Discussing families is a great way to get to know someone, and the subject gives you a wealth of topics when making small talk. Some people might even feel prompted to pull out the photos of family members they carry around in their wallets, although this is a far less popular practice in Germany than in America.

You should find all the members of your family tree in the following list. Even if you don't have kids or a sister-in-law, it's good to be familiar with these words so that you recognize them when discussing someone else's family:

✔ **der Mann** *(dehr mân)* (man / husband)

✔ **die Frau** *(dee frow)* (woman / wife)

✔ **der Junge** *(dehr yûn-ge)* (boy)

✔ **das Mädchen** *(dâs mad-Hên)* (girl)

✔ **die Eltern** *(dee êl-tern)* (parents)

✔ **der Vater** *(dehr fah-ter)* (father)

✔ **die Mutter** *(dee mû-ter)* (mother)

✔ **die Kinder** *(dee kîn-der)* (children, kids)

✔ **der Sohn** *(dehr zohn)* (son)

✔ **die Tochter** *(dee tôH-ter)* (daughter)

✔ **die Geschwister** *(dee ge-shvîs-ter)* (siblings)

- ✔ **die Schwester** *(dee shvês-ter)* (sister)
- ✔ **der Bruder** *(dehr broo-der)* (brother)
- ✔ **der Großvater** *(dehr grohs-fah-ter)* (grandfather)
- ✔ **die Großmutter** *(dee grohs-mû-ter)* (grandmother)
- ✔ **der Onkel** *(dehr ông-kel)* (uncle)
- ✔ **dic Tante** *(dee tân-te)* (aunt)
- ✔ **der Cousin** *(dehr koo-zeng)* (male cousin)
- ✔ **die Cousine** *(dee koo-zee-ne)* (female cousin)
- ✔ **die Schwiegereltern** *(dee shvee-ger-êl-tern)* (parents-in-law)
- ✔ **der Schwiegervater** *(dehr shvee-ger-fah-ter)* (father-in-law)
- ✔ **die Schwiegermutter** *(dee shvee-ger-mû-ter)* (mother-in-law)
- ✔ **der Schwiegersohn** *(dehr shvee-ger-zohn)* son-in-law
- ✔ **die Schwiegertochter** *(dee shvee-ger-tôH-ter)* daughter-in-law
- ✔ **der Schwager** *(dehr shvah-ger)* (brother-in-law)
- ✔ **die Schwägerin** *(dee shveh-ge-rîn)* (sister-in-law)

Saying that you have a certain type of relative involves the following simple phrase.

> **Ich habe einen / eine / ein . . .** *(îH hah-be ay-nen / ay-ne / ayn)* (I have a . . .)

In this phrase, you are using the accusative (direct object case), so it involves different forms of the indefinite article for both gender and the case. The feminine and the neuter indefinite articles happen to be the same in the nominative (subject case) and accusative (direct object case). The masculine indefinite article, however, takes a different form in the accusative.

- ✔ **Masculine nouns:** Nouns like **der Mann, der Bruder,** and **der Schwager** use the form **einen.**
- ✔ **Feminine nouns:** Family members like **die Frau, die Tochter,** and **die Schwägerin** use **eine.**
- ✔ **Neuter nouns: Das Mädchen** uses **ein.**

So what do you do if you want to express that you do not have siblings, a son, or a daughter or whatever it may be? In English, you would use "to do" for the negation and say "I don't have a daughter."

Adding the *s*

Just as in English, you can mark someone as the possessor of something (or someone) by adding *s* to their name — for example, Karen's apple, or Fred's lunch. There's just one difference in the German version: You drop the apostrophe. This method of showing possession can be used with family members and proper names. So the German translation of "Miller's daughter" would be **Müllers Tochter** *(muu-lers tôH-ter)* and "Michael's father" would be **Michaels Vater** *(mî-Hah-êls fah-ter).*

In German, you just use the negative form of the indefinite article **ein** *(masculine)* / **eine** *(feminine)* / **ein** *(neuter)* *(ayn / ay-ne / ayn)* (a), which is **kein / keine / kein** *(kyn / ky-ne / kyn)* (no). The good news is that the negative form — **kein / keine / kein** — works exactly like **ein / eine / ein**. You just add the letter 'k.'

- ✔ **Masculine nouns, such as der Sohn: Ich habe keinen Sohn.** *(îH hah-be ky-nen zohn)* (I don't have a son.)

- ✔ **Feminine nouns, such as die Tochter: Ich habe keine Tochter.** *(îH hah-be ky-ne tôH-ter)* (I don't have a daughter.)

- ✔ **Neuter nouns, such as das Kind: Ich habe kein Kind.** *(îH hah-be kyn kînt)* (I don't have a child.)

Talkin' the Talk

Herr Hanser and Frau Schneider are engaging in some small talk about their families to pass the time.

Herr Hanser: **Wohnen Sie in Frankfurt?**
voh-nen zee în frânk-fûrt
Do you live in Frankfurt?

Frau Schneider: **Nicht direkt. Mein Mann und ich haben ein Haus in Mühlheim. Und Sie?**
nîHt dee-rêkt. my-n mahn ûnt îH hah-bn ayn hows în muul-hym. ûnt zee
Not exactly, my husband and I have a house in Mühlheim. And you?

Herr Hanser:	**Wir haben eine Wohnung in der Innenstadt. Unser Sohn wohnt in München. Er studiert dort. Haben Sie Kinder?**
	veer hah-bn ay-ne voh-nûng în dehr în-nen-shtât. ûn-zer zohn vohnt în muun-Hen. ehr shtoo-deert dôrt. hah-bn zee kîn-der
	We have an apartment in the center of the city. Our son lives in Munich. He's studying there. Do you have kids?

Frau Schneider:	**Ja, zwei. Mein Sohn Andreas arbeitet bei Siemens und meine Tochter Claudia studiert in Köln.**
	yah, tsvy. myn zohn ân-dreh-âs âr-by-tet by zee-menss ûnt my-ne tôH-ter shtû-deert în kuoln
	Yes, two. My son Andreas works at Siemens, and my daughter Claudia is studying in Cologne.

Herr Hanser:	**Ach, meine Frau kommt aus Köln. Sie ist Juristin. Und was macht Ihr Mann beruflich?**
	âH, my-ne frow kômt ows kuoln. zee îsst yoo-rîs-tîn. ûnt vâss mâHt eer mân be-roof-lîH
	Oh, my wife is from Cologne. She is a lawyer. What kind of work does your husband do?

Frau Schneider:	**Er ist Lehrer.**
	ehr îst leh-rer
	He's a teacher.

Talking about the Weather

People everywhere love to talk about **das Wetter** *(dâs vê-ter)* (the weather). After all, it affects major aspects of life — your commute to work, your plans for any outdoor activities, and sometimes even your mood. And it often gives you something to complain about!

What's it like out there?

Your good friend, the phrase **Es ist** *(ês îst)* (It is), helps you describe the weather, no matter what the forecast looks like. You just supply the appropriate adjective at the end of the sentence. For example:

✔ **Es ist kalt.** *(ês îst kâlt)* (It is cold.)

✔ **Es ist heiß.** *(ês îst hys)* (It is hot.)

✔ **Es ist schön.** *(ês îst shuon)* (It is beautiful.)

The following words should allow you to describe almost any kind of weather:

✔ **bewölkt** *(be-_vuolkt_)* (cloudy)

✔ **neblig** *(_neh_-blîgk)* (foggy)

✔ **regnerisch** *(_rehgk_-ne-rîsh)* (rainy)

✔ **feucht** *(foyHt)* (humid)

✔ **windig** *(_vîn_-dîgk)* (windy)

✔ **kühl** *(kuuhl)* (cool)

✔ **frostig** *(_frôs_-tigk)* (frosty)

✔ **warm** *(vârm)* (warm)

✔ **sonnig** *(sô-nîgk)* (sunny)

You can also use the following phrases to give your personal weather report:

✔ **Die Sonne scheint.** *(dee _sôn_-ne shynt)* (The sun is shining.)

✔ **Es regnet / schneit.** *(êss _rehgk_-nêt / shnyt)* (It is raining / snowing.)

✔ **Es blitzt / donnert.** *(êss blîtst / _dô_-nert)* (It is lightning / thundering.)

✔ **Es wird hell / dunkel.** *(êss vîrt hêl / dûng-kel)* (It is getting light / dark.)

In German, you use two peculiar verbs to express that it begins or stops to rain: **anfangen** *(_ân_-fângn)* (to begin) and **aufhören** *(_owf_-huo-ren)* (to stop). These are *separable verbs,* meaning that when you use them in a sentence, their parts split and move around. This is how the verbs work:

✔ **Es fängt an zu regnen.** *(êss fêngkt ân tsoo _rehgk_-nen)* (It begins to rain.)

✔ **Es hört auf zu regnen.** *(êss huort owf tsu _rehgk_-nen)* (It stops to rain.)

See Chapter 14 for more information on separable verbs.

Talking about the temperature

Don't bring your winter coat when you're traveling to Germany and the forecast predicts 30-degree weather! In Germany, the temperature isn't measured in Fahrenheit but in Celsius *(tsêl-zî-ûs)* (Centigrade). If you want to convert Celsius to Fahrenheit and the other way around, this is the formula to use:

- ✔ **Celsius to Fahrenheit:** Multiply the Celsius temperature by 1.8, then add 32.

- ✔ **Fahrenheit to Celsius:** Subtract 32 from the Fahrenheit temperature and multiply the result by .5.

In general, it might help you to know that 0 degree Celsius corresponds to 32 degrees Fahrenheit, 20°C to 68°F, and 30°C to 86°F.

When the temperature is the topic of conversation, the following phrases are sure to come up:

- ✔ **Zehn Grad.** *(tsehn graht)* (Ten degrees.) Of course, you substitute the appropriate number before the word **Grad.** (See Chapter 2 for more information on numbers.)

- ✔ **Es ist minus zehn Grad.** *(ês îst mee-nûs tsehn graht)* (It is minus ten degrees.) Again, substitute the proper number before **Grad.**

- ✔ **Es ist zehn Grad unter Null.** *(ês îst tsehn graht ûn-ter nûl)* (It is ten degrees below zero.)

- ✔ **Die Temperatur fällt / steigt.** *(dee têm-pê-rah-toor fêlt / shtygkt)* (The temperature is dropping / climbing.)

Casting your vote on the day's weather

Any of the following phrases can get the ball rolling on a discussion of the weather:

- ✔ **Was für ein herrliches Wetter!** *(vâs fuur ayn hêr-lî-Hês vê-ter)* (What splendid weather!)

- ✔ **Was für ein schreckliches Wetter!** *(vâs fuur ayn shrêk-lî-Hês vê-ter)* (What horrible weather!)

- ✔ **Was für ein schöner Tag!** *(vâs fuur ayn shuo-ner tahgk)* (What a beautiful day!)

Talkin' the Talk

Anita and Rolf live across the hall from each other in the same apartment building. They have been planning to go to the park this Sunday afternoon. On Sunday morning, Rolf knocks on Anita's door to discuss their plans.

Rolf: **Was machen wir jetzt? Bei so einem Wetter können wir nicht in den Park gehen. Es ist regnerisch und windig.**
vâs mâ-Hen veer yêtst? by zoo ay-nem vê-ter kuon-nen veer nîHt în dehn pârk gehn. ês îst rehgk-ne-rîsh ûnt vîn-dîgk
What do we do now? We can't go to the park in this weather. It's rainy and windy.

Anita: **Ja, ja, ich weiß. Aber gegen Mittag soll es aufhören zu regnen.**
yah, yah, îH wys. ah-ber geh-gen mî-tahgk zoll ês owf-huo-ren tsu rehgk-nen
Yes, yes, I know. But around noon it is supposed to stop raining.

Rolf: **Na ja, ich sehe nur Wolken am Himmel . . .**
nâ yâ, îH zeh-he noor vôl-ken âm hî-mel . . .
Oh well, I only see clouds in the sky . . .

Anita: **Keine Panik! Heute Mittag scheint bestimmt wieder die Sonne.**
ky-ne pah-nîk! hoy-te mî-tahgk shynt be-stimmt vee-der dee zô-ne
No panic! Surely the sun will shine again around noon today.

Rolf: **Na gut. Vielleicht hast du recht.**
nâ goot. vee-lyHt hâst doo rêHt
Okay. Perhaps you're right.

Anita: **Bis später! Tschüs!**
bîs shpeh-ter! tshuuss
Till later! Bye!

Words to Know

machen	mâ-Hen	to do
sehen	zeh-hen	to see
wissen	vî-sen	to know
Recht haben	rêHt hah-bn	to be right
vielleicht	vee-lyHt	perhaps
bis später	bîs shpeh-ter	till later

Fun & Games

Fill in the missing words!

bewölkt   Sonne   Temperaturen   Regen   regnen   unter Null

1. Es friert, mit _____ **um 0 Grad Celsius.** *(ês freert, mît* _____ *ûm nûl graht <u>tsêl</u>-zee-ûss)* (It is freezing, with ___ around 0 degree Celsius.)

2. Am Sonntag fällt die Temperatur _____, **aber wir sehen auch ein bisschen** _____. *(âm zôn-tahgk falt dee <u>têm</u>-peh-rah-<u>toor</u>* _____, *<u>ah</u>-ber veer <u>zeh</u>-hen owH ayn <u>bîss</u>-Hen* _____) (On Sunday, the temperature will drop _____, but we will also see a little _____.)

3. Montag und Dienstag ist es wieder _____, **und es fängt an zu** _____. *(<u>mohn</u>-tahgk ûnt <u>deens</u>-tahgk îsst êss <u>vee</u>-der* _____, *ûnt êss fangkt ân tsoo* _____) (Monday and Tuesday it will be _____ again, and it will start to _____.)

4. In Berlin hört der _____ **nicht vor Donnerstag auf.** *(în bêr-<u>leen</u> huort dehr* _____ *nîHt fohr <u>dônr</u>-stahgk owf)* (In Berlin, the _____ won't stop before Thursday.)

Answer key: 1. Temperaturen; 2. unter Null; 3. bewölkt, regnen 4. Regen

Chapter 5

Guten Appetit! Dining Out and Going to the Market

*F*inding out about the food and eating habits in another country is one of the most pleasant ways of learning about its culture. Business lunch or casual dinner, eating out or cooking for yourself — you just have to know your way around food.

If you're eating out in Germany, you'll notice that the food variety is not too different from what you are used to. German "homestyle" cooking (which basically consists of meat, potatoes, and vegetables) is not particularly famous and has tended to be on the fatty side in the past, which has changed due to increasing health- and cholesterol-consciousness. Although there is a local cuisine, which varies from one part of the country to another, you also find a wide variety of international cuisine.

"Enjoy your meal," or **Guten Appetit** *(gûtn âpe-teet)*, as the Germans wish each other before they start to eat!

Is It Time to Eat Yet?

With the following phrases, you can voice your vote on when it's time to get something to eat or drink:

✔ **Ich habe Hunger / Durst.** *(îH hah-be hûngr / dûrst)* (I am hungry / thirsty.)

✔ **Ich bin hungrig / durstig.** *(îH bîn hûng-rigk / dûr-stigk)* (I am hungry / thirsty.)

To satisfy your hunger or thirst, you have to eat — **essen** *(êsn)* — and to drink — **trinken** *(trînkn)*.

Essen is an irregular verb (see Chapter 2 for more information on irregular verbs):

Conjugation	*Pronunciation*
ich esse	îH ê-se
du isst	doo îst
Sie essen	zee êsn
er, sie, es isst	ehr, zee, ês îst
wir essen	veer êsn
ihr esst	eer êst
Sie essen	zee êsn
sie essen	zee êsn

And so is **trinken** *(trînkn)*:

Conjugation	*Pronunciation*
ich trinke	îH trîng-ke
du trinkst	doo trînkst
Sie trinken	zee trînkn
er, sie, es trinkt	ehr, zee, ês trînkt
wir trinken	veer trînkn
ihr trinkt	eer trînkt
Sie trinken	zee trînkn
sie trinken	zee trînkn

All about Meals

German meal times and meals don't differ too much from their American counterparts. In most restaurants and hotels, breakfast is served from 7:00 to 10:00 a.m., and it is often more substantial than the typical Continental breakfast.

Lunch is usually served between 11:30 a.m. and 2:00 p.m. For Germans, lunch traditionally used to be the main meal of the day, which isn't necessarily the case any more.

The standard evening meal in German homes used to consist of bread with cold meats, cheeses, and maybe salad and cold dishes, but for more and more people, dinner has become the main meal, since many people work during the day and their work schedule often doesn't leave enough time for an extensive meal. In restaurants, a full menu is usually available between 6:30 and 9:00 p.m., and in larger cities and restaurants, it may be served until 10:00 or 11:00 p.m.

The three main **Mahlzeiten** *(mahl-tsy-ten)* (meals) of the day are the following:

- ✔ **das Frühstück** *(dâs fruuh-shtuuck)* (breakfast)
- ✔ **das Mittagessen** *(dâs mî-tahk-êsn)* (lunch)
- ✔ **das Abendessen** *(dâs ah-bnt-êsn)* (dinner)

You occasionally might hear people say **Mahlzeit!** as a greeting at lunchtime. If someone says this to you, just say the same — **Mahlzeit!** — back to them and smile.

Getting Set for the Table

The German table features all the same items that you find on your table at home, including the following:

- ✔ **das Glas** *(dâs glahs)* (glass)
- ✔ **die Tasse** *(dee tâ-se)* (cup)
- ✔ **der Teller** *(dehr tê-ler)* (plate)
- ✔ **der Suppenteller** *(dehr zû-pen-têl-ler)* (soup bowl)
- ✔ **die Serviette** *(dee sêrv-yet-te)* (napkin)
- ✔ **das Messer** *(dâs mê-ser)* (knife)
- ✔ **die Gabel** *(dee gah-bl)* (fork)

    ✔ **der Löffel** *(dehr luoffl)* (spoon)

    ✔ **das Besteck** *(dâs be-shtêk)* (a set of a knife, fork, and spoon)

If you are in a restaurant and need an item not found on the table (for example, a spoon, fork, or knife), call the waiter over by saying

> **Entschuldigen Sie bitte!** *(ênt-shûl-dî-gen zee bî-te)* (Excuse me, please.)

and ask

> **Kann ich bitte einen Löffel / eine Gabel / ein Messer haben?** *(kân îH bî-te ay-nen luoffl / ay-ne gah-bl / ayn mê-ser hah-bn)* (Can I please have a spoon / a fork / a knife?)

Going Out to a Restaurant

Eating out has become quite popular in Germany, and you will find that there is no big difference between going out to a restaurant in Germany and the U.S. In many German restaurants, you don't have to wait to be seated — although the waiter or waitress usually takes you to your table in more upscale places. Doggie bags also common practice, but an increasing number of restaurants (except the very fancy ones) let you take home leftovers.

Distinguishing places to eat

Most German dining establishments post a menu, making it easy to tell what kind of dining experience you can get there. This is helpful when you're just wandering around looking for a place to eat, but if you want to ask someone for a particular kind of eatery, it helps to know what different kinds are available:

    ✔ **das Restaurant** *(dâs rês-toh-rong)* (restaurant): You find the same variety of restaurants in Germany as in the U.S., ranging from simple to very fancy establishments with corresponding menus.

    ✔ **die Gaststätte** *(dee gâst-shta-te)* (local type of restaurant): This is a simpler type of restaurant where you can't expect a fancy menu and might find local specialties.

    ✔ **das Gasthaus** *(dâs gâst-hows)* / **der Gasthof** *(gâst-hohf)* (inn): You usually find these in the country. They often offer home cooking, and the atmosphere may be rather folksy.

    ✔ **die Raststätte** *(dee râst-shta-te)* (roadside restaurant): Usually found on highways and motorways with service station facilities and sometimes lodging. (Called **der Rasthof** *(dehr râst-hohf)* in Austria.)

✔ **der Ratskeller** *(dehr rahts-kê-ler):* This is a tough one to translate literally. These restaurants are named after an eatery in the cellar of the town hall **Rathaus** *(raht-hows).* You often find these in historic buildings.

✔ **die Bierhalle** *(dee beer-hâ-le)* / **die Bierstube** *(dee beer-shtoo-be)* / **der Biergarten** *(dehr beer-gâr-ten)* / **das Bierzelt** *(dâs beer-tzelt)* (beer hall / beer garden): Besides beer served from huge barrels, you can also order hot dishes (usually a few dishes-of-the-day), salads, and pretzels. The most and best-known beer halls are in Munich, Bavaria, where the **Oktoberfest** *(ok-toh-bêr-fêst)* takes place in late September. The nearest equivalent might be an English pub or an American sports bar, although the atmosphere may be very different.

✔ **die Weinstube** *(dee vyn-shtoo-be)* (wine hall): A cozy restaurant, usually found in wine-producing areas, where you can sample wine with bar food and snacks.

✔ **die Kneipe** *(dee kny-pe)* (bar-restaurant): This is the type of combination of bar and restaurant that you also find in the U.S., and it's usually not very fancy. You can have a drink at the bar or sit down at a table, where you can also order bar food.

✔ **das Café** *(dâs kâ-feh)* (café): This may range from a coffee shop to a more upscale establishment. Vienna and its café tradition are famous.

✔ **der (Schnell)imbiss** *(dehr shnêl-îm-bîs)* (snack bar, fast-food restaurant): Here you can get different types of food and peculiarities for take-out.

Making reservations

Just like in America, when you call a restaurant, the person who answers the phone is usually prepared to take your reservation. Of course, making reservations is not always necessary, and during the week you might be able to get a table without it, unless you pick a particularly trendy place or one with limited seating. (On weekends and in popular restaurants, however, reservations are recommended.) You usually don't make reservations at a **Kneipe** or **Gaststätte** (see the previous section) — you get a table on a first-come-first-serve basis.

When making a reservations, the following words and phrases come into play:

✔ **Ich möchte gern einen Tisch reservieren / bestellen.** *(îH muoH-te gêr-n ay-nen tîsh reh-zêr-vee-ren / be-shtê-len)* (I would like to reserve a table.)

✔ **Haben Sie um . . . Uhr einen Tisch frei?** *(hah-bn zee ûm . . . oor ay-nen tîsh fry)* (Do you have a table free around . . . o'clock?)

✔ **Ich möchte gern einen Tisch für . . . Personen um . . . Uhr.** *(îH muoH-te gêrn ay-nen tîsh fuor . . . pêr-zoh-nen ûm . . . oor)* (I would like a table for . . . people at around . . . o'clock.)

To get more specific about when you want the reservation, you can add the specific day of the week to your request, or one of the following appropriate phrases:

- **heute Abend** (*hoy-te ah-bnt*) (tonight)

- **morgen Abend** (*môr-gn ah-bnt*) (tomorrow night)

- **heute Mittag** (*hoy-te mî-tahgk*) (noon today)

- **morgen Mittag** (*môr-gn mî-tahgk*) (noon tomorrow)

So you would say:

- **Ich möchte gern für heute Abend einen Tisch reservieren.** (*îH muoH-te gêrn fuur hoy-te ah-bnt ay-nen tîsh reh-zêr-vee-ren*) (I would like to reserve a table for tonight.)

- **Haben Sie morgen Mittag um . . . Uhr einen Tisch frei?** (*hah-bn zee môr-gn mî-tahgk ûm . . . oor ay-nen tîsh fry*) (Do you have a table free tomorrow for lunch around . . . o'clock?)

Talkin' the Talk

 Mike and his friend Ute want to check out the hot new Restaurant Galleria. Mike calls the restaurant to make a reservation.

Restaurant: **Restaurant Galleria.**
rês-toh-rong gâ-le-ree-â
Restaurant Galleria.

Mike: **Guten Tag. Ich möchte gern einen Tisch für heute Abend bestellen.**
gûtn tahgk. îH muoH-te gêrn ay-nen tîsh fuor hoy-te ah-bnt be-shtê-len
Good day. I would like to reserve a table for tonight.

Restaurant: **Für wie viele Personen?**
fuor vee fee-le pêr-zoh-nen
For how many people?

Mike: **Zwei Personen, bitte. Haben Sie um acht Uhr einen Tisch frei?**
tzweye pêr-zoh-nen, bî-te. hah-bn zee ûm âHt oor ay-nen tîsh fry
Two people, please. Do you have a table free at eight o'clock?

Restaurant:	**Tut mir leid, um acht Uhr ist alles ausgebucht. Sie können aber um acht Uhr dreißig einen Tisch haben.** *toot meer lyt, ûm âHt oor îst <u>â</u>-lês <u>ows</u>-ge-booHt. zee <u>kuon</u>-en <u>ah</u>-bêr ûm âHt oor <u>dry</u>-sîk <u>ay</u>-nen tîsh <u>hah</u>-bn* I'm sorry. At 8:00 everything's booked. But you could have a table at 8:30.
Mike:	**Acht Uhr dreißig wäre auch gut.** *âHt oor <u>dry-sîgk</u> <u>vai</u>-re owH goot* 8:30 would be good, too.
Restaurant:	**Und Ihr Name, bitte?** *ûnt eer <u>nah</u>-me, <u>bî</u>-te* And your name, please?
Mike:	**Evans.**
Restaurant:	**Geht in Ordnung, ich habe den Tisch für Sie reserviert.** *geht în <u>ôrt</u>-nûngk, îH <u>hah</u>-be dehn tîsh fuur zee reh-zêr-<u>veert</u>* Okay, I have reserved the table for you.
Mike:	**Vielen Dank. Bis heute Abend.** *<u>fee</u>-lên dângk. bîs <u>hoy</u>-te <u>ah</u>-bnt* Thanks a lot. Until tonight.

In the preceding dialog, Mike was lucky and got a table. You may hear the following when making reservations:

> **Es tut mir leid. Wir sind völlig ausgebucht.** *(ês toot meer lyt. veer zînt <u>fuol</u>-ligk <u>ows</u>-ge-booHt)* (I'm sorry. We are totally booked.)

If you show up at the restaurant without making a reservation, expect to hear one of the following:

✔ **In . . . Minuten wird ein Tisch frei.** *(în . . . mî-<u>noo</u>-tn vîrt ayn tîsh fry)* (In . . . minutes a table will be free.)

✔ **Können Sie in . . . Minuten wiederkommen?** *(<u>kuon</u>-nen zee în . . . mî-<u>noo</u>-tn <u>vee</u>-dêr-kômn)* (Could you come back in . . . minutes?)

Sharing a table

Except maybe in a restaraunt, you'll find out that it's not unusual to share a table with other people. These places often tend to be crowded and some of them have pretty large tables. If there are still seats available at the table you're sitting at, someone might ask you **Ist hier noch frei?** *(îst heer nôH fry)* (Is this place still available?) or **Können wir uns dazu setzen?** *(kuo-nen*

veer ûns dâ-tsoo zêtsn) (May we sit down with you?). It is a very casual arrangement, and you're not obliged to start up a conversation with the party who is sharing the table with you. Some people might find the lack of privacy a little irritating, but it's also a good opportunity to meet the locals.

Arriving and being seated

After you arrive at a restaurant, you want to take your seat, **Platz nehmen** *(plâts neh-mn),* and get your **Speisekarte** *(shpy-ze-kâr-tê)* (menu). A waiter, **der Kellner** *(dehr kêl-nêr),* directs you to your table.

Talkin' the Talk

Mike and Ute have been looking forward to eating at Restaurant Galleria since Mike made the reservation. They arrive at the restaurant and are seated.

Mike: **Guten Abend. Mein Name ist Evans. Wir haben einen Tisch für zwei Personen bestellt.**
gûtn ah-bnt. myn nah-me îst evans. veer hah-bn ay-nen tîsh fuor ztweye pêr-zoh-nen be-shtêlt
Good evening. My name is Evans. We reserved a table for two people.

Kellner: **Guten Abend. Bitte, nehmen Sie hier vorne Platz.**
gûtn ah-bnt. bî-te neh-mn zee heer fôr-ne plâts
Good evening. Please take a seat over here.

Ute: **Könnten wir vielleicht den Tisch dort drüben am Fenster haben?**
kuon-tn veer fee-lyHt dehn tîsh dôrt druu-bn âm fên-stêr hah-bn
Could we perhaps have the table over there by the window?

Kellner:	**Aber sicher, kein Problem. Setzen Sie sich. Ich bringe Ihnen sofort die Speisekarte.**
	_ah_-ber _zî_-Her, kyn prô-_blehm_. zêtsn zee zîH. îH brînge _ee_-nen zô-_fôrt_ dee _shpy_-ze-kâr-tê
	But of course, no problem. Sit down. I'll bring you the menu right away.

Words to Know

bringen	brĭng-en	to bring
vielleicht	fee-lyHt	perhaps
hier vorne	heer fôr-ne	over here
dort drüben	dôrt druu-bn	over there
Setzen Sie sich!	zêtsn zee zîH	Sit down!
Tut mir leid!	toot meer lyt	I'm sorry!
In Ordnung!	în ôrt-nûngk	Okay!

Deciphering the menu

Now comes the fun part — deciding what you want to eat. Of course, what's on the menu depends entirely on what kind of eatery you're in.

If you go to a French, Spanish, or Chinese restaurant, the menu may be in the language of the respective country with a German translation below the original name of the dish. In some restaurants, you might even find an English translation.

The following sections tell you about foods you may find in German restaurants throughout the country. These sections don't tell you about local cuisine, which substantially differs from region to region; in fact, many areas have their local specialties. For example, there are certain dishes that you would commonly find on the menu in Bavaria or southern Germany but never in the northern parts of the country.

Breakfast

The following items may be offered **zum Frühstuck** *(tsûm fruuh-shtuuck)* (for breakfast):

- **das Brot** *(dâs broht)* (bread)
- **das Brötchen** *(dâs bruoht-Hên)* (roll)
- **der Toast** *(dehr tohst)* (toast)
- **der Aufschnitt** *(dehr owf-shnît)* (cold meats and cheese)
- **die Butter** *(dee bû-têr)* (butter)
- **die Cerealien** *(dee tseh-rê-ah-lî-en)* (cereal)
- **das Müsli** *(dâs muus-lee)* (muesli)
- **die Milch** *(dee mîlH)* (milk)
- **der Saft** *(dehr zâft)* (juice)
- **die Wurst** *(dee vûrst)* (sausage)
- **das Ei** *(dâs ay)* (egg)
- **das Spiegelei** *(dâs shpee-gêl-ay)* (fried egg)
- **die Rühreier** *(dee ruuhr-ay-êr)* (scrambled eggs)

In Germany, **Brötchen** are very popular for breakfast; however, you may also get all kinds of bread or croissants. It is still very common to eat cold cuts for breakfast, and if you order an egg without specifying that you want it scrambled or sunny side up, you will get it soft-boiled in an egg cup.

Appetizers

For **Vorspeisen** *(fohr-shpy-zen)* (appetizers), you might see the following:

- **Gemischter Salat** *(ge-mîsh-ter zâ-laht)* (mixed salat)
- **Grüner Salat** *(gruu-ner zâ-laht)* (green salad)
- **Melone mit Schinken** *(mê-loh-ne mît shing-ken)* (melon with ham)
- **Meeresfrüchtesalat mit Toastecken** *(meh-res-fruuH-te-zâ-laht mît tohst-êkn)* (seafood salad with toast halves)

Soups

You might see the following **Suppen** *(zû-pen)* (soups) on the menu:

- **Tomatensuppe** *(tô-mah-tn-zû-pe)* (tomato soup)
- **Bohnensuppe** *(boh-nen-zû-pe)* (bean soup)

✔ **Ochsenschwanzsuppe** *(ok-sên-shvânts-zûp-pe)* (oxtail soup)

✔ **Französische Zwiebelsuppe** *(frân-tsuo-zî-she tsvee-bêl-zû-pe)* (French onion soup)

Main dishes

Hauptspeisen *(howpt-shpy-zen)* (main dishes) are as diverse as they are in any culture; here are some you might find on a German menu:

✔ **Kalbsleber mit Kartoffelpüree** *(kâlps-leh-ber mît kâr-tofl-puu-reh)* (veal liver with mashed potatoes)

✔ **Frischer Spargel mit Kalbsschnitzel oder Räucherschinken / Kochschinken** *(frî-sher shpâr-gel mît kâlbs-shnî-tsel oh-der roy-Her-shîng-ken / kôH-shîng-ken)* (fresh asparagus with veal cutlet or smoked ham / ham)

✔ **Rindersteak mit Pommes Frites und gemischtem Gemüse** *(rîn-der-steak mît pôm frît ûnt ge-mîsh-tem ge-muu-ze)* (beef steak with french fries and mixed vegetables)

✔ **Lammkotelett nach Art des Hauses** *(lâm-kôt-lêt nahH ahrt dês how-zes)* (homestyle lamb chop)

✔ **Hühnerfrikassee mit Butterreis** *(huu-ner-frî-kâ-seh mît bû-ter-rys)* (chicken fricassee with butter rice)

✔ **Lachs an Safransoße mit Spinat und Salzkartoffeln** *(laks ân zâf-rahn-zoh-se mît shpî-naht ûnt zâlts-kâr-tofln)* (salmon in safran sauce with salt potatoes)

✔ **Fisch des Tages** *(fîsh dês tah-ges)* (fish of the day)

Side dishes

You can sometimes order **Beilagen** *(by-lah-gen)* (side dishes) separately from your main course:

✔ **Butterbohnen** *(bû-ter-boh-nen)* (butter beans)

✔ **Gurkensalat** *(gûr-ken-zâ-laht)* (cucumber salad)

✔ **Bratkartoffeln** *(braht-kâr-tôfln)* (fried potatoes)

Dessert

German restaurants commonly offer many fine dishes **zum Nachtisch** *(ztuhm naH-tîsh)* (for dessert), including the following:

✔ **Frischer Obstsalat** *(frî-sher ohbst-zâ-laht)* (fresh fruit salad)

✔ **Apfelstrudel** *(âpfl-shtroo-del)* (apple strudel)

✔ **Gemischtes Eis mit Sahne** *(ge-mish-tes ays mît zah-ne)* (mixed ice cream with whipped cream)

✔ **Rote Grütze mit Vanillesoße** *(roh-te gruu-tse mît vâ-nîle-zoh-se)* (red berry compote with vanilla sauce)

Drinks

When it comes to ordering **Wasser** *(vâ-ser)* (water), you have the choice between the carbonated or non-carbonated one, which is **ein Wasser mit Kohlensäure** *(ayn vâ-ser mît koh-len-zoy-re)* (carbonated water) or **ein Wasser ohne Kohlensäure** *(ayn vâ-ser oh-ne koh-len-zoy-re)* (non-carbonated water). If you ask the waiter or waitress for **ein Mineralwasser** *(mînê-rahl-vâ-sêr)* (mineral water), you usually get carbonated water.

Wine is usually offered by the bottle — **die Flasche** *(dee flâ-she)* — or by the glass — **das Glas** *(dâs glahs)*. Sometimes, you can also get a carafe of wine, which is **die Karaffe** *(dee kah-râ-fe)*.

In the following list, you find a couple of common drinks, **Getränke** *(geh-traing-ke)*, that you might see on a menu:

✔ **Bier** *(beer)* (beer)

✔ **das Export** *(dâs export)* / **das Kölsch** *(dâs kuolsh)* (less bitter, lager beer)

✔ **das Bier vom Fass** *(dâs beer fôm fâs)* (draft beer)

✔ **das Pils / Pilsener** *(dâs pîls / pîlze-ner)* (bitter, lager beer)

✔ **das Altbier** *(dâs âlt-beer)* (dark beer, similar to British ale)

✔ **Wein** *(vyn)* (wine)

✔ **der Weißwein** *(dehr vyss-vyn)* (white wine)

✔ **der Rotwein** *(dehr roht-vyn)* (red wine)

✔ **der Tafelwein** *(dehr tah-fl-vyn)* (table wine, lowest quality)

✔ **der Kaffee** *(dehr kâ-fê)* (coffee)

✔ **der Tee** *(dehr teh)* (tea)

Placing your order

As in English, you use a variety of common expressions to order your food. Luckily, they aren't too complicated, and you can use them both for ordering anything from food to drinks and for buying food at a store:

✔ **Ich hätte gern . . .** *(īH ha-te gêrn)* (I would like to have . . .)

✔ **Für mich bitte . . .** *(fuor mīH bî-te)* (For me . . . please)

✔ **Ich möchte gern . . .** *(īH muoH-te gêrn)* (I would like to have . . .)

When ordering, you may decide to be adventurous and ask the waiter

> **Können Sie etwas empfehlen?** *(kuon-nen zee êt-vâss êm-pfeh-len)* (Can you recommend something?)

Be prepared for him or her to respond at a rapid-fire pace, naming dishes you may have never heard of before. To avoid any confusion with the waiter's response, try holding out your menu for the waiter to point at while responding.

Using the conjunctive

Take a closer look at the verb forms **hätte, könnte,** and **würde** that you see in the previous section. Where do they come from and what are their functions?

The *conjunctive* is used to express a possibility, and you have a corresponding form in English. Basically, the conjunctive acts like the English "would." Let's take a look at how this forms works:

> **Ich hätte** *(īH ha-te)* (I would have) comes from **haben** *(hah-bn)* (to have)

The big difference between the German and the English conjunctive is that in German you can combine "would" and "have" into one word: **hätte. Ich hätte gern . . .** *(īH hat-te gêrn),* the form you use for ordering, is an easy way to say "I would like to have . . . ."

You also have **Ich würde** *(īH vuur-de)* (I would), which comes from **werden** *(wehr-den)* (to become / to get). It's quite simple: **würde** basically corresponds to the English "would" and is used in very a similar way:

> **Ich würde essen.** *(īH vuur-de êssn)* (I would eat.)

As in English, **würde** is always followed by the infinitive of a verb. And if you would like to have something? As above, we would use **gern** to express it:

> **Ich würde gern haben.** *(īH vuur-de gêrn hah-bn)* (I would like to have.)

The phrase **Ich könnte** *(īH kuon-te)* (I could) comes from the verb **können** *(kuon-nen)* (to be able to). **Könnte** calls for a similar construction as **würde:**

> **Ich könnte essen.** *(īH kuon-te êssn)* (I could eat.)

Talkin' the Talk

Mike and Ute have had a chance to look at the menu. The waiter returns to take their orders.

Kellner:	**Darf ich Ihnen etwas zu trinken bringen?** *dârf îH ee-nen êt-vâs tsû trîng-kn brîngn* May I bring you something to drink?
Mike:	**Ja, bitte. Ich möchte gern ein Glas Bier.** *yah, bî-te. îH muoH-te gêr-n ayn glahs beer* Yes, please. I'd like a glas of beer.
Kellner:	**Pils oder Export?** *Pilz oder export* A Pils or an Export?
Mike:	**Export, bitte.** *export, bî-te* Export, please.
Kellner:	**Ein Export. Und was darf es für Sie sein?** *ayn export. ûnt vâs dârf ês fuor zee zyn* One Export. And what would you like?
Ute:	**Ich hätte gern ein Glas Rotwein.** *îH ha-te gêrn ayn glahs roht-vyn* I would like to have a glass of red wine.

Using modals

You want to know a little more about the verb forms we use in the expressions **Darf ich . . .? / Ich möchte . . .?** Here's the story: These verbs help you to further determine the action expressed by another verb (that's why they are called *auxiliary modals*), and they work similar to the English "may" and "might."

Ich darf *(îH darf)* (I'm allowed to) comes from the verb **dürfen** *(duur-fn)* (to be allowed to):

- ✔ **Ich darf Bier trinken.** *(îH dârf beer trîng-ken)* (I'm allowed to drink beer.)

- ✔ **Darf ich Wein trinken?** *(dârf îH vyn trîng-ken)* (May I drink wine?)

- ✔ **Dürfen wir rauchen?** *(duur-fen veer row-Hen)* (May we smoke?)

Ich möchte *(īH muoH-te)* (I would like to) derives from the verb **mögen** *(muo-gen)* (to like):

- ✔ **Ich möchte Wein trinken.** *(īH muoH-te vyn trīng-ken)* (I would like to drink wine.)

- ✔ **Möchten Sie Wein trinken?** *(muoH-ten zee vyn tring-ken)* (Would you like to drink wine?)

You can also use **mögen** to simply express that you like something:

- ✔ **Ich mag Wein.** *(īH mahgk vyn)* (I like wine.)

- ✔ **Wir mögen Wein.** *(veer muo-gen vyn)* (We like wine.)

Ordering something special

You may need the following phrases to order something a little out-of-the-ordinary:

- ✔ **Haben Sie vegetarische Gerichte?** *(hah-bn zee veh-ge-tah-rī-she ge-rīH-te)* (Do you have vegetarian dishes?)

- ✔ **Ich kann nichts essen, was . . . enthält** *(īH kānn nīHts êsn, vās . . . ênt-hailt)* (I can't eat anything that contains . . .)

- ✔ **Haben Sie Gerichte für Diabetiker?** *(hah-bn zee ge-rīH-te fuor deeā-beh-tī-ker)* (Do you have dishes for diabetics?)

- ✔ **Haben Sie Kinderportionen?** *(hah-bn zee kīn-der-pôr-tseeo-nen)* (Do you have children's portions?)

Lighting up

In most of Europe, smoking in restaurants is still common practice, and Germany is no exception. Restaurants where you aren't allowed to light up at all are hard to find. Although smoking is increasingly restricted in public places, such as airports, there still are not too many restaurants that have a smoking and a non-smoking section (trains have compartments for smokers and non-smokers). If you go to a **Kneipe** *(kny-pe)*, you are forewarned that the person next to you might light a cigarette while you're eating.

How would you like it prepared?

If you order meat — steak, for example — the waiter may ask you **Wie hätten Sie das Steak gern?** *(vee hat-ten zee dâs steak gêrn)* (How would you like your steak?). You can respond with any of the following:

- **englisch** *(êng-lish)* (rare)
- **medium** *(meh-dee-ûm)* (medium)
- **durchgebraten** *(dûrH-ge-brah-ten)* (well-done)

Replying to "How did you like the food?"

After a meal, it's traditional for the waiter or waitress to ask if you liked the food:

> **Hat es Ihnen geschmeckt?** *(hât ês ee-nen ge-shmêkt)* (Did you like the food?)

Hopefully, you enjoyed your meal and feel compelled to answer that question with one of the following:

- **danke, gut** *(dâng-ke, goot)* (thanks, good)
- **sehr gut** *(zehr goot)* (very good)
- **ausgezeichnet** *(ows-ge-tsyH-net)* (excellent)

Getting the check

At the end of your meal, your waiter may ask you the following as a way to bring your meal to a close and to find out if you are ready for the check:

> **Sonst noch etwas?** *(zônst nôH êt-vâs)* (Anything else?)

Unless you'd like to order something else, it's time to pay **die Rechnung** *(rêH-nûngk)* (bill). You can ask for the bill in the following ways:

- **Ich möchte bezahlen.** *(îH muoH-te be-tsah-len)* (I would like to pay.)
- **Die Rechnung, bitte.** *(dee rêH-nûngk, bî-te)* (The check, please.)

You can pay together — **Alles zusammen, bitte.** *(â-les tsû-zâmn, bî-te)* (Everything together, please.) — or separately — **Wir möchten getrennt zahlen.** *(veer muoH-ten ge-trênt tsah-len)* (We would like to pay separately.).

CULTURAL WISDOM

Tipping

Wondering why the waiter or waitress is letting you sit at your table without ever bringing your check? In Germany, you have to ask for the check if you want to pay. It would be considered pushy and impolite to put the check on your table before you requested it. In more casual establishments, such as a **Kneipe**, it is pretty common to just let the waiter know that you want to pay, and the payment is then taken care of directly at the table. In Germany, waiters and waitresses receive a salary and don't live off the tip. If you're paying the waitress at your table, just round up the sum of money you're paying by 8 to 10 percent. The phrase **Stimmt so.** *(shtîmt zoh)* (Keep the change.) lets the waiter or waitress know that the sum added on to the bill is their tip.

TIP

Some German restaurants, especially upscale establishments, allow you to pay with a credit card — **die Kreditkarte** *(dee krê-dît-kâr-te)*. These restaurants have signs in the window or one at the door, indicating which cards they take (just like they do in American restaurants). If it's essential for you to pay with a credit card, look for these signs.

If you need a **Quittung** *(kvî-tûngk)* (a receipt) for tax or other purposes, just ask the waiter or waitress after you asked for the check:

> **Und eine Quittung, bitte.** *(ûnt ay-ne kvî-tûngk bî-te)* (And a receipt, please.)

Talkin' the Talk

Mike and Ute have enjoyed a great meal. They are ready for the check, and they plan to tip the waiter.

Mike: **Die Rechnung, bitte.**
dee _rêH_-nûngk, _bî_-te
The check, please.

Kellner: **Sofort. Das macht 85 Mark 80.**
zoh-_fôrt_. dâs mâHt fuunf-ûnt-aht-tsîgk mârk _âHt_-tsigk
Coming right up. That would be 85,80 Marks.

Mike puts 90 Marks on the table.

Mike:	**Stimmt so.**
	shtîmt zoh
	That's alright.
Kellner:	**Vielen Dank.**
	feeln dângk
	Thank you very much.
Mike:	**Bitte, bitte.**
	bî-te, bî-te
	You're welcome.

Words to Know

bezahlen	be-tsah-len	to pay
die Kreditkarte	dee krê-dît-'kâr-te	credit card
die Quittung	dee kvî-tûngk	receipt
in bar bezahlen	în bâr be-tsah-len	to pay cash
:die Rechnung	dee rêH-nûngk	bill
Stimmt so!	shtîmt zoh	That's alright!
Bitte, bitte.	bî-te, bî-te	You're welcome.

Shopping for Food

Sometimes you might not feel like eating out and might prefer to do the cooking yourself. The first thing you should know is where to go and what to buy where.

The following is a list of stores where you might have to shop and the food groups they sell:

- **das Lebensmittelgeschäft** (*dâs leh-bents-mît-tel-ge-shaift*) (grocery store)
- **der Supermarkt** (*dehr zoo-pêr-mârkt*) (supermarket)
- **der Markt** (*dehr mârkt*) (market)

- **die Metzgerei** *(dee <u>mêts</u>-ge-ry)* (butcher shop)
- **die Bäckerei** *(dee bai-ke-ry)* (bakery)
- **die Weinhandlung** *(dee vyn-hând-lûng)* (wine store)
- **die Backwaren** *(dee <u>bâk</u>-vah-ren)* (bakery goods)
- **das Gebäck** *(dâs ge-<u>baik</u>)* (pastry)
- **das Gemüse** *(dâs ge-<u>muu</u>-ze)* (vegetables)
- **der Fisch** *(dehr fîsh)* (fish)
- **das Fleisch** *(dâs flysh)* (meat)
- **das Obst** *(dâs ohpst)* (fruit)
- **die Spirituosen** *(dee shpî-rî-too-oh-zen)* (spirits)

Finding what you need

In the various shops you may find the following wares:

- **das Brot** *(dâs broht)* (bread)
- **das Brötchen** *(dâs <u>bruot</u>-Hen)* (roll)
- **das Schwarzbrot** *(dâs <u>shvârts</u>-broht)* (brown bread)
- **das Weißbrot** *(dâs vyss-broht)* (white bread)
- **der Kuchen** *(dehr <u>koo</u>-Hen)* (cake)
- **die Torte** *(dee <u>tôr</u>-te)* (tart)
- **die Butter** *(dee <u>bû</u>-têr)* (butter)
- **der Käse** *(dehr <u>kai</u>-ze)* (cheese)
- **die Milch** *(dee mîlH)* (milk)
- **die Sahne** *(dee <u>zah</u>-ne)* (cream)
- **die Flunder** *(dee <u>flûn</u>-der)* (flounder)
- **der Kabeljau** *(dehr <u>kah</u>-bel-yow)* (cod)
- **die Krabben** *(dee krâ-ben)* (shrimps)
- **der Krebs** *(dehr krehbs)* (crab)
- **die Muschel** *(dee <u>mû</u>-shel)* (mussel)
- **der Tunfisch** *(dehr <u>toon</u>-fîsh)* (tuna)
- **der Apfel** *(dehr âpfl)* (apple)
- **die Banane** *(dee bâ-nah-ne)* (banana)

- ✔ **die Birne** *(dee b*ir*-ne)* (pear)
- ✔ **die Erdbeere** *(dee ehrt-beh-re)* (strawberry)
- ✔ **die Orange** *(dee oh-rong-je)* (orange)
- ✔ **die Bratwurst** *(dee braht-v*u*rst)* (fried sausage)
- ✔ **das Rindfleisch** *(d*a*s r*i*nt-flysh)* (beef)
- ✔ **der Schinken** *(dehr sh*i*ng-ken)* (ham)
- ✔ **das Schweinefleisch** *(d*a*s shvy-ne-flysh)* (pork)
- ✔ **der Speck** *(dehr shp*ê*k)* (bacon)
- ✔ **die Wurst** *(dee v*u*rst)* (sausage)
- ✔ **das Hähnchen** *(d*a*s hain-Hen)* (chicken)
- ✔ **die Bohne** *(dee boh-ne)* (bean)
- ✔ **der Brokkoli** *(dehr broh-k*õ*lee)* (broccoli)
- ✔ **die Erbse** *(dee* ê*rp-se)* (pea)
- ✔ **die Gurke** *(dee g*u*r-ke)* (cucumber)
- ✔ **die Kartoffel** *(dee k*a*r-tof-fel)* (potato)
- ✔ **der Kohl** *(dehr kohl)* (cabbage)
- ✔ **der Kopfsalat** *(dehr kopf-z*a*-laht)* (lettuce)
- ✔ **die Möhre** *(dee muoh-re)* (carrot)
- ✔ **das Paprika** *(d*a*s p*a*p-ree-kah)* (green pepper)
- ✔ **der Pilz** *(dehr p*i*lts)* (mushroom)
- ✔ **der Reis** *(dehr ryss)* (rice)
- ✔ **der Salat** *(dehr z*a*-laht)* (salad)
- ✔ **das Sauerkraut** *(d*a*s zower-krowt)* (pickled cabbage)
- ✔ **der Spinat** *(dehr shpee-naht)* (spinach)
- ✔ **die Tomate** *(dee to-mah-te)* (tomato)
- ✔ **die Zucchini** *(dee tsu-kee-n*i*)* (zucchini)
- ✔ **die Zwiebel** *(dee tsvee-bel)* (onion)

If you go shopping at a supermarket in Germany, you might find out about an approach to recycling that you're not yet familiar with. Plastic bags for your groceries aren't something you just get for free. You either have to bring your own bag or pay a minimal amount to get a plastic bag at the cashier. So don't just throw away that plastic bag; it will save you money when you buy groceries the next time!

Measurements and weights

Asking someone in the open market or supermarket for something is just the same as ordering in a restaurant. You just say

Ich hätte gern . . . *(īH ha̱-te gêrn)* (I would like to have . . .)

At the end of that phrase, you get to tell the person what you want, which could include any of the following weights and measurements:

- ✔ **ein / zwei Kilo** *(ayn / tsvy ke̱e-loh)* (one kilogram / two kilograms)

- ✔ **ein / zwei Pfund** *(ayn pfûnt)* (one pound / two pounds)

- ✔ **ein / einhundert Gramm** *(ayn / ayn-hûn-dêrt grâm)* (one / one hundred gram)

- ✔ **ein / zwei Stück** *(ayn / tsvy shtuuk)* (one piece / two pieces)

- ✔ **eine Scheibe / zwei Scheiben** *(ay-ne shy̱-be / tsvy shy̱-ben)* (one slice / two slices)

To specify exactly what you want, simply add the appropriate word to the end of the whole phrase. For example, if you want one Kilo of apples, you would say

Ich hätte gern ein Kilo Äpfel. *(īH ha̱-te gêrn ayn ke̱e-loh ap̱fl)* (I would like to have one kilogram of apples.)

Talkin' the Talk

Frau Bauer buys all her produce at the open market. Today she needs apples and tomatoes. After shopping the various stalls, she approaches one where she has bought before.

Verkäuferin: **Guten Tag. Was darf es sein?**
gûtn tahgk. vâs dârf ês zyn
Good day. What would you like?

Frau Bauer: **Ein Kilo Äpfel und ein Pfund Tomaten.**
ayn ke̱e-loh apfl ûnt ayn pfûnt toh-ma̱h-ten
One kilogram of apples and one pound of tomatoes.

Verkäuferin: **Sonst noch etwas?**
zônst nôH e̱t-vâs
Anything else?

Frau Bauer: **Danke, das ist alles.**
dâng-ke, dâs îst â-lês
Thank you, that's all.

Next, Frau Bauer goes to a stand which sells dairy and cold meats.

Frau Bauer: **Ich hätte gern etwas von dem Gouda.**
îH ha-te gêrn êt-vâs fôn dehm gow-dâ
I would like to have some Gouda.

Verkäuferin: **Wie viel hätten Sie denn gern?**
vee-feel ha-tn zee dên gêrn
How much would you like?

Frau Bauer: **Zweihundert Gramm, bitte.**
tsvy-hûn-dert grâm, bitte
Two hundred grams, please.

Verkäuferin: **Sonst noch etwas?**
zônst nôH êt-vâs
Anything else?

Frau Bauer: **Nein, danke. Das wär's.**
nyn dâng-ke. dâs vêhrs
No thank you. That's it.

Words to Know

das Kilo	dâs kee-loh	kilogram
das Pfund	dâs pfûnt	pound
das Gramm	dâs grâm	gram
wie viel	vee-feel	how much
wie viele	vee-feeleh	how many
Das wär's.	dâs vêhrs	That's it.
Was darf es sein?	vâs dârf ês zyn	What would you like?
Sonst noch etwas?	zônst nôH êt-vâs	Anything else?

FUN & GAMES

You have just ordered a glass of water, coffee, soup, salad, steak, and mashed potatoes for lunch at a café. Identify everything on the table to make sure that your waiter hasn't forgotten anything, using the indefinite articles der, die, or das:

A. _____

B. _____

C. _____

D. _____

E. _____

F. _____

G. _____

H. _____

I. _____

J. _____

Answer key: A. die Suppe; B. die Serviette; C. die Gabel; D. der Teller; E. das Steak; F. das Kartoffelpüree; G. das Messer; H. die Tasse Kaffee; I. das Glas Wasser; J. der Löffel. (The waiter forgot der Salat.)

Chapter 6

Shopping Made Easy

• •

In This Chapter

▶ Discovering where to shop

▶ Asking for help

▶ Browsing

▶ Trying on and buying clothes

▶ Picking the right size, color, and material

• •

Shopping in another country can be a fun part of diving into the culture and a great opportunity for rubbing elbows with the locals. In European cities, you have a choice of discovering the wares of enticing specialty stores, or if you're in the mood for one-stop shopping, you can head into the major department stores found in all the larger cities.

City centers tend to be rather compact, inviting you out for a leisurely stroll, the ideal setting for window shopping — **Schaufensterbummel** (*shaû-fêns-ter-bû-ml*).

Places to Shop the Town

When in Europe, you will find myriad shopping opportunities in all kinds of venues, including the following:

✔ **das Kaufhaus** (*dâs kowf-hows*) (department store)

✔ **das Fachgeschäft** (*dâs fâH-ge-shêft*) (specialty store)

✔ **die Boutique** (*dee boo-teek*) (a small, often elegant store generally selling clothes or gifts)

✔ **die Buchhandlung** (*dee booH-hând-lûng*) (book store)

✔ **die Fußgängerzone** (*dee foos-gêng-er-tsoh-ne*) (pedestrian zone)

✔ **der Kiosk** (*dehr kee-ôsk*) (news stand)

✔ **der Flohmarkt** (*dehr floh-mârkt*) (flea market)

Finding Out about Opening Hours

CULTURAL WISDOM

Shopping hours are not quite what you're used to in America. Opening hours are regulated by law. In Germany, stores may open at 6:00 a.m., and they close by 8:00 p.m. (in Austria, they close at 7.30 p.m.). In small towns, some stores may close between noon and 2:00 or 3:00 p.m. for lunch.

Don't count on banks being open after 4:00 p.m., though you may get lucky on Thursdays when some banks stay open until about 6:00 p.m.

On Saturdays, stores stay open until 4:00 p.m. (Regionally, stores may stay open until 6:00 p.m. on the first Saturday of the month and the four Saturdays leading up to Christmas.) On Sundays, stores may be open in some resort towns; everywhere else they remain closed, except sometimes for bakeries, which can be open for three hours. (Sunday hours for bakeries are a Swiss traditon. It's a lucky break for the Germans though, who have only recently been able to enjoy fresh rolls, or **Brötchen** (_bruot_-Hen), on Sunday.)

The best way to know when a store is open is to call the store, or stop by, and ask the following questions:

- ✔ **Wann öffnen Sie?** *(vân _uof_-nen zee)* (When do you open?)

- ✔ **Wann schließen Sie?** *(vân _shlee_-sn zee)* (When do you close?)

- ✔ **Haben Sie mittags geöffnet?** *(_hah_-bn zee _mî_-tahgks ge-_uof_-net)* (Are you open during lunch?)

- ✔ **Um wie viel Uhr schließen Sie am Samstag?** *(ûm _wee_-feel oor _shlee_-sn zee âm _zâms_-tahgk)* (At what time do you close on Saturdays?)

Getting around the Store

If you need help finding a certain item or section in a department store, you can consult the information desk — **die Auskunft** *(dee _ows_-kûnft)* or **die Information** *(dee în-fôr-mâ-_tsyohn_)*. They have all the answers, or at least some of them.

If you're searching for a certain item, you can ask for it by name with either of these phrases (at the end of the phrase, just fill in the plural form of the item you're looking for):

- ✔ **Wo bekomme ich . . .?** *(voh be-_kô_-me îH)* (Where do I get . . .?)

- ✔ **Wo finde ich . . .?** *(voh _fîn_-de îH)* (Where do I find . . .?)

CULTURAL WISDOM

What ever happened to the first floor?

German speakers look at buildings differently. They don't count the ground floor, **das Erdgeschoss** *(dâs êrt-geshôs)*, as the first floor. They start numbering with the floor above ground floor. That system makes the American second floor to the German first floor, and so on, all the way to the top.

The people at the information desk will either say **. . . führen wir nicht** *(. . . fuu-ren veer nîHt)* (We don't carry . . .), or they will point you to the appropriate section of the store, using one of the following phrases:

- **Im Erdgeschoss.** *(îm êrt-ge-shôs)* (On the ground floor.)
- **Im Untergeschoss.** *(îm ûn-ter-ge-shôs)* (In the basement.)
- **In der . . . Etage.** *(în dêr . . . ê-ta-jhe)* (On the . . . floor.)
- **Im . . . Stock.** *(îm . . . shtôk)* (On the . . . floor.)
- **Eine Etage höher.** *(ay-ne ê-tah-jhe huo-her)* (One floor above.)
- **Eine Etage tiefer.** *(ay-ne ê-tah-jhe tee-fer)* (One floor below.)

If you'd like to browse through a section of the store, or investigate a special feature of the store, you can use the phrase **Wo finde ich . . .?** *(voh fîn-de îH)* (Where do I find . . .?), ending the phrase with one of the following department or feature names:

- **Haushaltsgeräte** *(hows-hâlts-ge-ra-te)* (domestic appliances)
- **die Herrenabteilung** *(dee hê-ren-âp-ty-lûng)* (men's department)
- **die Damenabteilung** *(dee dah-mên-âp-ty-lûng)* (ladies' department)
- **die Kinderabteilung** *(dee kîn-der-âp-ty-lûng)* (children's department)
- **die Schuhabteilung** *(dee shoo-âp-ty-lûng)* (shoe department)
- **die Schmuckabteilung** *(dee shmûk-âp-ty-lûng)* (jewelry department)
- **den Aufzug / den Fahrstuhl** *(dehn owf-tsûk / dehn fâr-shtool)* (elevator)
- **die Rolltreppe** *(dee rôl-trê-pe)* (escalator)

Asking Nicely

Saying please and excuse me can get you a long way in almost any situation. When you're shopping, these magic words may mean the difference between a calm, slowly spoken answer and not-so-good service.

Saying please

When asking somebody for help (or anything else, for that matter), it pays to add **bitte** *(bĭ-te)* (please) to your request. You can add **bitte** to most any question, including the phrases mentioned in the preceding sections. It can go in various places, but it's easiest and, in terms of grammar, reasonably safe to stick it at the end of your request. For example:

- ✔ **Wo finde ich Schuhe, bitte?** *(voh fĭn-de ĭH shoo-e, bĭ-te)* (Where do I find shoes, please?)
- ✔ **Wo ist der Aufzug, bitte?** *(voh ĭst dehr owf-tsoogk, bĭ-te)* (Where is the elevator, please?)

Saying excuse me

When asking for help, you can be especially nice and say **Entschuldigen Sie, bitte . . .** *(ênt-shŭl-dĭ-gen zee, bĭ-te)* (Excuse me, please . . .) at the beginning of your request. Doesn't roll off the tongue easily? Don't worry, people will understand that one immediately. Plus, your opening gives the person you're addressing time to focus and listen, and by the time you say what you actually want to find out, they're tuned in to you.

Here are a few examples of how you can use this phrase at the beginning of a question:

- ✔ **Entschuldigen Sie, bitte, wo sind die Toiletten?** *(ênt-shŭl-dĭ-gen zee, bĭ-te, voh zĭnt dee tô-ah-lê-tn)* (Excuse me please, where are the bathrooms?)
- ✔ **Entschuldigen Sie bitte, wo finde ich Wintermäntel?** *(ênt-shŭl-dĭ-gen zee, bĭ-te, voh fĭn-de ĭH vĭn-ter-mên-tel)* (Excuse me please, where do I find winter coats?)

If that's too long for you, stick the word **Entschuldigung** *(ênt-shŭl-dee-gûng)* (which actually translates as the noun "excuse") in front of whatever you're going to ask:

Entschuldigung. Wo ist der Ausgang, bitte? *(ênt-shŭl-dee-gûng, voh ĭst dehr ows-gâng, bĭ-te)* (Excuse me, where is the exit, please?)

Browsing with Style

Sometimes you just want to check out the merchandise on your own without anybody's assistance. However, store assistants may offer their help by saying something like the following:

- **Suchen Sie etwas Bestimmtes?** *(zoo-Hen zee êt-vâs be-shtîm-tes)* (Are you looking for something in particular?)

- **Kann ich Ihnen behilflich sein?** *(kân îH eeh-nen be-hîlf-lîH zyn)* (Can I help you?)

When all you want to do is browse, this phrase can help you politely turn down help:

> **Ich möchte mich nur umsehen.** *(îH muoH-te mîH noor ûm-zehn)* (I just want to look around.)

The store assistant will probably let you know it's okay to keep browsing by saying either of the following:

- **Aber natürlich. Sagen Sie Bescheid, wenn Sie eine Frage haben.** *(ah-ber nâ-tuur-lîH. zah-gn zee be-shyt, vên zee ay-ne frah-ge hah-bn)* (Of course. Just let me know if you need help.)

- **Rufen Sie mich, wenn Sie eine Frage haben.** *(roo-fn zee mîH, vên zee ay-ne frah-ge hah-bn)* (Call me if you have a question.)

Getting Assistance

In some situations, you may want or need some assistance. Here are some useful phrases you may say or hear:

- **Würden Sie mir bitte helfen? Ich suche . . .** *(vuur-dn zee meer bî-te hêl-fn. îH zoo-He . . .)* (Would you help me please? I'm looking for . . .)

- **Aber gern, hier entlang bitte.** *(ah-ber gêrn, heer ênt-lâng bî-te)* (But with pleasure. This way please.)

- **Welche Größe suchen Sie?** *(vêl-He gruo-se zoo-Hn zee)* (What size are you looking for?)

- **Welche Farbe soll es sein?** *(vêl-He fâr-be zôl ês zyn)* (What color do you want?)

- **Wie gefällt Ihnen diese Farbe?** *(vee ge-fêlt ee-nen dee-ze fâr-be)* (How do you like this color?)

You will find sales help in most Austrian, German, and Swiss stores competent and knowledgeable. That's due in part to the education system. Salespeople, as is true for most trades, pass a three-year apprenticeship that combines on-the-job training with trade school instruction.

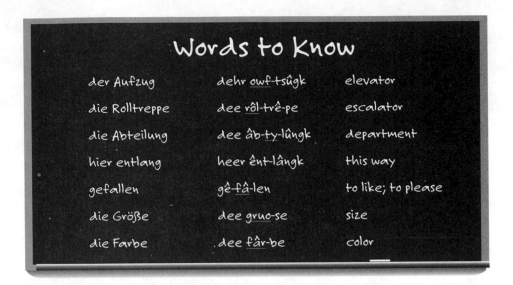

Words to Know

der Aufzug	dehr <u>owf</u>-tsûgk	elevator
die Rolltreppe	dee rôl-trê-pe	escalator
die Abteilung	dee âb-<u>ty</u>-lûngk	department
hier entlang	heer ênt-lângk	this way
gefallen	gê-<u>fâ</u>-len	to like; to please
die Größe	dee <u>gruo</u>-se	size
die Farbe	dee <u>fâr</u>-be	color

Shopping for Clothes

What is your heart's desire? Many terms for clothing are unisex, but some are usually reserved for one gender.

Some items usually meant for women include the following:

- **die Bluse** *(dee <u>bloo</u>-ze)* (blouse)
- **das Kleid** *(dâs klyt)* (dress)
- **das Kostüm** *(dâs kôs-<u>tuum</u>)* (suit)
- **der Hosenanzug** *(dehr <u>hoh</u>-zn-<u>ân</u>-tsûgk)* (pant suit)
- **der Rock** *(dehr rôk)* (skirt)

The following words usually apply to clothing for men:

- **das Oberhemd** *(dâs <u>oh</u>-ber-hêmt)* (button-down shirt)
- **der Anzug** *(dehr <u>ân</u>-tsoog)* (suit)

The following items are generally considered to be worn by both men and women:

- **der Pullover** *(dehr pû-<u>loh</u>-ver)* (sweater)
- **die Jacke** *(dee <u>yâ</u>-ke)* (cardigan, jacket)
- **das Jackett** *(dâss jhâ-kêt)* (jacket / sports coat)

- **der Blazer** *(dehr bleh-zer)* (blazer)
- **die Weste** *(dee vês-te)* (vest)
- **die Krawatte** *(dee krâ-vâ-te)* (tie)
- **der Mantel** *(dehr mân-tl)* (coat)
- **die Hose** *(dee hoh-ze)* (pants)
- **das Hemd** *(dâss hêmt)* (shirt)
- **das T-Shirt** *(dâs t-shirt)* (t-shirt)

Of course, these items can come in any number of fabrics and styles, including the following:

- **die Seide** *(dee zy-de)* (silk)
- **die Wolle** *(dee vô-le)* (wool)
- **die Baumwolle** *(dee bowm-vô-le)* (cotton)
- **das Leinen** *(dâss ly-nen)* (linen)
- **das Leder** *(dâs leh-der)* (leather)
- **gestreift** *(ge-shtryft)* (striped)
- **kariert** *(kâ-reert)* (checkered)
- **geblümt** *(ge-bluumt)* (with flowers)
- **gepunktet** *(ge-pûnk-tet)* (with dots)
- **einfarbig** *(ayn-fâr-bîgk)* (solid color)
- **sportlich** *(shpôrt-lîH)* (sporty, casual)
- **elegant** *(ê-le-gânt)* (elegant)

Color me German

The basic **Farben** *(fâr-bn)* (colors) are:

- **schwarz** *(shvârts)* (black)
- **weiß** *(vyss)* (white)
- **rot** *(roht)* (red)
- **grün** *(gruun)* (green)
- **gelb** *(gêlp)* (yellow)
- **blau** *(blâû)* (blue)

These words are all adjectives. If you want to find out more about how to fit them into phrases and sentences, go to Chapter 2.

Knowing your size

Finding the right size can be a headache in any shopping situation. In Europe, the problem is compounded by the fact that clothes sizes are not the same as in America. For German-speaking countries, the following charts might be a useful guideline to help you crack the code.

Here are the rough equivalents for sizes of women's clothes:

American	4	6	8	10	12	14	16	18	20
German	34	36	38	40	42	44	46	48	50

For men's jacket and suit sizes, use the following approximate conversions:

American	38	40	42	44	46	48	50
German	48	50	52	54	56	58	60

Talkin' the Talk

 Frau Schulte is in the ladies' section of a department store. She wants to buy a blouse and is talking to a saleswoman.

Verkäuferin: **Kann ich Ihnen behilflich sein?**
kân îH ee-nen be-hîlf-liH zyn
Can I help you?

Frau Schulte: **Ja bitte. Ich suche eine Bluse.**
yah bî-te. îH zoo-He ay-ne bloo-ze
Yes please. I'm looking for a blouse.

Verkäuferin: **Hier entlang, bitte. Welche Farbe soll es denn sein?**
heer ênt-lang bî-te. vêl-He fâr-be zôl ês dên zyn
Please come this way. What color do you want?

Frau Schulte: **Weiß.**
vyss
White.

Verkäuferin: **Suchen Sie etwas Sportliches?**
zoo-Hn zee êt-vâs shpôrt-lî-Hes
Are you looking for something casual?

Frau Schulte: **Nein, eher etwas Elegantes.**
                nyn, ê-her êt-vâs eh-le-gân-tes
                No, rather for something elegant.

Verkäuferin: **Gut. Welche Größe haben Sie?**
                goot, vêl-He gruo-se hah-bn zee
                Good. What is your size?

Frau Schulte: **Größe 38.**
                gruo-se âH-tûn-dry-ssîk
                Size 38.

Verkäuferin: **Wie gefällt Ihnen dieses Modell?**
                vee ge-fêlt ee-nen dee-zes mô-dêl
                How do you like this style?

Frau Schulte: **Sehr gut.**
                zehr goot
                Very much.

Trying it on

When you find something that looks promising, you may wish to try it on. You can ask the sales assistant the following question, supplying the name of the article that you want to try:

> **Kann ich . . . anprobieren?** *(kân îH . . . ân-prô-bee-ren)* (Can I try on . . .?)

A sales assistant may jump the gun and ask you

> **Möchten Sie . . . anprobieren?** *(muoH-ten zee . . . ân-prô-bee-ren)* (Would you like to try . . . on?)

In either case, the object of the game is to get to the dressing rooms, which you can ask about by saying

> **Wo sind die Umkleidekabinen?** *(voh zînt dee ûm-kly-de-kâ-bee-nen)* (Where are the fitting rooms?)

After you try your item on, the sales assistant may ask you any of the following questions to find out if you liked what you saw in the dressing room:

✔ **Passt . . .?** *(pâst . . .)* (Does . . . fit?)

✔ **Wie passt Ihnen . . .?** *(wie past ee-nen . . .)* (How does . . . fit you?)

✔ **Gefällt Ihnen . . .?** *(ge-fêlt ee-nen . . .)* (Do you like . . .?)

You can answer with any of the following, depending on how things went when you tried on your item:

✔ **Nein, . . . ist zu lang / kurz / eng / weit / groß / klein.** *(nyn, . . . îst tsû lâng / kûrts / êng / vyt / grohss / klyn)* (No, — . . . is too long / short / tight / loose / big / small.)

✔ **Können Sie mir eine andere Größe bringen?** *(kuo-nen zee meer ay-ne ân-de-re gruo-se brîngen)* (Can you get me another size?)

✔ **. . . passt sehr gut.** *(. . . pâst zehr goot)* (. . . fits very well.)

✔ **. . . steht mir.** *(. . . shteht meer)* (. . . suits me.)

✔ **. . . gefällt mir.** *(. . . ge-fêlt meer)* (I like . . .)

✔ **Ich nehme . . .** *(ÎH neh-me . . .)* (I'll take . . .)

Words to Know

eng	êng	tight
weit	vyt	loose
lang	lâng	long
kurz	kûrts	short
groß	grohs	big
klein	klyn	small
das Modell	dâs mô-dêl	style
anprobieren	ân-prô-bee-ren	to try on
bringen	brîn-gn	to bring
passen	pâ-sen	to fit
stehen	steh-en	to suit
gefallen	ge-fâ-len	to like
. . . gefällt mir	ge-fêlt meer	I like
die Umkleidekabine	dee ûm-kly-de-kâ-bee-ne	fitting room
kaufen	kow-fen	to buy

Talkin' the Talk

 Frau Schulte likes the blouse the saleswoman has shown her and wants to try it on.

Frau Schulte: **Ich möchte die Bluse anprobieren. Wo sind die Umkleidekabinen, bitte?**
îH <u>muoH</u>-te dee <u>bloo</u>-ze <u>ân</u>-prô-bee-ren. voh zînt dee <u>ûm</u>-kly-de-kâ-<u>bee</u>-nen, <u>bî</u>-te
I would like to try this blouse on. Where are the fitting rooms, please?

Verkäuferin: **Ja, natürlich. Hier entlang, bitte.**
yah nâ-<u>tuur</u>-lîH. heer ênt-<u>lâng</u>, <u>bî</u>-te
Of course. This way, please.

(A few minutes later Frau Schulte returns.)

Verkäuferin: **Passt die Bluse?**
pâst dee <u>bloo</u>-ze
Does the blouse fit?

Frau Schulte: **Ja. Ich nehme die Bluse!**
jah. îH <u>neh</u>-me dee <u>bloo</u>-ze
Yes. I'll take the blouse.

Paying the Bill

Most of the time, when you go shopping, the merchandise has a tag on it that tells you exactly how much something costs. The price you see on a price tag is what you pay for the merchandise at the cash register, including sales tax-VAT. If you don't reside in a country of the European Union, you can usually get a value added tax (VAT) refund when leaving the EU. VAT is called **die Mehrwertsteuer** (Mwst) *(dee <u>mêr</u>-vêrt-<u>stoy</u>-er)* in German. Your VAT refund is **die Mehrwertsteuerrückerstattung** *(dee <u>mêr</u>-vêrt-stoy-er-<u>ruuk</u>-êr-shtâ-tûng)*.

Although the word might look a bit daunting, getting your VAT back is usually simple. Just ask for a VAT refund form when you pay at the register. Collect all the receipts for merchandise you're taking out of the European Union, as well as the forms, and have the lot approved by a customs agent before you leave the EU to return home. If you have time you can head to the VAT refund counter at the airport, where you can get the refund (minus a service charge) in cash. Or you can mail in your receipts and receive a refund check drawn on an American bank.

Once in a while, you may find yourself in a situation where you need to ask about the price (**der Preis**) *(dehr prys)* of a piece of merchandise. Price tags, being the devious little critters that they are, have a way of falling off or being indecipherable, especially when handwritten. Case in point, the German number one can look awfully like the American number seven when scrawled by hand. The following simple phrases take care of the price question:

- ✔ **Was kostet . . .?** *(vâs kôs-tet)* (What does . . . cost?)
- ✔ **Wie viel kostet . . .?** *(vee feel kôs-tet)* (How much does . . . cost?)

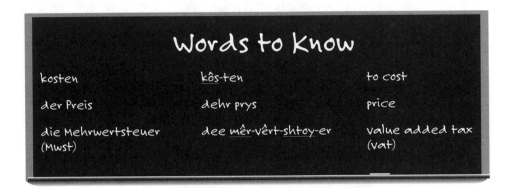

Words to Know

kosten	kôs-ten	to cost
der Preis	dehr prys	price
die Mehrwertsteuer (Mwst)	dee mêr-vêrt-shtoy-er	value added tax (vat)

Talkin' the Talk

Frau Schulte goes over to the cash register to pay for her purchase.

Kassiererin:	**Das macht 69.90 DM.**
	dâs mâHt noyn-ûnt-zêH-tsîgk mârk noyn-tsîgk
	69.90 Marks, please.

Frau Schulte:	**Nehmen Sie Kreditkarten?**
	nam-en see kreh-dît-kâr-ten
	Can I pay by credit card?

Kassiererin:	**Kein Problem.**
	kyn prô-blehm
	No problem.

Frau Schulte:	**Hier bitte.**
	heer bî-te
	Here.

Kassiererin:	**Danke. Würden Sie bitte unterschreiben? Und hier its Ihre Quittung.**
	dâng-ke. Wuur-den zee bî-te unter-<u>schry</u>-ben? <u>ûnt</u> heer îst ee-re <u>qui</u>-toong
	Thanks. Would you please sign here? And here is your receipt.
Frau Schulte:	**Danke!**
	<u>dâng</u>-ke
	Thanks!

Comparatively Speaking

In English, when you want to compare two things, you use the word "than" and an appropriate adjective or adverb. For example, in English, you could make the following comparisons:

- ✔ Mick Jagger is older than the hills.
- ✔ Cod is a tastier fish than scrod.

Comparisons in German are made in exactly the same way — all you need is the word **als** *(âls)* (than) plus the appropriate adverb or adjective. For example:

- ✔ **Die grünen Schuhe sind teurer als die weißen.** *(dee <u>gruu</u>-nen <u>shoo</u>-e zînt <u>toy</u>-rer âls dee <u>vy</u>-sn)* (The green sneakers are more expensive than the white ones.)

- ✔ **Das blaue Kleid gefällt mir besser als das grün-weiß gestreifte.** *(dâs <u>blâû</u>-e klyt ge-<u>fêlt</u> meer <u>bê</u>-ser âls dâs <u>gruun</u>-vys ge-<u>stryf</u>-te)* (I like the blue dress better than the one with the green and white stripes.)

- ✔ **Der gelbe Rock ist länger als der schwarze.** *(dehr <u>gêl</u>-be rôk îst <u>lên</u>-ger âls dehr <u>shvâr</u>-tse)* (The yellow skirt is longer than the black one.)

- ✔ **Hamburg ist größer als Düsseldorf.** *(<u>hâm</u>-bûrg îst <u>gruo</u>-ser âls <u>duu</u>-sel-dôrf)* (Hamburg is larger than Düsseldorf.)

Fun & Games

The following German words have been scrambled. They are all color words. Unscramble them!

1. UABL _____

2. ZRSAHWC _____

3. BLEG _____

4. TRO _____

5. NUARB _____

6. ÜRGN _____

1. BLAU 2. SCHWARZ 3. GELB 4. ROT 5. BRAUN 6. GRÜN

Chapter 7

Going Out on the Town

In This Chapter
▶ Telling time
▶ Getting information about movies, museums, and the theater
▶ Talking about entertainment
▶ Going to a party

T his chapter is all about having a good time — whether that means going out to a movie, attending an art show, or going to a party.

Performance spaces, museums, galleries, and exhibits abound in Germany, where cultural institutions receive state and federal funds to support their efforts. To experience German culture, you should check out these entertainments. Just like in America, the local newspapers offer weekly guides of events in the area (**der Veranstaltungskalender**) *(dehr fêr-__an__-shtâl-tûngks-kâ-lên-der).*

Before heading out for a day of fun or a night on the town, you need to know the days of the week and how to tell time in German. After all, you need to know when the fun starts.

Telling Time

In the classic movie *Casablanca,* an old German-speaking couple decides to practice their English by talking about the time. The man asks the woman, "What watch?" to which she replies, "One watch." The couple's English sounds a little off-beat because they tried to translate German literally into English. Read on to find out how you can avoid making a similar mistake when talking about the time in German.

Asking for the time

Most people make a point of wearing a watch so that they don't have to ask someone what time it is — why make life more complicated than it needs to be, right? However, you should know the following two phrases about asking for the time just in case your watch gets away from you:

- ✔ **Wie viel Uhr ist es?** *(vee feel <u>oor</u> îst ês)* (What time is it?)
- ✔ **Wie spät ist es?** *(vee <u>shpeht</u> îst ês)* (What time is it?)

When approaching somebody to ask the time you can, as usual, make the request a little more polite by adding the phrase **Entschuldigen Sie, bitte** *(ênt-<u>shûl</u>-dî-gen zee <u>bî</u>-te)* (Excuse me, please) to the beginning of your question.

Telling time the "old-fashioned" way: From 1 to 12

German speakers can use one of two systems for telling time: the "old-fashioned" way that uses the numbers on a standard clock (1 to 12); or by a 24-hour format, which is discussed in the following section.

Whether you adopt the 12-hour or the 24-hour routine is a matter of choice. Many German speakers use the 12-hour format when talking casually and revert to the 24-hour format when they want to make absolutely sure there's no room for misunderstandings, for example when discussing schedules. Many speakers prefer to use the 24-hour format at all times, and businesses like airlines, train and bus operators, as well as theaters and movie houses all adhere to the 24-hour system in their schedules.

On the hour

At the top of the hour, telling the time is very easy. You just say

Es ist . . . Uhr. *(ês îst . . . oor)* (It's . . . o'clock.)

substituting the number of the appropriate hour. (See Chapter 2 for more information on German numbers.)

On the quarter or half hour

The time gets a little more complicated when it's a quarter before or after the hour, but not too complicated. The following phrases show you how to use the German word for quarter (of course, you need to insert the appropriate hour in the phrases):

✔ **Es ist Viertel nach . . .** *(ês îst fîr-tl nâH . . .)* (It's a quarter past . . .)

✔ **Es ist Viertel vor . . .** *(ês îst fîr-tl fohr . . .)* (It's a quarter to . . .)

The half hour deserves a little extra explanation. German speakers are truly forward thinking when it comes to telling time on the half hour. They always refer to it being a half hour before the next hour, rather than it being half an hour after the last hour. For example, in German, when it's 4:30, you say that it's half an hour before 5:00 rather than it being half an hour after 4:00. In German, to say 4:30, you say **Es ist halb fünf** *(ês îst hâlp fuunf)*.

Es ist halb . . . *(ês îst hâlp . . .)* (It's half an hour before . . .)

A few minutes before and after

As we all know, sometimes things don't happen according to schedule. You may need to express a time that isn't directly on the hour, half hour, or quarter hour. In these cases, you can break down the time in terms of minutes before or after the hour. For example:

✔ **Es ist fünf Minuten vor zwölf.** *(ês îst fuunf mî-noo-tn fohr tsvuolf)* (It's five minutes to twelve.)

✔ **Es ist zwanzig Minuten nach sechs.** *(ês îst tsvân-tsîk mi-noo-tn nâH sêks)* (It's twenty minutes past six.)

It's very common to leave out the word **Minuten** in phrases such as those in the preceding list. Don't get confused if you hear someone say **Es ist fünf vor zwölf** instead of **Es ist fünf Minuten vor zwölf.** Both phrases mean the same thing.

Using the 24-hour routine: 0 to 24

For situations where it's important to avoid any chance of misunderstanding, German speakers use the 24-hour system (which is commonly known as military time in the United States). You see this system used commonly in any type of schedule, such as train timetables, movie house schedules, and so on.

With the 24-hour system, once you've reached 12, you keep on adding hours until you get to 24 or **Mitternacht** *(mî-ter-nâHt)* (midnight), which is also referred to as **null Uhr** *(nûl oor)* (literally: zero hour).

In this system of telling time, there are no phrases like half-past or a quarter before the hour. Everything is expressed in terms of minutes after the hour. Note in the following examples how the hour comes first and then the minutes:

✔ **Es ist 15 Uhr dreißig.** *(ês îst fuunf-tsehn oor dry-ssîgk)* (It's fifteen (hundred hours) and thirty.) This corresponds to 3:30 p.m.

✔ **Es ist 21 Uhr fünfzehn.** *(ês îst ayn-ûn-tsvân-tzîgk oor fuunf-tsehn)* (It's twenty one (hundred hours) and fifteen.) That's 9:15 p.m. to you and me.

✔ **Es ist 22 Uhr vierundvierzig.** *(ês îst tsvy-ûn-tsvân-tsîgk oor feer-ûn-fîr-tsîgk)* (It's twenty two (hundred hours) and forty-four.) You got it — it's 10:44 p.m.

✔ **Es ist null Uhr siebenundreißig.** *(ês îst nûl oor zee-bn-ûn-dry-sîgk)* (It's zero hours and thirty-seven.) You're up early this morning — it's 12:37 a.m!

Times of the day

This is how the day gets divided up in German. Don't take the following time periods too literally, though; they are meant as a guideline. Just as in English, different speakers may have slightly different ideas about when one part of the day starts and another ends.

✔ **der Morgen** *(dehr môr-gn)* (morning; 4:00 a.m. to noon)

✔ **der Vormittag** *(dehr fohr-mî-tahgk)* (morning; 9:00 a.m. to noon)

✔ **der Mittag** *(dehr mî-tahgk)* (noon; 12 noon to 2:00 p.m.)

✔ **der Nachmitag** *(dehr nâH-mî-tahgk)* (afternoon; 2:00 p.m. to 6:00 p.m.)

✔ **der Abend** *(dehr ah-bnt)* (evening; 6:00 p.m. to 12:00 p.m.)

✔ **die Nacht** *(dee nâHt)* (tonight; 12:00 p.m. to 4:00 a.m.)

Days of the week

Newspaper listings can tell you at what times a movie or a play is showing on different days, but unless you know the names of the days of **die Woche** *(dee wô-He)* (the week), you may end up sitting in the dark.

Your basic days

Some words in the German calendar actually sound and look similar to their English equivalents, which hopefully makes them fairly easy to remember.

The following days of the week are all the same gender, masculine (**der**), but generally they are used without an article. For example, if you want to say that today is Monday, you'd say **Heute ist Montag** *(hoy-te îst mohn-tahgk)*.

Without further ado, here are the days of the week:

✔ **Montag** *(mohn-tahgk)* (Monday)

✔ **Dienstag** *(deens-tahgk)* (Tuesday)

- **Mittwoch** *(mĭt-vôH)* (Wednesday)

- **Donnerstag** *(dônrs-tahgk)* (Thursday)

- **Freitag** *(fry-tâgk)* (Friday)

- **Samstag** / **Sonnabend** *(zâmss-tahgk / zôn-ah-bênt)* (Saturday)

- **Sonntag** *(zôn-tahgk)* (Sunday)

The following forms are used to indicate that something always happens on a particular day of the week. For example, you may get to a museum or a restaurant and find it closed. They may have a sign on the door reading **montags geschlossen** *(mohn-tahgks ge-shlôsn)* (closed on Mondays):

- **montags** *(mohn-tahgks)* (Mondays)

- **dienstags** *(deens-tahgks)* (Tuesdays)

- **mittwochs** *(mĭt-vôHs)* (Wednesdays)

- **donnerstags** *(dônrs-tahgks)* (Thursdays)

- **freitags** *(fry-tahgks)* (Fridays)

- **samstags** / **sonnabends** *(zâms-tahgks / zôn-ah-bênts)* (Saturdays)

- **sonntags** *(zôn-tahgks)* (Sundays)

Speaking of days . . .

In English, you don't always talk about days in terms of their proper names. For example, if today is Monday, and you want to refer to an event that will happen on Tuesday, you don't say, "That's happening on Tuesday." Rather, you say, 'That's happening tomorrow." It's the same in German, which uses the following words to help refer to specific days:

- **heute** *(hoy-te)* (today)

- **gestern** *(gês-tern)* (yesterday)

- **vorgestern** *(fohr-gês-tern)* (day before yesterday)

- **morgen** *(môr-gn)* (tomorrow)

- **übermorgen** *(uu-ber-môr-gn)* (day after tomorrow)

To speak precisely about a particular time on a specific day, you can combine the preceding words with the times of day discussed in the section "Times of the day" earlier in this chapter. Try the following examples on for size:

- **heute Morgen** *(hoy-te môr-gn)* (this morning)

- **heute Vormittag** *(hoy-te vohr-mĭ-tahgk)* (this morning)

- **gestern Abend** *(gês-tern ah-bnt)* (yesterday evening / last night)

GRAMMATICALLY SPEAKING

Pulling double duty

The word **morgen** *(môr-gn)* shows up in two different versions. Written with a lower case 'm,' **morgen** means *tomorrow.* The noun **der Morgen** written with upper case 'm' means *morning.* Theoretically, you could say **morgen Morgen** to mean *tomorrow morning,* but German speakers don't do that. Instead, they say **morgen früh** *(môr-gen fruu).*

Morgen, morgen does, however, exist. It's the beginning of a German proverb, and sometimes only the auspicious beginning is invoked. The complete proverb is

Morgen, morgen, nur nicht heute, sagen alle faulen Leute. *(môr-gn, môr-gn, nûr nîHt hoy-te zâ-gn â-le fow-len loy-te)* (Tomorrow, tomorrow, just not today, that's what all lazy folk say.)

What Would You Like to Do?

Sometimes you like to go out by yourself, and sometimes you would like company. If you want to brainstorm ideas with someone for the social calendar, you can ask:

> **Was wollen wir unternehmen?** *(vâs vô-len veer ûn-ter-neh-men)* (What do we want to do?)

This is a common way of asking somebody what you want to do together.

Use the following phrases if you want to find out about somebody's plans. These phrases are also very useful if you want to know if somebody is available:

- ✔ **Haben Sie (heute Abend) etwas vor?** *(hah-bn zee [hoy-te ah-bênt] êt-vâs fohr)* (Do you have anything planned [for tonight]?)

- ✔ **Hast du (morgen Vormittag) etwas vor?** *(hâst dû [môr-gn fohr-mî-tahgk] êt-vâs fohr)* (Do you have anything planned [for tomorrow morning]?)

- ✔ **Haben Sie (heute Abend) Zeit?** *(hah-bn zee [hoy-te ah-bênt] tsyt)* (Do you have time [tonight]?)

Going to the Movies

Watching films in a language you want to learn helps you assimilate new words, acquire useful expressions, and generally get a glimpse of some facets of the culture lurking behind the language. At the same time, you can get used to understanding many different speakers.

When you want to go to the movies, use the following phrases to let everyone know:

- ✔ **Ich möchte ins Kino gehen.** *(îH <u>muoH</u>-te îns <u>kee</u>-nô gehn)* (I would like to go to the movies.)

- ✔ **Ich möchte einen Film sehen.** *(îH muoH-te ay-nen fîlm zehn)* (I would like to see a film.)

Getting to the show

If you're searching for a movie to go to, newspaper listings are the easiest way to find out what's around. The listings usually tell you everything you need to know about **die Vorstellung** *(dee <u>vohr</u>-stê-lûng)* (the show): when and where the show is playing; who's in the show; and whether the show is in its original language — **im Original** *(îm ô-rî-gî-<u>nahl</u>)* (in the original language) — or if it's been dubbed — **synchronisiert** *(zyn-krô-nee-<u>zeert</u>)* (dubbed). (See the sidebar "What a strange voice you have" in this chapter for more information on language in movies.)

Sometimes you may not have the benefit of a newspaper listing to give you all of this information. The following phrases can help you when you need to ask about information for a movie:

- ✔ **In welchem Kino läuft . . .?** *(în <u>vêl</u>-Hêm <u>kee</u>-nô loyft . . .)* (In which movie house is . . . showing?)

- ✔ **Um wie viel Uhr beginnt die Vorstellung?** *(ûm <u>vee</u>-feel oor be-<u>gînt</u> dee <u>vohr</u>-stê-lûng)* (At what time does the show start?)

- ✔ **Läuft der Film im Original oder ist er synchronisiert?** *(loyft dehr fîlm îm ô-rî-gî-<u>nahl</u> <u>oh</u>-der îst ehr zyn-krô-nee-<u>zeert</u>)* (Is the film shown in the original (language) or is it dubbed?)

CULTURAL WISDOM

What a strange voice you have

Most foreign films shown in Germany are dubbed into German. Once in a while, especially in art film houses, foreign films are shown in the original language with German subtitles — **Originalfassung mit deutschen Untertiteln** *(ô-rî-gî-nahl-fâ-sûng mît doy-tshen ûn-têr-tî-teln)*. So if you're not keen on the mind-altering experience of listening to your favorite actors assuming strange voices and speaking in tongues, keep an eye open for the undubbed version of the film or go see movies filmed in German exclusively.

In multilingual Switzerland, you won't have to worry. Films are generally shown in the original language with subtitles in German, Italian, and French, as the case may be.

Purchasing tickets

You can use the following phrase whenever you want to buy tickets, be it for the opera, the movies, or the museum:

>**Ich möchte . . . Karten für . . .** *(īH muoH-te . . . kârtn fuur . . .)* (I would like . . . tickets for . . .)

After asking the attendant for your tickets, you may get some information about the show, including the following:

- ✔ **Die Vorstellung hat schon begonnen.** *(dee fohr-shtê-lûng hât shohn be-gô-nen)* (The show has already started.)

- ✔ **Die . . .-Uhr-Vorstellung ist leider ausverkauft.** *(dee . . .-oor-fohr-stê-lûng īsst ly-der ows-fêr-kowft)* (The show at . . . o'clock is unfortunately sold out.)

- ✔ **Wir haben noch Karten für die Vorstellung um . . . Uhr.** *(veer hah-bn nôH kâr-tn fuur dee fohr-shtê-lûng ûm . . . oor)* (There are tickets left for the show at . . . o'clock.)

These phrases work for any type of show or performance; they are not limited to the movie house.

Talkin' the Talk

Antje is talking to her friend Robert on the phone. Antje wants to go to the movies. After greeting her friend, Antje gets right to the point.

Antje:	**Der neue Sciencefictionfilm von Spielberg soll super spannend sein.** *dehr noy-e science-fic-tion-fîlm fon spiel-berg sôl soo-per shpâ-nent zayn* The new science-fiction film by Spielberg is supposed to be incredibly suspenseful.
Robert:	**Wann willst du gehen?** *vân vîlst dû gehn* When do you want to go?
Antje:	**Morgen Abend habe ich Zeit.** *môr-gn ah-bent hah-be îH tsyt* I have time tomorrow evening.

Robert: **Morgen passt mir auch.**
            môr-gn pâst meer owH
            Tomorrow works for me as well.

            In welchem Kino läuft der Film?
            în vêl-Hêm kee-nô loyft dehr fîlm
            In which movie house is the film showing?

Antje: **Im Hansatheater. Die Vorstellung beginnt um 20 Uhr.**
            îm hân-sâ-teh-ah-ter. dee fôr-shtê-lûng be-gînt ûm
            tsvân-tsîgk oor
            In the Hansa Theater. The show starts at 8:00.

Robert: **Gut, treffen wir uns um Viertel vor acht am Hansa.**
            goot, trê-fn veer ûns ûm fîr-tl fohr âHt âm hân-sâ
            Okay. Let's meet at a quarter to eight at the Hansa.

Antje: **Prima. Bis morgen dann.**
            pree-mâ. bîs môr-gn dân
            Great. Until tomorrow then.

Words to Know

das Kino	dâs kee-nô	movie house
der Spielfilm	dehr shpeel-fîlm	feature film
die Vorstellung	dee fohr-shtê-lûng	show
die Karte	dee kâr-te	ticket
die Eintrittskarte	dee ayn-trîts-kâr-te	ticket
der Platz	dehr plâts	seat
spannend	shpâ-nent	suspenseful
sehen	zeh-en	to see
laufen	low-fen	to show

What Was That? The Simple Past Tense of Sein

You may already be familiar with the present tense of **sein** *(zayn)* (to be): **Ich bin / du bist** *(îH bîn / dû bîst)* (I am / you are), and so on. (Turn to Chapter 2 for more information about the verb **sein**.) When talking about things past — such as I was, you were, they were — you put the verb **sein** into the simple past tense. (The simple past tense is called **Imperfekt** *[îm-pêr-fêkt]* in German. Not that you need to know that.) The simple past tense of the verb **sein** looks like this:

Conjugation	Pronunciation	English
ich war	îH vahr	I was
du warst	dû vârst	you were
Sie waren	zee <u>vah</u>-ren	you were
er, sie, es war	ehr, zee, ês vahr	he, she, it was
wir waren	veer <u>vah</u>-ren	we were
ihr wart	eer vârt	you were
Sie waren	zee <u>vah</u>-ren	you were
sie waren	zee <u>vah</u>-ren	they were

You can use the simple past tense of **sein** to express many different ideas and questions. Have a look at the past tense of **sein** in action:

- ✔ **Ich war gestern im Kino.** *(îH vahr <u>gês</u>-tern îm <u>kee</u>-nô)* (I was at the movies yesterday.)

- ✔ **Vorgestern war Sonntag.** *(<u>fohr</u>-gês-tern vahr <u>zôn</u>-tahgk)* (The day before yesterday was Sunday.)

- ✔ **Wie war der Film?** *(vee vahr dehr film)* (How was the film?)

- ✔ **Wir waren heute Morgen im Kunstmuseum.** *(veer <u>vah</u>-ren <u>hoy</u>-te <u>môr</u>-gn îm <u>kûnst</u>-mû-<u>zeh</u>-ûm)* (We were at the art museum this morning.)

- ✔ **Warst du letzte Woche in der Schule?** *(vârst dû <u>lêts</u>-te <u>vô</u>-He în dehr <u>shoo</u>-le)* (Were you at school last week?)

- ✔ **Wo waren Sie am Freitag?** *(vô <u>vâ</u>-ren zee âm <u>fry</u>-tahgk)* (Where were you on Friday?)

Going to the Museum

Germany has a long and fruitful museum tradition with many venerable institutions sprinkled liberally across the country. Most German museums receive state or federal funds and, as a consequence, charge comparatively low entrance fees.

If you're into art, you might keep an eye open for the **Kunstmuseum** *(kûnst-mû-zeh-ûm)* (art museum). If you want to find out more about the treasures of a certain area, go to the **Landesmuseum** *(lân-des-mû-zeh–ûm)* found in the capital of each state.

For history buffs, there is the **Historisches Museum** *(hîs-toh-rî-shes mû-zeh-ûm)* (Historical Museum), and if you're fascinated by natural history, you should look for the **Naturgeschichtliches Museum** *(nâ-toor-ge-shîHt-lî-Hes mû-zeh-ûm)* (Museum of Natural History). There are museums for virtually everything a human being might fancy.

Next time somebody asks you what you would like to do, just tell them

> **Ich möchte ins Museum gehen.** *(îH muoH-te îns mû-zeh-ûm gehn)*
> (I would like to go to the museum.)

When you want to catch an exhibition — **Ausstellung** *(ows-shtê-lûng)*, some of the following phrases should come in handy:

- **Ich möchte die . . . Ausstellung sehen.** *(Ich muoH-te dee ows-shtê-lûng zehn)* (I would like to see the . . . exhibition.)

- **In welchem Museum läuft die . . . Ausstellung?** *(în vêl-Hem mû-zeh-ûm loyft dee . . . ows-shtê-lûng)* (At which museum is the . . . exhibit running?)

- **Ist das Museum sonntags geöffnet?** *(îsst dâs mû-zeh-ûm zôn-tahgks ge-ûof-net)* (Is the museum open on Sudays?)

- **Um wie viel Uhr öffnet das Museum?** *(ûm vee-feel oor uof-net dâs mû-zeh-ûm)* (At what time does the museum open?)

- **Haben Sie eine Sonderausstellung?** *(hah-bn zee ay-ne zôn-der-ows-shtê-lûng)* (Do you have a special exhibit?)

Closed on Mondays

Museum mavens beware: Many European museums and other cultural institutions remain closed on Mondays, **montags geschlossen** *(mohn-tahgks ge-shlôssn)*. Make sure to check the opening hours, **die Öffnungszeiten** *(dee uof-nûngs-tsy-ten)*, before heading out.

Talkin' the Talk

Jan and Mona are planning a trip to a museum. They invite their friend Ingo to join them.

Jan: **Hallo Ingo. Wir wollen morgen ins Städtische Museum.**
hâ-lô în-gô. veer vô-len môr-gn îns shtê-tî-she mû-zeh-ûm
Hi Ingo. We want to go to the city museum tomorrow.

Mona: **Wir wollen uns die Ausstellung über die Bronzezeit ansehen.**
veer vô-len ûns dee ows-shtê-lûng uu-ber dee brôn-tse-tsyt ân-zehn
We want to see the exhibit about the Bronze Age.

Kommst du mit?
kômst dû mît
Do you want to come along?

Ingo: **Hmm, ich weiß nicht. Die Ausstellung habe ich gestern schon gesehen.**
hmm, îH vyss nîHt. dee ows-shtê-lûng hah-be îh gêss-tern shohn ge-zehn
Hmm, I don't know. I already saw the exhibit yesterday.

Mona: **Hat sie dir gefallen?**
hât zee deer ge-fâ-len
Did you like it?

Ingo: **Ja. Vielleicht komme ich noch einmal mit.**
yah. fee-lyHt kô-me îH nôH ayn-mahl mît
Yes. Maybe I'll come along for a second time.

Jan: **Wir wollen morgen um 10.00 Uhr in die Ausstellung.**
veer vô-len môr-gn ûm tsehn oor în dee ows-shtê-lûng
We want to go to the exhibit tomorrow at ten o'clock.

Ingo: **Gut. Ich treffe euch dort.**
goot. îH trê-fe oyH dohrt
Good. I'll meet you there.

Talking about Action in the Past

Earlier in this chapter, we show you how to use the simple past tense of the verb **sein** in order to say things like "I was at the musuem yesterday" or "It was cold yesterday." To communicate a full range of actions in the past tense, you need a different set of words.

The perfect tense — **Perfekt** (_pêr-fêkt_) — is just the set of words that you need. To form the perfect tense, you need two things:

✔ The appropriate present-tense form of either **haben** (_hah-ben_) or **sein** (_zayn_). If the sentence is a question, this present tense form appears as the first word of the sentence. If your sentence is a straightforward statement, it appears as the second word of the sentence.

✔ The past participle of the action verb, which goes at the end of the sentence. Whether you use **haben** or **sein** with the past participle of the action verb depends on which action verb you're working with. Simply put, most verbs require **haben**, and some use **sein**. You just have to memorize which action verbs use **haben** and which use **sein**. (More on how to form the past particple of a verb in the next section.)

You should consider the perfect tense a real lifesaver. This tense is very versatile in German, and you can use it to refer to most actions and situations that took place in the past. There are many other tenses you can use to describe past actions, but if you have perfect tense under your belt, you won't need the other tenses until you're writing your first book in German or are preparing to address the German Parliament. Hey — it could happen! But not for a while.

Forming the past participle

The past participle is a form you might want to learn with each new verb. However, there are a few rules that make life easier. In order to apply them, you need to know which category the verb in question falls into.

Weak verbs

Weak verbs, also known as regular verbs, form the largest group of German verbs. When forming the past participle of a weak verb, use the following formula:

ge + **verb stem** (the infinitive minus -en) + **(e)t** = **past participle**

Okay, this isn't really as hard as algebra! Look at how the formula plays out on the common verb **fragen** *(frah-gen)* (to ask).

> **ge + frag + t = gefragt**

Now check out a verb that has the ending **-et** instead of **–t**, like **reden** *(reh-den)* (to talk):

> **ge + red + et = geredet**

In this case, you add **-et** so you can actually pronounce the word ending.

Another verb that follows this pattern is **öffnen** *(uof-nen)* (to open):

> **ge + öffn + et**

Without the **e** it would be hard to pronounce the consonant cluster.

Strong verbs

Other verbs, the so-called strong verbs, also known as irregular verbs, follow a different pattern. They add **ge-** in the beginning and **-en** at the end. Forming the past participle of a strong verb entails the following:

> **ge + verb stem** (the infinitive minus -en) **+ en = past participle**

The verb **kommen** *(kô-men)* (to come) is a good example for this:

> **ge + komm + en = gekommen**

Pesky critters that they are, some strong verbs change their verb stem when forming a past participle. For example, a stem vowel, and sometimes even a stem consonant, can change.

The verb **helfen** *(hêl-fen)* (to help) changes its stem vowel:

> **ge + holf + en = geholfen**

The verb **gehen** *(geh-en)* (to go) changes a vowel and a consonant!

> **ge + gang + en = gegangen**

Gehen, a verb indicating a change of place, is one of the verbs conjugated (or used) with **sein**. All the verbs conjugated with **sein** are strong verbs. So you need to remember a vowel and possibly a consonant change for each of those. But on the sunny side, remember: One tense gets you really far in German, since perfect tense is used all the time in the spoken language.

Using haben in the perfect tense

Because the present-tense forms of **haben** are so important to forming the perfect tense with many verbs, here's a quick reminder of the conjugation of **haben** in the present tense:

Conjugation	*Pronunciation*
ich habe	îH hah-be
du hast	dû hâst
Sie haben	zee hah-bn
er / sie / es hat	ehr / zee / ês hât
wir haben	veer hah-bn
ihr habt	eer hahpt
Sie haben	zee hah-bn
sie haben	zee hah-bn

Table 7-1 shows you some very common German verbs that use **haben** in the perfect tense.

Table 7-1	Verbs That Use haben in the Perfect Tense
Verb	*Past Participle*
hören *(huo-ren)* (to hear)	gehört
kaufen *(kow-fen)* (to buy)	gekauft
lachen *(lâ-Hen)* (to laugh)	gelacht
lesen *(leh-zen)* (to read)	gelesen
nehmen *(neh-men)* (to take)	genommen
sehen *(zeh-en)* (to see)	gesehen

Take a look at some examples of how the verb **haben** combines with a past participle to make the perfect tense:

- ✔ **Ich habe den Film gesehen.** *(îH hah-be dehn fîlm ge-zehn)* (I have seen the film.)

- ✔ **Hast du eine Theaterkarte bekommen?** *(hâst dû ay-ne teh-ah-ter-kâr-te be-kô-men)* (Did you get a theater ticket?)

> ✔ **Wir haben das Kino verlassen.** *(veer hah-ben dâs kee-nô vêr-lâ-sn)* (We left the movie house.)

> ✔ **Habt ihr Karten für die Matinee gekauft?** *(hâpt eer kâr-tn fuur dee mâ-tee-neh ge-kowft)* (Did you buy tickets for the matinee?)

> ✔ **Hat euch der Film gefallen?** *(hât oyH dehr film ge-fâ-len)* (Did you like the movie?)

Using sein in the perfect tense

Some verbs don't use the present tense of **haben** to form the perfect tense, but use **sein** instead.

As a reminder, here are the present tense forms of sein:

Conjugation	*Pronunciation*
ich bin	îH bîn
du bist	dû bîst
Sie sind	zee zînt
er / sie / es ist	ehr /zee / ês îst
wir sind	veer zînt
ihr seid	eer zyt
Sie sind	zee zînt
sie sind	zee zînt

Verbs in that category include the verb **sein** itself and generally verbs that indicate a change of place or a change of state. Sounds a bit theoretical? Table 7-2 shows you some common verbs that take **sein** in the perfect tense.

Incidentally, all verbs conjugated with **sein** are strong verbs, that's to say their past participles are irregular. It's best to memorize the past participle whenever you pick up a new verb that's used with **sein**.

Table 7-2	Verbs That Use sein in the Perfect Tense
Verb	*Past Participle*
gehen *(geh-en)* (to go)	gegangen
fahren *(fah-ren)* (to drive / ride)	gefahren
fliegen *(flee-gen)* (to fly)	geflogen
kommen *(kô-men)* (to come)	gekommen

Verb	Past Participle
laufen *(low-fen)* (to run)	gelaufen
sein *(zyn)* (to be)	gewesen

Have a look at these examples of verbs forming the present perfect tense with the present tense of **sein** and the past participle.

- **Ich bin ins Theater gegangen.** *(îH bîn îns teh-ah-ter ge-gân-gen)* (I went to the theater.)

- **Bist du mit dem Auto gekommen?** *(bîst dû mît dehm ow-tô ge-kô-men)* (Did you come by car?)

- **Sie ist mit dem Zug gefahren.** *(zee îst mît dehm tsoogk ge-fah-ren)* (She went by train.)

- **Wir sind letzte Woche ins Kino gegangen.** *(veer zînt lêts-te wô-He îns kee-nô ge-gân-gen)* (We went to the movies last week.)

- **Seid ihr durch den Park gelaufen?** *(zyt eer dûrH dehn pârk ge-low-fen)* (Did you run through the park?)

- **Sie sind gestern im Theater gewesen.** *(zee zînt gês-tern îm teh-ah-ter ge-veh-zen)* (They were at the theater yesterday.)

Bringing Down the House

Wherever you might be staying in Europe, you're probably just a short trip away from cultural institutions presenting **Oper** *(oh-per)* (opera), **Konzert** *(kôn-tsêrt)* (concert), and **Theater** *(teh-ah-ter)* (theater). Performing arts centers abound in Europe, so if you're in a festive mood, you should say **Ich möchte heute Abend ausgehen.** *(îH muoH-te hoy-te ah-bênt ows-gehn)* (I would like to go out tonight.)

Worried about the dress code? It's very liberal, so you can wear what you wish. Often, people dress up for **Premiere** *(prem-yeh-re)* (opening night) or **Galavorstellung** *(gâ-lâ-fohr-shtê-lûng)* (gala performance), but other than that, almost anything goes.

The following words and phrases may help you out on a trip to the opera or theater:

- **Ich möchte ins Theater / Konzert gehen.** *(îH muoH-te îns teh-ah-ter / Kôn-tsert geh-en)* (I would like to go to the theater / a concert.)

- **Ich möchte in die Oper gehen.** *(îH muoH-te în dee oh-per geh-en)* (I would like to go to the opera.)

✔ **Gehen wir ins Theater / Konzert.** *(gehn veer îns teh-ah-ter / kôn-tsert)* (Let's go to the theater / a concert.)

✔ **Gehen wir in die Oper.** *(gehn veer în dee oh-per)* (Let's go to the opera.)

✔ **Wann ist die Premiere von . . .?** *(vân îst dee prêm-yeh-re fôn . . .)* (When is the opening night of . . .?)

✔ **In welchem Theater spielt . . .?** *(în vêl-Hem teh-ah-ter shpeelt . . .)* (In which theater is . . . showing?)

✔ **Gibt es noch Orchesterplätze für die Matinee?** *(gîpt ês nôH ôr-kês-ter-plê-tse fuur dee mâ-tî-neh)* (Are there any orchestra seats left for the matinee?)

Words to Know

das Theater	dâs teh-ah-ter	theater
die Oper	dee oh-per	opera / opera house
das Ballett	dâs bâ-lêt	ballet
die Pause	dee pow-ze	intermission
der Sänger / die Sängerin	dehr zên-ger / dee zên-ge-rîn	singer
der Schauspieler / die Schauspielerin	dehr show-shpee-ler / dee show-spee-le-rîn	actor/actress
der Tänzer / die Tänzerin	dehr tên-tser / dee tên-tse-rîn	dancer
singen	zîn-gen	to sing
tanzen	tân-tsen	dance
klatschen	klât-shen	to clap
der Beifall	dehr by-fâl	applause
die Zugabe	dee tsoo-gah-be	encore
die Kinokasse / Theaterkasse	dee kee-nô-kâ-sse / teh-ah-ter-kâ-sse	box office (movies) and theater
der Platz	dehr plâts	seat

How Was It? Talking about Entertainment

When it comes to entertainment, everybody seems to have an opinion. So why miss out on the fun?

Asking your opinion

Someone might ask you one of the following questions, or you might pose one of them to someone else, in order to start a conversation about an exhibition, film, or performance (the first version is for speaking with someone formally; the second is for informal speaking):

✔ **Hat Ihnen die Ausstellung / der Film / die Oper gefallen?** *(hât ee-nen dee ows-shtê-lûng / dehr film / dee oh-per ge-fâ-len)* (Did you like the exhibition / the movie / the opera?)

✔ **Hat dir die Ausstellung / der Film / die Oper gefallen?** *(hât deer dee ows-shtê-lûng / dehr film / dee oh-per ge-fâ-len)* (Did you like the exhibition / the movie / the opera?)

Telling people what you think

Now comes the fun part — telling someone what you think about a film or show you've just seen. For starters, you can say whether you liked or didn't like the entertainment. Try one of the following on for size:

✔ **Die Ausstellung / der Film / die Oper hat mir (sehr) gut gefallen.** *(dee ows-shtê-lûng / dehr film / dee oh-per hât meer zehr goot ge-fâ-len)* (I liked the exhibition / the movie / the opera (a lot).)

✔ **Die Ausstellung / der Film / die Oper hat mir (gar) nicht gefallen.** *(dee ows-shtê-lûng / dehr film / dee oh-per hât meer (gâr) nîHt ge-fâ-len)* (I didn't like the exhibition / the movie / the opera (at all).)

You may want to follow up that statement with a reason. Start out by saying:

Die Ausstellung / Der Film / Die Oper war wirklich . . . *(dee ows-shtê-lûng / dehr film / dee oh-per vahr vîrk-lîH . . .)* (The exhibition / the movie / the opera was really . . .)

Then you can finish the thought with any of the following adjectives that might apply. (You can always string a few of these adjectives together with the conjunction **und** (*ûnd*) (and) if you like):

- **aufregend** (*owf-reh-gent*) (exciting)

- **wunderschön** (*vûn-der-shuon*) (beautiful)

- **phantastisch** (*fân-tâs-tîsh*) (fantastic)

- **ausgezeichnet** (*ows-ge-tsyH-net*) (excellent)

- **spannend** (*shpâ-nênt*) (suspenseful)

- **unterhaltsam** (*ûn-ter-hâlt-zahm*) (entertaining)

- **sehenswert** (*zeh-êns-vehrt*) (worth seeing)

- **enttäuschend** (*ênt-toy-shênt*) (disappointing)

- **langweilig** (*lâng-vy-lîg*) (boring)

Talkin' the Talk

Frau Peters went to the theater last night. Today, at the office, she tells her colleague Herr Krüger about the show.

Herr Krüger: **Sind Sie nicht gestern im Theater gewesen?**
zînt zee nîHt gês-tern îm theh-ah-ter ge-weh-zen
Weren't you at the theater last night?

Frau Peters: **Ich habe das neue Ballet gesehen.**
îH hah-be dâs noy-e bâ-lêt ge-zehn
I saw the new ballet.

Herr Krüger: **Wie hat es Ihnen gefallen?**
vee hât ês ee-nen ge-fâ-len
How did you like it?

Frau Peters: **Die Tänzer sind phantastisch. Die Vorstellung hat mir ausgezeichnet gefallen.**
dee tên-tser zînt fân-tâs-tîsh. dee vôr-shtê-lûng hât meer ows-ge-tsyH-net ge-fâ-len
The dancers are fabulous. I liked the performance very much.

Herr Krüger: **War es einfach, Karten zu bekommen?**
vahr ês ayn-fâH, kâr-tn tsû be-kô-men
Was it easy to get tickets?

Frau Peters: **Ja. Ich habe die Karte gestern Morgen an der Theaterkasse gekauft.**
yah, îH hah-be dee kâr-te gês-têrn môrgn ân dehr teh-ah-ter-kâ-se ge-kowft
Yes, I bought the ticket at the box office yesterday morning.

Going to a Party

Just as in America, different people have different ideas about what makes a good party. Some folks like to plan an event months ahead, and they work hard to make sure that everything falls neatly into place. Others prefer their parties to be impromptu events where the host has no more idea about the way things are going to shape up than the guests, some of whom might just be friends of friends of friends tagging along.

In case you're invited to a rather formal gathering at somebody's private residence, it would be polite to bring a small gift, such as a bottle of wine.

If you receive a written **Einladung** *(ayn-lah-dûng)* (invitation), make sure to check if you're expected to RSVP. In that case, the invitation may hold the cryptic message **U. A. w. g.,** which is short for **Um Antwort wird gebeten** *(ûm ânt-vôrt vîrt ge-beh-ten)*, a request to respond to the invitation.

If you're asked to a rather informal party that could very well include dancing, your host may ask you to contribute a bottle. You can also take the initiative and ask if you should bring anything by asking **Soll ich etwas mitbringen?** *(zôl îH êt-vâs mît-brîn-gen)* (Do you want me to bring anything?).

If you're invited to **Kaffee und Kuchen** *(kâ-feh ûnt koo-Hen)*, coffee and cake in the afternoon, a German institution, don't expect to be asked for dinner. You may well be, but you shouldn't count on it.

Getting an invitation

You may hear any of the following common phrases when receiving an invitation — **die Einladung** *(dee ayn-lah-dûng)* — to a party:

- ✔ **Ich würde Sie gern zu einer Party einladen.** *(îH vuur-de zee gêrn tsû ay-ner pâr-tee ayn-lah-den)* (I would like to invite you to a party.)

- ✔ **Wir wollen eine Party feiern. Hast du Lust zu kommen?** *(veer vô-len ay-ne pâr-tee fy-ern. hâst dû lûst tsû kô-men)* (We want to have a party. Do you feel like coming?)

You may need to ask when and where the party is going to take place before you can accept or decline the invitation. These simple phrases can get you the information you need:

> ✔ **Wann findet die Party statt?** *(vân fin-det dee pâr-tee shtât)* (When does the party take place?)

> ✔ **Wo findet die Party statt?** *(vô fin-det dee pâr-tee shtât)* (Where does the party take place?)

Declining

If you can't make it (or don't want to go for some reason), you can politely turn down the invitation by saying the following:

> ✔ **Nein, tut mir leid, ich kann leider nicht kommen.** *(nyn, tût meer lyt, îH kân ly-der nîHt kô-men)* (No, sorry. Unfortunately, I won't be able to make it.)

> ✔ **Nein, da kann ich leider nicht. Ich habe schon etwas anderes vor.** *(nyn, dâ kân îH ly-der nîHt. îH hah-be shohn êt-vâs ân-de-res fohr)* (No, unfortunately, I won't be able to make it. I have other plans.)

Accepting

If the time, place, and your mood are right, you can accept an invitation with the following phrases:

> ✔ **Vielen Dank. Ich nehme die Einladung gern an.** *(fee-len dângk. îH neh-me dee ayn-lah-dûng gêrn ân)* (Thank you very much. I'll gladly accept the invitation.)

> ✔ **Gut, ich komme gern. Soll ich etwas mitbringen?** *(goot, îH kô-me gêrn. zôl îH êt-vâs mît-brîn-gen)* (Good, I'd like to come. Would you like me to bring anything?)

To the question of whether you can bring something with you, your host may respond:

> ✔ **Nicht nötig. Für Essen und Trinken ist gesorgt.** *(nîHt nuo-tîg. fuur êsn ûnt trîn-ken îst ge-zôrgt)* (Not necessary. Food and drink are taken care of.)

> ✔ **Es wäre schön, wenn Sie . . . mitbringen.** *(ês vê-re shuon, vên zee . . . mît-brîn-gen)* (It would be nice if you brought . . . along.)

> ✔ **Es wäre schön, wenn du . . . mitbringst.** *(ês vê-re shuon, vên dû . . . mît-brîn-gst)* (It would be nice if you brought . . . along.)

Talking about a party

When someone asks you **Wie war die Party am Samstag?** *(vee vahr dee pâr-tee âm zâms-tahgk)* (How was the party on Saturday?), here are some possible responses:

- ✔ **Toll, wir haben bis . . . Uhr gefeiert.** *(tôl, veer hah-bn bîs . . . oor ge-fy-êrt)* (Great. We partied until . . . o'clock.)

- ✔ **Wir haben uns ausgezeichnet unterhalten.** *(veer hah-bn ûns ows-ge-tsyH-net ûn-ter-hâl-ten)* (We had a great time.)

- ✔ **Die Party war . . .** *(dee pâr-tee vahr)* (The party was . . .)

Check in the list of adjectives in the section "Telling people what you think" earlier in this chapter for the appropriate descriptions to fill in the preceding phrases.

Fun & Games

In the following statements, you want to talk about something fun that you or someone else did in the past. Fill in the appropriate forms of **haben** or **sein**, choosing from the following list.

habe   hat   haben   seid   hast   sind

1. Wir _____ letzte Woche eine Party gefeiert.

2. _____ du schon den neuen Western im Kino gesehen?

3. _____ ihr am Wochenende im Kino gewesen?

4. Ich _____ mir die Sonderausstellung im Museum angesehen.

5. Herr und Frau Munster _____ ins Theater gegangen.

6. Alexander _____ eine Kinokarte gekauft.

Answer key: 1. haben 2. Hast 3. Seid 4. habe 5. sind 6. hat

Chapter 8

Recreation and the Outdoors

●●

In This Chapter

▶ Discussing hobbies and interests

▶ Playing sports

▶ Exploring the outdoors: animals and plants

●●

*I*n this chapter, we look at the fun things people do when they are not working. Europeans receive an average of between 25 and 30 vacation days per year, and they like to make the most of them. They enjoy visiting foreign places as well as the many beautiful spots inside their own countries. Whether sailing on one of many lakes, skiing in the mountains, or simply enjoying nature while walking on one of the many well-marked hiking trails, Europeans like to keep busy, even in leisure, and they like to have fun.

Talking about Hobbies and Interests

During the course of conversation, the topic often turns to people's various interests, including collecting and other hobbies. In this section, we tell you what you need to know to join in the conversation.

Collecting

People like to collect anything and everything. Maybe you'll get inspired, too, or are an avid collector already. You can tell people about your particular area of interest by saying either of the following:

✔ **Ich sammele . . .** *(îH zâm-le . . .)* (I collect . . .)

✔ **Ich interessiere mich für . . .** *(îH în-te-re-see-re mîH fuur . . .)* (I'm interested in . . .)

At the end of these phrases, you name the thing you like to collect. For example, you could finish with any of the following:

- **Briefmarken** *(breef-mâr-ken)* (stamps)

- **Münzen und Medaillen** *(muun-tsen ûnt mê-dâl-yen)* (coins and medals)

- **antikes Glas und Porzellan** *(ân-tee-kes glahs ûnt pôr-tse-lahn)* (antique glass and porcelain)

- **Antiquitäten und Trödel** *(ân-tî-kvî-teh-ten ûnt truo-dl)* (antiques and bric-a-brac)

- **Puppen** *(pû-pen)* (dolls)

Telling people about your hobby

Some people enjoy making things with their hands. Whether it is something to eat or something to wear, the rewards are obvious — as are the rewards of knowing how to describe your favorite hobby in German. Just use this simple phrase to introduce the topic:

> **Mein Hobby ist . . .** *(myn hô-bee îst . . .)* (My hobby is . . .)

At the end of this phrase, you supply the necessary information.

For example:

- **Basteln** *(bâs-teln)* (crafts)

- **Malen** *(mah-len)* (painting)

- **Kochen** *(kô-Hen)* (cooking)

- **. . . sammeln** *(. . . zâ-meln)* (collecting . . .)

- **Gärtnerei** *(gêrt-ne-ry)* (gardening)

Getting Reflexive

German verbs have a reputation for acting a bit strangely. They do things that English verbs just don't do — for example, German verbs can go at the end of a sentence. And sometimes they split in two, with only one part of the verb going to the end of a sentence! (See Chapter 14 for more on verbs that split.) Hold on to your socks. We are about to tell you something about German verbs that you may find truly riveting.

Some German verbs just can't make it on their own. Certain verbs always need a helper with them in the sentence in order to work. They are always accompanied by a pronoun in the accusative case. The pronoun reflects back (just like a mirror) on the subject. That's why these verbs are usually called *reflexive verbs* and the pronouns are called *reflexive pronouns*.

Accusing your pronouns

Hold up here! What are these so-called reflexive pronouns in the accusative case? Well, most of them may sound familiar. Table 8-1 shows you the accusative reflexive pronouns.

Table 8-1	Accusative Reflexive Pronouns
Personal Pronoun	*Reflexive Pronoun*
ich	mich (mîH)
du	dich (dîH)
Sie	sich (zîH)
er	sich (zîH)
sie	sich (zîH)
es	sich (zîH)
wir	uns (ûns)
ihr	euch (oyH)
Sie	sich (zîH)
sie	sich (zîH)

The reflexive pronoun goes after the conjugated verb in a normal sentence. In a question starting with a verb, the reflexive pronoun goes after the subject. (See Chapter 2 for more information on forming questions in German.) Take a look at some of these reflexive verbs and accusative reflexive pronouns doing their thing in the following sentences:

- **Ich interessiere mich für Bildhauerei.** *(îH în-te-re-see-re mîH fuur bîlt-howê-ry)* (I am interested in sculpting.) Literally, this sentence translates as: I interest myself in sculpting. The subject **ich** (I) is reflected in the pronoun **mich** (myself).

- **Freust du dich auf deinen Urlaub?** *(froyst dû dîH owf dy-nen oor-lowp)* (Are you looking forward to your vacation?)

- **Herr Grobe meldet sich für einen Fotokurs an.** *(hêr groh-be mêl-det zîH fuur ay-nen foh-tô-kûrs ân)* (Mr. Grobe is registering for a photography class.)

- **Herr und Frau Weber erholen sich im Urlaub an der Küste.** *(hêr ûnt frow veh-ber êr-hoh-len zîH îm oor-lowp ân dehr kuus-te)* (Mr. and Mrs. Weber are relaxing during their vacation on the coast.)

> ✔ **Stellen Sie sich vor, wen ich gerade getroffen habe!** (_shtê_-len zee zîH
> fohr, vehn îH ge-_rah_-de ge-_trô_-fn _hah_-be) (Imagine who I just ran into!)

Some common reflexive verbs

If you're wondering how in the world you're supposed to know which verbs
are reflexive and which ones aren't, good for you — it's an excellent question.
Unfortunately, our answer is one you may not look forward to: You just have
to memorize them.

To give you a leg up, we can tell you some of the most common reflexive
verbs you may run into. Take **sich freuen** (_zîH froy_-en) (to be happy) as an
example.

Conjugation	Pronunciation
ich freue mich	îH froy-e mîH
du freust dich	dû froyst dîH
Sie freuen sich	zee froy-en zîH
er, sie, es freut sich	êr, zee, ês froyt zîH
wir freuen uns	veer froy-en ûns
ihr freut euch	eer froyt oyH
Sie freuen sich	zee froy-en zîH
sie freuen sich	zee froy-en zîH

Other very common reflexive verbs include:

> ✔ **sich freuen auf** (_zîH froy_-en owf) (to look forward to)
>
> ✔ **sich freuen über** (_zîH froy_-en _uu_-ber) (to be glad about)
>
> ✔ **sich aufregen** (_zîH owf_-reh-gen) (to get excited or upset)
>
> ✔ **sich beeilen** (_zîH bê-_ay_-len) (to hurry)
>
> ✔ **sich entscheiden** (_zîH ênt-_shy_-den) (to decide)
>
> ✔ **sich erinnern** (_zîH êr-_in_-ern) (to remember)
>
> ✔ **sich gewöhnen an** (_zîH ge-_vuo_-nen ân) (to get used to)
>
> ✔ **sich interessieren für** (_zîH în-te-rê-_see_-ren fuur) (to be interested in)
>
> ✔ **sich setzen** (_zîH zê_-tsen) (to sit down)
>
> ✔ **sich unterhalten** (_zîH ûn-têr-_hâl_-ten) (to talk, to enjoy oneself)
>
> ✔ **sich verspäten** (_zîH fêr-_shpeh_-ten) (to be late)
>
> ✔ **sich vorstellen** (_zîH fohr_-shtê-len) (to introduce oneself, to imagine)

Talkin' the Talk

 Anke runs into her friend Jürgen at the supermarket. The two are talking about Anke's vacation plans.

Jürgen: **Hallo Anke. Wie gehts? Wir haben uns lange nicht gesehen.**
hâ-lô âng-ke. wee gates. veer hah-bn ûns lân-ge nîHt ge-zehn
Hallo Anke. How are you? We haven't seen each other in a long time.

Anke: **Ich hatte viel zu tun. Aber jetzt habe ich endlich Urlaub.**
îH hâ-te feel tsû toon. ah-ber yêtst hah-be îH ênt-lîH oor-lowp
I had a lot of work. But now I finally have vacation.

Jürgen: **Wie schön. Hast du was vor?**
vee shuon. hâst dû vâs fohr
How nice. Do you have anything planned?

Anke: **Ich fahre in die Toskana. Ich nehme an einem Malkurs teil.**
îH fah-re în dee tôs-kah-nâ. îH neh-me ân ay-nem mahl-kûrs tyl
I am going to Tuscany. I am taking part in a painting class.

Jürgen: **Wie lange bleibst du?**
vee lân-ge blypst dû
How long are you staying?

Anke: **Zwei Wochen. Ich freue mich riesig auf den Kurs.**
tsvy vô-Hen. îH froy-e mîH ree-zîgk owf dehn kûrs
Two weeks. I'm really looking forward to the course.

Jürgen: **Ich hoffe, du erholst dich gut.**
îH hô-fe, dû êr-hohlst dîH goot
I hope you'll get a good rest.

Words to Know

teilnehmen an	tyl-neh-men ân	to participate
sich für etwas interessieren	zîH fuur êt-vâs în-te-re-see-ren	to be interested in something
sich auf etwas freuen	zîH owf êt-vâs froy-en	to be looking forward to something
sich sehen	zîH zeh-en	to see each other
dauern	dow-ern	to last
der Malkurs	dehr mahl-kûrs	painting class

Playing Sports

Europeans, like people all over the world, have been getting a lot more health conscious in recent years. Many people try to eat healthier foods and to exercise more. They want to keep fit, whether it means hitting and kicking balls, peddling up steep hills, or hanging loose and feeling the spray of the surf against them. With the words and phrases we show you in this section, you'll be able to share your interest in sports with other people.

Playing around with the verb spielen

You can express your interest in playing many sports by using the verb **spielen** *(shpee-len)* (to play) in the following phrase:

> **Ich spiele gern . . .** *(îH shpee-le gêrn . . .)* (I like to play . . .)

You can insert the names of the following sports at the end of the sentence, and then, let the games begin!

- **Fußball** *(foos-bâl)* (soccer)
- **Handball** *(hânt-bâl)* (handball)
- **Basketball** *(bahs-ket-bâl)* (basketball)
- **Golf** *(gôlf)* (golf)
- **Tennis** *(tê-nîs)* (tennis)

With some sports, it's the verb

Use the following expression to communicate what you're in the mood for:

Ich möchte gern . . . *(īH muoH-te gêrn . . .)* (I would like to . . .)

Here are a few activities, which, again, you can insert at the end of the sentence:

- ✔ **joggen** *(jô-gen)* (jogging)
- ✔ **Fahrrad fahren** *(fah-rât fah-ren)* (bike riding)
- ✔ **ski laufen** *(shee low-fen)* (skiing)
- ✔ **schwimmen** *(shvî-men)* (swimming)
- ✔ **segeln** *(zeh-geln)* (sailing)
- ✔ **Wind surfen** *(vînt surfen)* (wind surfing)

This construction will get you far when discussing favorite activities:

Ich . . . gern. *(īH . . . gêrn)* (I like to . . .)

Here you need to remember to conjugate the verb you fill in the blank. Check it out:

- ✔ **Ich schwimme gern.** *(īH shvî-me gêrn)* (I like swimming.)
- ✔ **Ich fahre gern Fahrrad.** *(īH fah-re gêrn fah-rât)* (I like bicycling.)

Inviting someone to play

If you'd like to ask someone to join you in an activity, use one of the following expressions:

- ✔ **Lass uns . . . gehen!** *(lâs ûns . . . geh-en)* (Let's go . . .!)
- ✔ **Spielst du . . .?** *(shpeelst dū . . .)* (Do you play . . .?)

Talkin' the Talk

Karl is heading to the pub to meet his colleague Michael.

Karl: **Hallo Michael.**
          hâ-lô mî-Hâ-ehl
          Hallo Michael.

Michael: **Grüß dich Karl. Du humpelst ja!**
gruus dîH kârl. dû <u>hûm</u>-pelst yâ
Hi Karl. But you are limping!

Karl: **Ich habe mich gestern beim Fußballspiel verletzt.**
îH <u>hah</u>-be mîH <u>gês</u>-tern baym <u>foos</u>-bâl-shpeel fêr-<u>lêtst</u>
I hurt myself yesterday at the soccer match.

Michael: **Das tut mir leid. Wie habt ihr denn gespielt?**
dâs tût meer lyt. vee hahpt eer dên ge-<u>shpeelt</u>
I am sorry. How did you play?

Karl: **Wir haben 2 zu 0 gewonnen.**
veer <u>hah</u>-bn tsvy tsû nûl ge-<u>vô</u>-nen
We won two to nothing.

Michael: **Da gratuliere ich natürlich. Bisher habt ihr nicht so gut gespielt, oder?**
dâ grâ-tû-<u>lee</u>-re îH nâ-<u>tuur</u>-lîH. bîs-<u>hehr</u> hahpt eer nîHt zoh guht ge-<u>shpeelt</u>, <u>oh</u>-der
I congratulate you, naturally. Up to now you hadn't been playing too well, right?

Karl: **Bis gestern hat unsere Mannschaft jedes Spiel verloren.**
bîs <u>gês</u>-têrn hât <u>ûn</u>-ze-re <u>mân</u>-shâft <u>yeh</u>-des shpeel fêr-<u>loh</u>-ren
Until yesterday our team had lost every match.

Michael: **Da habt ihr euch sicher besonders gefreut.**
dâ hahpt eer oyH <u>zî</u>-Her be-<u>zôn</u>-ders ge-<u>froyt</u>
You were probably especially happy, then.

Words to Know

das Spiel	dâs shpeel	game
sich verletzen	zîH fêr-lê-tsen	to get hurt
tut mir leid	toot meer lyt	I'm sorry
gewinnen	gê-vî-nen	to win
die Mannschaft	dee mân-shâft	team

Exploring the Outdoors

Had a hectic week at work? Tired of waiting for your turn in the shower after the soccer match? Maybe you just want to get away from it all and experience the great outdoors alone or with your family and friends. So it's time to lace up your hiking boots and grab your binoculars and guide book. And don't forget to pack lunch, because there might not be a snack bar at the end of the trail.

Getting out and going

When it comes to walking and hiking, the following phrases should get you on your way:

- **Wollen wir spazieren / wandern gehen?** (*vô-len veer shpâ-tsee-ren / vân-dêrn gehn*) (Should we take a walk?)
- **Ich möchte spazieren / wandern gehen.** (*îH muoH-te shpâ-tsee-ren / vân-dern gehn*) (I would like to take a walk / go hiking.)

Things to see along the way

When you return from your tour of the great outdoors, you can tell people about what you saw by saying:

- **Ich habe . . . gesehen.** (*îH hah-be . . . gê-zehn*) (I saw . . .)
- **Ich habe . . . beobachtet.** (*îH hah-be . . . bê-ohp-âH-tet*) (I was watching . . .)

Just fill in the blanks. You may encounter any of the following on your tour:

- **der Vogel** (*dehr foh-gl*) (bird)
- **der Baum** (*dehr bowm*) (tree)
- **das Gebirge** (*dâs ge-bîr-ge*) (mountains)
- **der Fluss** (*dehr flûss*) (river)
- **das Meer** (*dâs mehr*) (sea, ocean)
- **der See** (*dehr zeh*) (lake)
- **die Kuh** (*dee koo*) (cow)
- **das Pferd** (*dâs pfêrt*) (horse)
- **das Reh** (*dâs reh*) (deer)
- **das Schaf** (*dâs shaaf*) (sheep)

Remember that you'll need to use the accusative case when completing these sentences. (See Chapter 2 for more information on the accusative case.) This is how you tell it for masculine nouns:

> **Ich habe einen Vogel gesehen.** *(îH hah-be ay-nen foh-gl ge-zehn)* (I saw a bird.)

For feminine nouns:

> **Ich habe eine Kuh gesehen.** *(îH hah-be ay-ne koo ge-zehn)* (I saw a cow.)

For neuter nouns:

> **Ich habe ein Reh gesehen.** *(îH hah-be ayn reh ge-zehn)* (I saw a deer.)

Or you may want to use plural, which is generally easier:

> **Ich habe Vögel gesehen.** *(îH hah-be fuo-gl ge-zehn)* (I saw birds.)

Talkin' the Talk

 Mr. and Mrs. Paulsen are in a small town in the mountains. Today they want to go hiking. They are speaking with Frau Kreutzer at the local tourist information office to find out about hiking trails in the area.

Frau Paulsen: **Guten Morgen. Wir möchten eine Wanderung machen.**
goo-ten môr-gn. veer muoH-ten ay-ne vân-de-rûng mâ-Hen
Good morning. We would like to go hiking.

Frau Kreutzer: **Ich kann Ihnen eine Wanderkarte für diese Gegend geben.**
îH kân ee-nen ay-ne vân-dêr-kâr-te fuur dee-ze geh-gend geh-bn
I can give you a hiking map of this area.

Herr Paulsen: **Das ist genau das, was wir brauchen.**
dâs îst ge-now dâs, vâs veer brow-hen
That's exactly what we need.

Frau Kreutzer: **Wie wäre es mit dem Blauen See. Und wenn Sie Lust haben, können Sie sogar schwimmen gehen.**
vee veh-re ês mît dehm blow-en zeh. ûnt vên zee lûst hah-bn, kuo-nen zee zoh-gâr shvî-men gehn
How about the Blue Sea. And if you feel like it, you can even go for a swim.

Herr Paulsen:	**Das klingt gut. Können Sie uns den Weg auf der Karte markieren?**
	dâs klîngkt gût. kuo-nen zee ûns dehn vêg owf dehr kâr-te mâr-kee-ren
	Sounds good. Can you mark the trail for us on the map?
Frau Kreutzer:	**Ja natürlich.**
	yah, nâ-tuur-lîH
	Yes, of course.
Frau Paulsen:	**Vielen Dank für ihre Hilfe.**
	fee-len dângk fuur ee-re hîl-fe
	Thank you very much for your help.

Going to the mountains

Whether it's the ever popular Alps, or one of the other mountain ranges that you're planning to visit, you are sure to meet the locals, because frolicking in the mountains is definitely a favorite pastime. And before you join them, fortify yourself with some sustaining vocabulary:

- ✔ **Wir fahren in die Berge.** *(veer fah-ren în dee bêr-ge)* (We are going to the mountains.)

- ✔ **Wir wollen wandern gehen.** *(veer vô-len vân-dêrn geh-en)* (We want to go hiking)

- ✔ **Ich will bergsteigen.** *(îH vîl bêrg-shty-gen)* (I want to go rock climbing.)

- ✔ **der Berg** *(dehr bêrg)* (mountain)

- ✔ **das Gebirge** *(dâs ge-bîr-ge)* (mountain range)

- ✔ **der Gipfel** *(dehr gîp-fel)* (peak)

- ✔ **der Hügel** *(dehr huu-gel)* (hill)

- ✔ **das Tal** *(dâs tahl)* (valley)

- ✔ **das Naturschutzgebiet** *(dâs nâ-toor-shûts-ge-beet)* (nature preserve)

Words to Know

wandern	vân-dêrn	to go hiking
spazieren gehen	shpâ-<u>tsee</u>-ren gehn	to take a walk
die Wanderung	dee vân-de-rûng	hike
die Karte	dee <u>kâr</u>-te	map
der Weg	dehr vehgk	trail, path, way
die Gegend	dee <u>geh</u>-gent	area

Talkin' the Talk

Herr Mahler is meets Frau Pohl on his way home from work. They start talking about their travel plans.

Frau Pohl: **Tag Herr Mahler. Na, haben Sie schon Urlaubspläne gemacht?**
tahgk hêr <u>mah</u>-ler. nah, <u>hah</u>-bn zee shôn <u>oor</u>-lowps-<u>pleh</u>-ne ge-<u>mâHt</u>
Hi, Mr. Mahler. Have you made plans for your vacation yet?

Herr Mahler: **Aber ja, meine Frau und ich werden wieder in die Berge fahren.**
<u>ah</u>-ber yah, <u>my</u>-ne frow ûnt îH <u>vêr</u>-den <u>vee</u>-der în dee <u>bêr</u>-ge <u>fah</u>-ren
Oh yes, my wife and I will go to the mountains again.

Frau Pohl: **Wieder in die Alpen?**
<u>vee</u>-der în dee <u>âl</u>-pen
Back to the Alps?

Herr Mahler: **Nein, diesmal gehen wir in den Pyrenäen wandern. Und Sie?**
nyn, <u>dees</u>-mahl <u>geh</u>-en veer în dehn puu-re-<u>neh</u>-en <u>vân</u>-dêrn. ûnt zee
No, this time we will go hiking in the Pyrenees. And you?

Frau Pohl:	**Wir wollen im Herbst in die Dolomiten zum Bergsteigen.**
	veer <u>vô</u>-len îm hêrpst în dee dô-lô-<u>mee</u>-ten tsûm <u>bêrg</u>-shty-gen
	We want to go mountain climbing in the Dolomite Alps in the fall.
Herr Mahler:	**Haben Sie schon ein Hotel gebucht?**
	<u>hah</u>-bn zee shôn ayn hô-<u>têl</u> ge-<u>booHt</u>
	Did you book a hotel yet?
Frau Pohl:	**Nein, wir werden in Berghütten übernachten.**
	nyn, veer <u>vêr</u>-den în <u>bêrg</u>-huu-tn uu-bêr-<u>nâH</u>-ten
	No. We are going to stay in mountain huts.

Going to the country

The mountains are not your idea of fun? How about some fresh country air then? Despite a population of close to 80 million people, you will still find quiet rural areas and out-of-the-way places in Germany, sometimes suprisingly close to bustling urban centers. And that you can find peace and quiet in the Austrian and Swiss countrysides goes without saying. All you need to get started is the right language:

- **Wir fahren aufs Land.** *(veer <u>fah</u>-ren owfs länt)* (We are going to the country.)

- **Wir machen Urlaub auf dem Bauernhof.** *(veer <u>mâ</u>-Hn <u>oor</u>-lowp owf dehm <u>bow</u>-êrn-hohf)* (We are vacationing on a farm.)

- **Ich gehe im Wald spazieren.** *(îH <u>geh</u>-e îm vâlt shpâ-<u>tsee</u>-ren)* (I am going for a walk in the woods.)

- **das Land** *(dâs länt)* (countryside)

- **der Wald** *(dehr vâlt)* (forest)

- **das Dorf** *(dâs dôrf)* (village)

- **das Feld** *(dâs fêlt)* (field)

- **die Wiese** *(dee <u>vee</u>-ze)* (meadow)

- **der Bauernhof** *(dehr <u>bow</u>-êrn-hohf)* (farm)

Talkin' the Talk

 Daniel runs into his friend Ellen. After greeting each other, Daniel tells Ellen about his upcoming vacation.

Daniel:	**Ich werde im Oktober eine Woche aufs Land fahren.**
	îH vêr-de îm ôk-toh-ber ay-ne vô-He owfs lânt fah-ren
	I am going to go to the country for a week in October.

Ellen:	**Fährst du allein?**
	fehrst dû ah-lyn
	Are you going alone?

Daniel:	**Nein, ich werde zusammen mit meiner Schwester und ihren Kindern verreisen.**
	nyn, îH vêr-de tsû-sâ-men mît my-ner shvês-ter ûnt ee-ren kîn-dêrn fêr-ry-zen
	No, I am going to travel together with my sister and her children.

Ellen:	**Habt ihr eine Ferienwohnung gemietet?**
	hahpt eer ay-ne feh-rî-ên-voh-nûng ge-mee-tet
	Did you rent a vacation apartment?

Daniel:	**Wir werden auf einem Bauernhof in einem kleinen Dorf übernachten.**
	veer vêr-den owf ay-nem bow-êrn-hohf în ay-nem kly-nen dôrf uu-bêr-nâH-ten
	We are going to stay on a farm in a small village.

Ellen:	**Die Kindern freuen sich sicher.**
	dee kîn-der froy-en zîH zî-Her
	The kids are probably very happy.

Daniel:	**Und wie.**
	ûnt vee
	Oh yes.

Going to the sea

If all this sounds somewhat dry and tame to you, maybe what you need is a stiff nor'easter and some waves crashing around you. Whether you decide to brave the wild North Sea or settle for the more serene Baltic Sea, you'll be able to enjoy nature and meet the locals at the same time using the following words:

- **das Meer** *(dâs mehr)* (sea)
- **die Ostsee** *(dee ôst-zeh)* (Baltic Sea)
- **die Nordsee** *(dee nôrt-zeh)* (North Sea)
- **die Küste** *(dee kuus-te)* (coast)

- **der Wind** *(dehr vînt)* (wind)
- **der Sturm** *(dehr shtûrm)* (storm)
- **die Welle** *(dee vê-le)* (wave)
- **die Gezeiten** *(dee gê-tsy-tn)* (tides)
- **die Ebbe** *(dee ê-be)* (low tide)
- **die Flut** *(dee floot)* (high tide)

Talkin' the Talk

Udo and Karin are talking about their holiday trips. They both like the seaside but have different ideas about what's fun.

Udo: **Wir wollen dieses Jahr an die Ostsee.**
veer vô-len dee-zes yahr ân dee ôst-zeh
We want to go to the Baltic Sea this year.

Karin: **Werdet ihr mit dem Auto fahren?**
vêr-det eer mît dehm ow-tô fah-ren
Will you go by car?

Udo: **Nein, wir haben eine Pauschalreise mit dem Bus gebucht.**
nyn, veer hah-bn ay-ne pow-shahl-ry-ze mît dehm bûs ge-booHt
No, we booked a package bus tour.

Karin: **Wir werden auf eine Nordseeinsel fahren. Wir wollen im Watt wandern gehen.**
veer vêr-den owf ay-ne nôrt-zeh-în-zel fah-ren. veer vô-len îm vât vân-dêrn geh-en
We will go to a North Sea island. We want to go walking in the mud flats.

Udo: **Ist das nicht gefährlich?**
îst dâs nîHt ge-fehr-lîH
Isn't that dangerous?

Karin: **Nein, man geht bei Ebbe los, und dann hat man einige Stunden Zeit, bevor die Flut kommt.**
nyn, mân geht by ê-be lohs, ûnt dân hât mân ay-nee-ge shtûn-den tsyt, bê-fohr dee floot kômt
No, you set out at low tide, and then you have several hours before high tide sets in.

FUN & GAMES

Fill in the boxes with the correct German words. The answers are in Appendix D.

Across

1. Coast
5. You (informal)
7. Hi
8. Cow
9. Yes
10. Ocean
12. Crafts
14. Good

15. Lake
18. I
19. Ski
20. Trail

Down

2. And
3. Article (neuter)
4. Cooking
6. Vacation

8. Class
10. Coin
11. Article (masculine)
13. Antique
15. She
16. It
17. Hint

Chapter 9

Talking on the Phone and Sending Mail

*T*alking to people in person is just one aspect of communication — you also want to be able to handle everything that is covered by that nice term *telecommunications,* be it talking to people on the phone or sending faxes and e-mail (and we shouldn't forget about what is now known as snail mail). Dealing with the phone involves quite a lot of topics, ranging from making appointments and leaving messages to phone cards.

Phoning Made Simple

When German speakers pick up **das Telefon** *(dâs tê-le-fohn)* (phone), they usually answer the call by stating their last name — particularly when they are at their office. If you call somebody at home, you sometimes might hear a simple **Hallo?** *(hâ-loh)* (Hello?).

If you want to express that you're going to call somebody or that you want somebody to call you, you use the verb **anrufen** *(ân-roo-fen)*. It is a separable verb, so the prefix **an** *(ân)* gets seperated from the stem **rufen** *(roo-fen)* (to call), when you conjugate it:

Conjugation	*Pronunciation*
ich rufe an	îH roo-fe ân
du rufst an	doo roo-fst ân
Sie rufen an	zee roofn ân
er, sie, es ruft an	ehr, zee, ês rooft ân
wir rufen an	veer roofn ân
ihr ruft an	eer rooft ân
Sie rufen an	zee roofn ân
sie rufen an	zee roofn ân

Asking for your party

If the person you wish to speak to doesn't pick up the phone, it's up to you to ask for your party. As in English, you have quite a few options when it comes to expressing that you want to speak with somebody:

- ✔ **Ich möchte gern Herrn / Frau . . . sprechen.** (*îH muoH-te gêrn hêrn / frow . . . shprê-Hen*) (I would like to talk to Mr. / Mrs. . . .)

- ✔ **Ist Herr / Frau . . . zu sprechen?** (*îst hêr / frow . . . tsoo shprê-Hen*) (Is Mr. / Mrs. . . . available?)

- ✔ **Kann ich bitte mit Herrn / Frau . . . sprechen?** (*kân îH bî-te mît hêrn / frow . . . shprê-Hen*) (Can I speak to Mr. / Mrs. . . . , please?)

- ✔ **Herrn / Frau . . . , bitte.** (*hêrn / frow . . . , bî-te*) (Mr./Mrs. . . . , please.)

If you find that somebody talks too fast for you to understand, you can ask the person:

- ✔ **Können Sie bitte langsamer sprechen?** (*kuo-nen zee bî-te lâng-zah-mer sprê-Hen*) (Could you please talk more slowly?)

- ✔ **Können Sie das bitte wiederholen?** (*kuo-nen zee dâs bî-te vee-der-hoh-len*) (Could you repeat that, please?)

And if the person on the other end starts speaking English in response to your question, it's not a failure on your part — it just means that the person wants to practice his or her English!

Saying goodbye on the phone

Does **auf Wiederhören!** *(owf vee-der-huo-ren!)* somehow sound familiar? It is the phone equivalent to **auf Wiedersehen** *(owf vee-der-zeh-en)*, the expression you use if you say goodbye to somebody you've just seen in person.

Auf Wiedersehen combines **wieder** *(vee-der)* (again) with the verb **sehen** *(zeh-en)* (to see), and **auf Wiederhören** uses the verb **hören** *(huo-ren)* (to hear), so it literally means "hear you again."

Making the connection

After you've asked to speak to a specific person, you could hear any number of responses depending on who you're calling and where they are:

- ✔ **Am Apparat.** *(âm <u>ap</u>a-raht)* (Speaking.)

- ✔ **Einen Moment bitte, ich verbinde.** *(<u>ay</u>-nen moh-<u>mênt</u> <u>bî</u>-te, îH fêr-<u>bîn</u>-de)* (One moment please, I'll put you through.)

- ✔ **Er / sie telefoniert gerade.** *(ehr / zee <u>tê</u>-le-foh-<u>neert</u> ge-<u>rah</u>-de)* (He / she is on the phone right now.)

- ✔ **Die Leitung ist besetzt.** *(dee <u>ly</u>-tûng îst <u>be</u>-zêtst)* (The line is busy.)

- ✔ **Können Sie später noch einmal anrufen?** *(<u>kuo</u>-nen zee <u>speh</u>-ter nôH <u>ayn</u>-mahl <u>ân</u>-roo-fen)* (Could you call again later?)

- ✔ **Kann er / sie Sie zurückrufen?** *(kân ehr / zee zee tsoo-<u>ruuk</u>-roo-fen)* (Can he / she call you back?)

- ✔ **Hat er / sie Ihre Telefonnummer?** *(hât ehr / zee eeh-re <u>tê</u>-le-fohn-nû-mer)* (Does he / she have your phone number?)

Here are some expressions that might be helpful if something goes wrong with your connection:

- ✔ **Es tut mir leid. Ich habe mich verwählt.** *(ês toot meer lyt. îH <u>hah</u>-be mîH fer-<u>vehlt</u>)* (I'm sorry. I have dialed the wrong number.)

- ✔ **Ich kann Sie schlecht verstehen.** *(îH kân zee shlêHt fêr-<u>shtehn</u>)* (I can't hear you very well.)

- ✔ **Er / sie meldet sich nicht.** *(ehr / zee <u>mêl</u>-det zîH nîHt)* (He / she doesn't answer the phone.)

Talkin' the Talk

 The following is a conversation between Frau Bauer, the secretary of Herr Huber, and Herr Meißner, a potential client of the company.

Frau Bauer:	**Firma TransEuropa, Bauer. Guten Morgen!** *fîr-mah <u>trâns</u>-oy-<u>roh</u>-pah, bowr. gûtn <u>môr</u>-gn* TransEuropa company, Bauer speaking. Good morning!
Herr Meißner:	**Guten Morgen! Herrn Huber, bitte.** *gûtn <u>môr</u>-gn! hêrn <u>hoo</u>-ber, <u>bî</u>-te* Good morning. Mr. Huber, please.
Frau Bauer:	**Tut mir leid. Herr Huber ist in einer Besprechung. Kann er Sie zurückrufen?** *toot meer lyt. hêr <u>hoo</u>-ber îst în <u>ay</u>-ner be-<u>shprê</u>-Hûng. kân ehr zee tsoo-<u>ruuk</u>-roo-fen* I'm sorry. Mr. Huber is in a meeting. Can he call you back?
Herr Meißner:	**Selbstverständlich.** *zêlpst-fêr-<u>shtant</u>-lîH* Of course.
Frau Bauer:	**Wie ist noch einmal Ihr Name?** *vee îst nôH <u>ayn</u>-mahl eer <u>nah</u>-me* What is your name again?
Herr Meißner:	**Meißner, mit ß.** *<u>mys</u>-ner, mît ês-tsêt* Meißner, with ß.
Frau Bauer:	**Gut, Herr Meißner.** *goot, hêr <u>mys</u>-ner* Good, Mr. Meißner.
Herr Meißner:	**Vielen Dank. Auf Wiederhören!** *fee-len dângk. owf <u>vee</u>-der-huo-ren* Thanks a lot. Good bye.

CULTURAL WISDOM

Phone cards

If you want to make a call from a public phone — **die Telefonzelle** *(dee tê-le-fohn-tsê-le)* — in Germany, you should be prepared: Only a few of them accept coins these days. The majority take only phone cards, or **Telefonkarten** *(tê-le-fohn-kâr-tn)*. You can purchase these cards at the post office or get them from small vending machines attached to public mailboxes. These machines are miniversions of the stamp machines found at U.S. post offices. They take coins and bills, and you may buy both phone cards and stamps. Some department stores and newsstands also sell phone cards.

Words to Know

das Telefon	dâs tê-le-fohn	phone
anrufen	ân-roo-fen	to call
zurückrufen	tsoo-ruuk-roo-fen	to call back
auf Wiederhören!	owf vee-der-huo-ren	Good-bye! (on the phone)
das Telefonbuch	dâs tê-le-fohn-booH	phone book
das Telefongespräch	dâs tê-le-fohn-ge-shprehH	phone call
die Telefonnummer	dee tê-le-fohn-nû-mer	phone number
der Anrufbeantworter	dehr ân-roof-be-ânt-vôrtr	answering machine

Making Appointments

You hardly get to see anybody without making an appointment, so take a look at some of the vacabulary that may help you get through the door:

- ✔ **Ich möchte gern einen Termin machen.** *(îH muoH-te gêrn ay-nen têr-meen mâ-Hen)* (I would like to make an appointment.)

- ✔ **Kann ich meinen Termin verschieben?** *(kân îH my-nen têr-meen fêr-shee-ben)* (Can I change my appointment?)

And here are some of the answers you might hear:

- **Wann passt es Ihnen?** *(vân pâst ês ee-nen)* (What time suits you?)

- **Wie wäre es mit . . .?** *(vee veh-re ês mît . . .)* (How about . . .?)

- **Heute ist leider kein Termin mehr frei.** *(hoy-te îst ly-der kyn têr-meen mehr fry)* (Unfortunately, there is no appointment available today.)

Talkin' the Talk

 Frau Bauer has to make an appointment at the doctor's office. She is talking to the the doctor's assistant, Liza.

Liza:	**Praxis Dr. Eggert.** *prâ-ksîs dôc-tôr êgert* Dr. Eggert's office.
Frau Bauer:	**Guten Tag, Anita Bauer. Ich möchte einen Termin für nächste Woche machen.** *gûtn tahgk, â-nee-tâ bowr. îH muoH-te ay-nen têr-meen fuur nehH-ste vô-He mâ-Hen* Good day. This is Anita Bauer. I would like to make an appointment for next week.
Liza:	**Wann passt es Ihnen?** *vân pâst ês ee-nen* What time suits you?
Frau Bauer:	**Mittwoch wäre gut.** *mît-vôH veh-re goot* Wednesday would be good.
Liza:	**Mittwoch ist leider kein Termin mehr frei. Wie wäre es mit Donnerstag?** *mît-vôH îst ly-der kyn têr-meen mehr fry. vee veh-re ês mît dônr-stahgk* Unfortunately, there is no appointment available on Wednesday. How about Thursday?
Frau Bauer:	**Donnerstag ist auch gut. Geht fünfzehn Uhr?** *dônr-stahgk îst owH goot. geht fuunf-tsehn oor* Thursday is good, too. Does 3:00 p.m. work?

Liza:	**Kein Problem. Dann bis Donnerstag!** *kyn proh-blehm. dân bîs dônr-stahgk* No problem. Until Thursday.
Frau Bauer:	**Bis dann. Auf Wiederhören.** *bîs dân. owf vee-der-huo-ren* See you then. Good-bye.

Leaving Messages

Unfortunately, you often don't get through to the person you're trying to reach, and you have to leave a message. In that case, some of the following expressions might come in handy (Some of these phrases use dative pronouns, which you can read about in the following section.):

- **Kann ich ihm / ihr eine Nachricht hinterlassen?** *(kân îH eem / eer ay-ne nahH-rîHt hîn-ter-lâsn)* (May I leave him / her a message?)

- **Kann ich ihm etwas ausrichten?** *(kân îH eem êt-vâs ows-rîH-ten)* (Can I leave him a message?)

- **Möchten Sie eine Nachricht hinterlassen?** *(muoH-ten zee ay-ne naH-rîHt hîn-ter-lâsn)* (Would you like to leave a message?)

- **Ich bin unter der Nummer . . . zu erreichen.** *(îH bîn ûn-ter dehr nû-mer . . . tsoo êr-ry-Hen)* (I can be reached at the number . . .)

A Few Words about Dative Pronouns

Ihm *(eem)* and **ihr** *(eer)* are personal pronouns in the dative case. In German — as in English — you use the dative case of these pronouns if you want to express that you want to talk to or speak with a person (him or her):

> **Ich möchte gern mit ihm / ihr sprechen.** *(îH muoH-te gêrn mît eem / eer shprê-Hen)* (I would like to speak with him / her.)

But watch out — in German, you don't leave a message *for* somebody; you just leave somebody a message:

> **Ich hinterlasse Ihnen / dir / ihm / ihr eine Nachricht.** *(îH hîn-ter-lâ-se ee-nen / deer / eem / eer ay-ne nahH-rîHt)* (I'm leaving a message for you (formal / informal) / him / her.)

Talkin' the Talk

Frau Bauer, an assistant at the company TransEuropa, gets a phone call from Hans Seibold, an old friend of Herr Huber.

Frau Bauer: **Firma TransEuropa, guten Tag!**
fîr-mâ <u>trâns</u>-oy-<u>roh</u>-pâ, gûtn tahgk
TransEuropa company, good day!

Herr Seibold: **Guten Tag, Seibold hier. Kann ich bitte mit Herrn Huber sprechen?**
<u>gûtn</u> tahgk, <u>zy</u>-bôldt heer. kân îH <u>bî</u>-te mît hêrn <u>hoo</u>-ber <u>shprê</u>-Hen
Good day, Seibold here. Can I please speak to Mr. Huber?

Frau Bauer: **Guten Tag, Herr Seibold. Einen Moment bitte, ich verbinde.**
<u>gûtn</u> tahgk, hêr <u>zy</u>-bôldt. <u>ay</u>-nen moh-<u>mênt</u> <u>bî</u>-te, îH fêr-<u>bîn</u>-de
Good day, Mr. Seibold. One moment, please. I'll connect you.

(After a short moment)

Herr Seibold? Herr Huber spricht gerade auf der anderen Leitung. Möchten Sie ihm eine Nachricht hinterlassen?
hêr <u>zy</u>-bôldt? hêr <u>hoo</u>-ber shprîHt ge-<u>rah</u>-de owf dehr <u>ân</u>-de-ren <u>ly</u>-tûngk. <u>muoH</u>-ten zee eem <u>ay</u>-ne <u>nahH</u>-rîHt hîn-ter-<u>lâssn</u>
Mr. Seibold? Mr. Huber is on the other line. Would you like to leave him a message?

Herr Seibold: **Ja bitte. Ich bin unter der Nummer 57 36 48 zu erreichen.**
yah, <u>bî</u>-te. îH bîn <u>ûn</u>-têr dehr <u>nû</u>-mer fuunf zeebn dry zeks feer âHt tsoo êr-<u>ry</u>-Hen
Yes, please. I can be reached at the number 57 36 48.

Frau Bauer: **Ich werde es ausrichten!**
îH <u>vehr</u>-de ês <u>ows</u>-rîH-ten
I'll forward the message.

Herr Seibold: **Vielen Dank! Auf Wiederhören!**
<u>vee</u>-len dângk. owf <u>vee</u>-der-<u>huo</u>-ren
Thanks a lot! Good-bye!

Sending a Letter, Fax, or E-Mail

As pervasive as phones are these days, when it seems like everyone and her uncle has at least one mobile phone, people still like to, and need to, send written correspondence from time to time.

Just as in English, there are certain conventions that people use to write letters in German. For example, in English, it's customary to end a letter with "Sincerely." In German, the phrase most used to sign off a letter is **Mit freundlichen Grüßen** *(mît froynt-lî-Hen gruu-sen)* (With friendly greetings).

Entire books have been written about the art of writing letters in German; here, we just want to give you enough information so that you can send your correspondence where it needs to go.

Sending a letter or postcard

Post offices in German-speaking countries tend to be busy places. Besides dispensing postage, a number of other services are typically available at post offices, making them centers of a lot of activity. (See the sidebar "Making phone calls at the post office" in this chapter for more information.)

With people standing in line behind you, it pays to be prepared with some simple phrases that will get you in and out of the post office, **das Postamt** *(dâs pôst-âmt),* as quickly and hassle-free as possible. (And get your letter, **der Brief** *(dehr breef),* and postcard, **die Postkarte** *(dee pôst-kâr-te),* or package, **das Paket** *(dâs pâ-keht),* on their merry way.)

Buying stamps

In Germany, you usually buy stamps — **die Briefmarke** *(dee breef-mâr-ke)* (stamp) / **die Briefmarken** *(dee breef-mâr-kn)* (stamps) — at the post office. (You can also get them from the small vending machines attached to public mailboxes.) To get your stamps, this is what you say to the postal worker:

> **Ich möchte gern Briefmarken kaufen.** *(îH muoH-te ger-n breef-mâr-kn kow-fen)* (I would like to buy stamps.)

To specify how many stamps and what value you would like, you can say the following (and insert the number of stamps and the value you want):

> **5-mal 1 DM, 10-mal 20 Pfennig, und 6-mal 50 Pfennig.** *(fuunf-mahl ay-ne mârk, tsehn-mahl tsvân-tsîgk pfê-nîgk, ûnt sêks-mahl fuunf-tsîgk pfê-nîgk)* (5 times one Mark, 10 times 20 Pfennigs, and 6 times 50 Pfennigs.)

Making phone calls at the post office

You don't have a phone card and just found out that your hotel charges exorbitant rates for a call? There's one more possibility you might want to explore: In Germany, phone service is also provided by most post offices. Just go to the counter and tell the postal worker that you want to make a call — **Ich möchte gern telefonieren** *(îH muoH-te gêr-n tê-le-foh-nee-ren)* (I would like to make a phone call). He or she will let you know which phone booth is available, and you'll go back to pay after you're done with your call.

Putting your mail in the mail box

As in the U.S., you can give your mail to a postal worker, drop it into one of the receptacles at the post office (look for those slits in the wall), or put it into one of the yellow mailboxes — **Briefkästen** *(breef-kêstn)* (pl) / **der Briefkasten** *(dehr breef-kâstn)* — you find on street corners or in front of post offices. Sometimes there are separate mailboxes for the city you're in, and its surroundings, and for other cities. So the mailboxes might have a sign saying, for example, **Köln und Umgebung** *(kuoln ûnt ûm-geh-bûngk)* (Cologne and surrounding area) and **Andere Orte** *(ân-de-re ôr-te)* (Other places).

Asking for special services

If you want to send an express letter, airmail, certified mail, or a package, you need to be familiar with these words:

- ✔ **der Eilbrief** *(dehr ayl-breef)* (express letter)
- ✔ **die Luftpost** *(dee lûft-pôst)* (airmail)
- ✔ **das Einschreiben** *(dâs ayn-shrybn)* (registered letter / certified mail)
- ✔ **das Paket** *(dâs pâ-keht)* (package)

To get these pieces of mail on their way, you just tell the postal worker:

- ✔ **Ich möchte diesen Brief per Eilzustellung / per Luftpost / per Einschreiben schicken.** *(îH muoH-te dee-zen breef pêr ayl-tsoo-shtê-lûngk / pêr lûft-pôst /pêr ayn-shrybn shî-ken)* (I would like to send this letter express / by air mail / by registered mail.)
- ✔ **Ich möchte dieses Paket aufgeben.** *(îH muoH-te dee-zes pâ-keht owf-geh-ben)* (I would like to send this package.)

The following words are helpful when it comes to sending mail (and you'll also find them on the form you will have to fill out when you're sending certified mail):

- ✔ **der Absender** *(dehr a̰p-zên-der)* (sender)
- ✔ **der Empfänger** *(dehr êm-pfên-ger)* (addressee)
- ✔ **das Porto** *(dâs pôr-toh)* (postage)

Sending a fax

If you're not going to Germany on business and can't conveniently use some-body's fax machine — **das Faxgerät** *(dâs fâks-ge-reht)* — you will be able to send a fax — **das Fax** *(dâs fâks)* — from most hotels and post offices. Just walk up to the reception or counter and tell the receptionist or postal worker:

> **Ich möchte etwas faxen.** *(îH muoH-te êt-vâss fâ-ksen)* (I would like to fax something.)

After you've found a place that can send your fax, the person operating the machine may ask you for the fax number, **die Faxnummer** *(dee fâks-nū-mer)*. Do yourself a favor: If you plan to send a fax, write the number on a piece of paper beforehand, so that when you're asked for the fax number, you can just hand it over with a cool smile.

Just as in America, it's a courtesy to call the recipient of a fax and let them or their assistant know that a fax is on the way. (See "Phoning Made Simple" earlier in this chapter to find out how to make a call and get somone on the phone.) To inform someone of an impeding fax arrival, just say

> **Ich schicke Ihnen ein Fax.** *(îH shî-ke ee-nen ayn fâks)* (I'm sending you a fax.)

Sending an e-mail

If you want to send e-mail and haven't brought a computer with you, you might want to find out where the next Internet café is located. However, bigger hotels might also offer Internet access.

The great thing about e-mail and the Internet is that it involves an international language — the language of computers. If you understand that language, then you know enough to send an e-mail from just about any country in the world. However, it is still handy to know a few words connected with e-mailing:

- ✔ **der Computer** *(dehr com-pjuh-ter)* (computer)
- ✔ **das Internet** *(dâs în-ter-nêt)* (Internet)

✏ **die E-mail** *(dee ee-mail)* (e-mail)

✏ **die E-mail-Adresse** *(dee ee-mail ah-drê-se)* (e-mail address)

✏ **Ich schicke eine E-mail.** *(îH shî-ke ay-ne ee-mail)* (I'm sending an e-mail.)

Talkin' the Talk

Frau Bauer's work day is almost over, she only has to mail one letter at the post office. Listen in on her conversation with **der Postbeamte** *(dehr pôst-be-âm-te)* (the postal worker).

Frau Bauer:	**Guten Tag. Ich möchte den Einschreibebrief hier aufgeben. Wann kommt der Brief in München an?** *gûtn tahgk. îH muoH-te dehn ayn-shry-be-breef heer owf-geh-ben. vân kômt dehr breef în muun-Hen ân* Good day. I would like to send this registered letter. When will the letter arrive in Munich?
Der Postbeamte:	**Heute ist Dienstag — vielleicht am Donnerstag, aber ganz bestimmt am Freitag.** *hoy-te îst deens-tahgk — fee-lyHt âm dônr-stahgk, ah-ber gânts bê-shtîmt âm fry-tahgk* Today is Tuesday — perhaps on Thursday, but certainly on Friday.
Frau Bauer:	**Das ist zu spät. Kommt er übermorgen an, wenn ich ihn als Eilbrief schicke?** *dâs îst tsoo shpait. kômt ehr uuber-môr-gn an, vên îH een âls ayl-breef shî-ke* That's too late. Will it arrive the day after tomorrow, if I send it as an express letter?
Der Postbeamte:	**Garantiert!** *gârân-teert* Guaranteed.
Frau Bauer:	**Gut, dann schicken Sie das Einschreiben bitte per Eilzustellung.** *goot, dân shî-ken zee dahs ayn-shry-ben bî-te pêr ayl-tsoo-shtê-lûng* Good, please send the registered letter per express.
Der Postbeamte:	**In Ordnung.** *în ôrd-nûng* Okay.

FUN & GAMES

Fill in the boxes with the correct German words. The answers are in Appendix D.

Across

1. Mail
2. Package
5. Company
6. Then
7. Problem
10. To send
12. Mrs.
13. Name
15. Here
16. Please

Down

1. Postage
3. Can
4. Phone
6. Deutschmark (abbreviation)
8. Line
9. In
11. German city
12. Free
14. with

FUN & GAMES

• •

You called the office of a company, but you got their answering machine. Complete the announcement you heard using the following words.

schicken   Fax   rufen   Anrufbeantworter   hinterlassen   Nummer   Nachricht

Guten Tag, hier ist der _____.der Firma TransEuropa. Bitte
_____.Sie eine _____.oder _____.Sie ein
_____.an die _____.68 74 93. Wir _____.Sie zurück.

Answer key: Anrufbeanworter–hinterlassen–Nachricht–schicken–Fax–Number–rufen

• •

Chapter 10

At the Office and Around the House

In This Chapter

▶ Renting an apartment

▶ Working in an office

*I*n this chapter, we take a look at the real estate section of a paper, check out rental apartments, and learn the basics of office life.

Renting an Apartment or House

To look for places to rent, you can search in newspapers' real estate sections or hire an agent or realtor, which is more expensive. Finding an apartment or house usually isn't a problem, but getting an affordable one can be very difficult, particularly if you're looking for an apartment in the center of bigger cities. If you're looking for a space in the center of Berlin, Frankfurt, or Hamburg, for example, be prepared to pay substantial rent. Single-standing houses in city centers are rare, but you may find them for rent in the suburbs, smaller cities, or the country side.

Describing what you want

Looking for a place to live is hard work even when you know the language — so imagine trying to find a place to your liking when you can't even describe what your liking is. That's why we're here — right? Here is the lingo you need to help you describe the kind of house or apartment you want:

✔ **die Wohnung** (*dee voh-nûng*) (apartment)

✔ **das Zimmer** (*dâs tsî-mer*) (room)

✔ **die 2-Zimmer-Wohnung** *(dee tsvy-tsî-mer-voh-nûng)* (1-bedroom apartment)

✔ **der Quadratmeter / die Quadratmeter** (pl) *(dehr kvâ-draht-meh-ter)* (square meter)

✔ **die Nebenkosten** *(dee neh-bn-kôss-tn)* (additional costs like electricity and heat)

✔ **ab sofort** *(âp zoh-fôrt)* / **sofort frei** *(zoh-fôrt fry)* (immediately available / free)

✔ **möbliert** *(muo-bleert)* (furnished)

✔ **das Bad** *(dâs baht)* (bathroom)

✔ **der Balkon** *(dehr bâl-kông)* (balcony)

✔ **die Küche** *(dee kuu-He)* (kitchen)

✔ **das Esszimmer** *(dâs êss-tsî-mer)* (dining room)

✔ **das Wohnzimmer** *(dâs vohn-tsî-mer)* (living room)

✔ **das Schlafzimmer** *(dâs shlahf-tsî-mer)* (bed room)

Deciphering newspaper ads

It's hard enough to read a newpaper ad, **die Anzeige** *(dee ân-tsy-ge)*, in your native tongue — just try reading one in a language that's new to you! It's those pesky abbreviations that make reading ads so difficult. Here, in Table 10-1, we take the mystery and teeth-nashing out of deciphering these abbreviations. (For the pronunciations and translations of the full versions of these words, see the previous section.)

Table 10-1	Common Abbreviations in Apartment Ads
Abbreviation	*Full Word*
Blk.	**der Balkon**
Kü	**die Küche**
möbl.	**möbliert**
qm / m2	**der Quadratmeter**
sof.	**sofort**
2 Zi. Whg. / 2-ZW	**die 2-Zimmer-Wohnung**

Counting rooms

When it comes to counting and advertising the rooms in an apartment, Germans use a slightly different method. What Americans would call a one-bedroom apartment is a **2-Zimmer-Wohnung** *(tsvy tsî-mer voh-nûng)*, a two-room apartment, in Germany. You count the actual rooms, minus the kitchen and bath. As to the kitchen, watch out: German kitchens don't come with a stove and refrigerator. You have to bring your own!

Asking the right questions

There's nothing more depressing than showing up to look at an apartment, only to find out that the place has been rented, or the rent, **die Miete** *(dee mee-te)*, is too high, or the rent doesn't include heat and hot water (very common in Germany). These points of information can easily be obtained over the telephone (if they aren't already listed in an ad). This is what you might say when you're responding to an ad advertising an apartment:

- ✔ **Ich interessiere mich für Ihre Wohnung.** *(îH în-te-re-see-re mîH fuur ee-re voh-nûng)* (I'm interested in your apartment.)

- ✔ **Ist die Wohnung noch frei?** *(îst dee voh-nûng nôH fry)* (Is the apartment still available?)

- ✔ **Ist die Wohnung schon vermietet?** *(îst dee voh-nûng shohn fêr-mee-tet)* (Is the apartment already rented?)

- ✔ **Wie hoch ist die Miete?** *(vee hohH îst dee mee-te)* (How high is the rent?)

- ✔ **Wie hoch sind die Nebenkosten?** *(vee hohH zînt dee nê-bn-kôs-tn)* (How high are the additional costs for heating and electricity?)

- ✔ **Wann wird die Wohnung frei?** *(vân vîrt dee voh-nûng fry)* (When will the apartment be available?)

- ✔ **Kann ich mir die Wohnung ansehen?** *(kân îH meer dee voh-nûng ân-zehn)* (Can I take a look at the apartment?)

Talking about an apartment

You may hear or say the following about an apartment:

- **Die Wohnung hat eine schöne Lage.** *(dee voh-nûng hât ay-ne shuo-ne lah-ge)* (The apartment has a good location.)

- **Die Wohnung liegt zentral.** *(dee voh-nûng leekt tsên-trahl)* (The apartment is centrally located.)

- **Die Wohnung kostet . . . DM im Monat kalt.** *(dee voh-nûng kôs-tet . . . deh-mârk îm moh-naht kâlt)* (The apartment costs DM . . . per month cold = without heating and electricity.)

- **Die Wohnung ist zu klein / zu dunkel / zu teuer.** *(dee voh-nûng îst tsoo klyn / tsoo dûn-kl / tsoo toy-êr)* (The apartment is too small / too dark / too expensive.)

If you like the apartment and would like to rent it, you can say:

- **Ich nehme die Wohnung.** *(îH neh-me dee voh-nûng)* (I'll take the apartment.)

- **Ich möchte die Wohnung gern mieten.** *(îH muoh-te dee voh-nûng gêrn mee-ten)* (I would like to rent the apartment.)

Sealing the deal

After you decide to rent a place, you will be asked by the landlord or landlady — **der Vermieter / die Vermieterin** *(dehr fêr-mee-ter/ dee fêr-mee-te-rîn)* — to sign the lease, which is called **der Mietvertrag** *(der meet-fêr-trahgk)*. You will need a German-speaking advisor to help you understand this agreement — just like contracts that are made out in English, these rental agreements are crammed full of legalese that even we have a hard time understanding.

If you would like some time to evaluate the contract, you can say **Ich möchte mir den Vertrag gern noch einmal genauer ansehen.** *(îH muoH-te meer dehn fêr-trahgk gêrn nôH ayn-mahl ge-nowr ân-sehn)* (I would like to take a closer look at the contract again.).

Talkin' the Talk

Paul Fraser is looking for an apartment. He calls the numbers of a few places whose ads he saw in the newspaper.

Vermieter:	**Köbel.** *kuo-bl* Köbel.
Paul:	**Guten Tag, mein Name ist Paul Fraser. Sie haben eine Anzeige in der Zeitung. Ist die Wohnung noch frei?** *gûtn <u>tahgk</u>, myn <u>nah</u>-me îst powl fraser. zee <u>hah</u>-bn <u>ay</u>-ne <u>ân</u>-tsy-ge în dehr <u>tsy</u>-tûng. îst dee <u>voh</u>-nûng nôH fry* Good morning, my name is Paul Fraser. You have an ad in the paper. Is the apartment still available?
Vermieter:	**Es tut mir leid, aber die Wohnung ist schon weg.** *ês toot meer lyt, <u>ah</u>-bêr dee <u>voh</u>-nûng îst shohn vêgk* I'm sorry, but the apartment is gone.
Paul:	**Schade. Vielen Dank. Auf Wiederhören.** *<u>shah</u>-de. <u>fee</u>-len dângk owf <u>vee</u>-der-<u>huo</u>-ren* Too bad. Thank you very much. Good-bye.

What a bummer. But there are more ads of apartments for rent. Paul dials another number.

Vermieterin:	**Albrecht.** *<u>âl</u>-brêHtt*
Paul:	**Fraser. Guten Tag! Ich interessiere mich für die Wohnung in der Zeitung.** *Fraser gûtn <u>tahgk</u>! îH în-te-re-<u>see</u>-re mîH fuur dee <u>voh</u>-nûng în dehr <u>tsy</u>-tûng* Fraser. Hi. I'm interested in the apartment in the paper.
	Wie hoch ist denn die Miete? *vee hohH îst dên dee <u>mee</u>-te* How high is the rent?
Vermieterin:	**1500 Mark im Monat kalt.** *fuunf-zehn-<u>hûn</u>-dêrt mark îm <u>moh</u>-nât kâlt* Fifteen hundred marks a month, cold.

Möchten Sie die Wohnung sehen?
muoH-tn zee dee voh-nûng zehn
Would you like to see the apartment?

Paul: **Ja. Wann passt es Ihnen?**
Yah. vân pâsst êss ee-nen
Yes. When is a good time for you?

Vermieterin: **Sagen wir heute abend um halb 7?**
zah-gn veer hoy-te ah-bent ûm hâlp zeebn
Shall we say tonight at 6:30?

Paul: **Gut. Bis heute abend. Auf Wiederhören!**
goot. bîs hoy-te ah-bnt. owf vee-der-huo-ren
Good. Until tonight then. Good-bye!

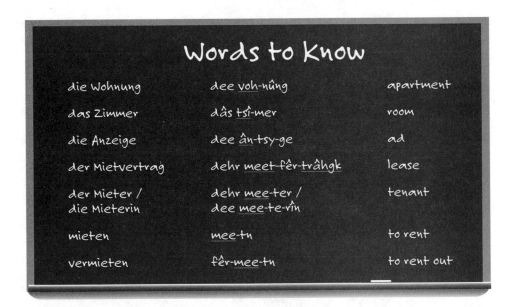

Words to Know

die Wohnung	dee voh-nûng	apartment
das Zimmer	dâs tsî-mer	room
die Anzeige	dee ân-tsy-ge	ad
der Mietvertrag	dehr meet-fêr-trâhgk	lease
der Mieter / die Mieterin	dehr mee-ter / dee mee-te-rîn	tenant
mieten	mee-tn	to rent
vermieten	fêr-mee-tn	to rent out

Getting Around at the Office

Germans have a reputation for being rather productive and efficient, but you might be surprised to find out that, statistically speaking, they don't work as much as Americans. Not that people never work late, but a lot of businesses and state and government agencies in particular, stick to a strict nine-to-five work schedule. And on Fridays, many companies close early.

When you're working in a German-speaking office, which is called **das Büro** *(dâs buu-roh)*, you will give out assignments or receive them — **die Büroarbeit** *(dee buu-roh-âr-byt)* (office work).

You need to know the basics, like what all that stuff on your desk is called, or all the goodies in the supply closet. After you've got those down, you need to know how to describe what to do with them. Time to get to work!

Mastering your desk and supplies

Typically, you might find, or hope to find, the following items on or around your desk, which is called **der Schreibtisch** *(dehr shryp-tîsh)*:

- ✔ **das Telefon** *(dâs tê-le-fohn)* (telephone)
- ✔ **der Computer** *(dehr com-pjuh-ter)* (computer)
- ✔ **die Schreibmaschine** *(dee shryp-mâ-shee-ne)* (typewriter)
- ✔ **das Faxgerät** *(dâs fâks-gê-reht)* (fax machine)
- ✔ **der Kopierer** *(dehr kô-pee-rêr)* (copier)
- ✔ **die Unterlagen** *(dee ûn-têr-lahgn)* (documents or files)
- ✔ **der Brief** *(dehr breef)* (letter)

Don't forget the question **Wo ist . . . ?** *(voh îst)* (Where is . . . ?) if you need to ask someone for help finding something around the office.

Sooner or later, you're going to come up short of one of the following supplies:

- ✔ **der Briefbogen** *(dehr breef-boh-gn)* (letterhead)
- ✔ **das Papier** *(dâs pâ-peer)* (paper)
- ✔ **der Bleistift** *(dehr bly-shtîft)* (pencil)
- ✔ **der Kugelschreiber** *(dehr koo-gel-shry-ber)* (pen)
- ✔ **der Umschlag** *(dehr ûm-shlahgk)* (envelope)

When you need some of these supplies, and you can't find them on your own (you brave soul), you can ask a colleague to help you find them by saying:

- ✔ **Haben Sie einen Kugelschreiber / einen Umschlag für mich?** *(hah-ben zee ay-nen koo-gel-shry-ber / ay-nen ûm-shlahgk fuur mîH)* (Could you give me a pen / envelope. Literally: Do you have a pencil / envelope for me?)
- ✔ **Können Sie mir sagen, wo ich Umschläge / Briefbögen / Papier finde?** *(kuo-nen zee meer zah-gen, voh îH ûm-shlê-ge / breef-buo-gen / pâ-peer fîn-de)* (Could you tell me where I would find envelopes / stationary / paper?)

Elsewhere in the office . . .

Just as in English, German-speaking countries have their business world with its own culture and specialized language. Nonnative speakers study for many years, taking special courses on writing business letters and giving speeches, in order to do business in German. As you might imagine, we don't have the space (and you probably don't have the time) to study enough German to communicate at the business level. Instead, we suggest that you do the following if you plan to perform some business with German speakers:

✔ **Call ahead (see Chapter 9) and ask if a translator, who is called der Übersetzer** *(dehr uu-ber-zê-tsêr)* / **die Übersetzerin** *(dee uu-ber-zê-tsê-rîn)* **can be made available to you.** Make sure that the translator will take notes — **die Notizen** *(dee noh-tî-tsên)* — in English during any meetings so that you have a written record of the goings-on. Don't feel the slightest bit bad about asking for a translator. Business people all over the world respect someone who knows when it's time to delegate.

✔ **Study up on the formal introductions we tell you about in Chapter 3.** Nailing the introductions shows your interest in the proceedings, even if you don't understand another word that's said.

✔ **Read the section "Talking about your job" in Chapter 4.** This will arm you with a few words you need to make small talk about your job.

✔ **Learn the terms and phrases we show you in the previous section, "Mastering your desk and supplies," and in the next section, "Commanding the Command Form."**

✔ **Acquaint yourself with the following common office terms:**

- **die Besprechung** *(dee be-shprê-Hûng)* (meeting)

- **der Termin** *(dehr têr-meen)* (appointment)

- **die Sekretärin / der Sekretär** *(dee zê-krê-teh-rîn / dehr zê-krê-tehr)* (secretary)

- **der Chef / die Chefin** *(dehr shêf / die shê-fîn)* (boss)

- **der Direktor / die Direktorin** *(dehr dî-rêk-tohr / dee dî-rêk-toh-rîn)* (director)

- **der Mitarbeiter / die Mitarbeiterin** *(dehr mît-âr-by-ter / dee mît-âr-by-te-rîn)* (colleague / employee)

- **anrufen** *(ân-roo-fen)* (to phone)

- **diktieren** *(dîk-tee-ren)* (to dictate)

- **faxen** *(fâk-sen)* (to fax)

- **kopieren** *(kô-pee-ren)* (to copy)

- **schicken** *(shî-ken)* (to send)

CULTURAL WISDOM

A vacationer's paradise

Germans get far more vacation time than Americans: 30 work days of vacation plus paid holidays, which amounts to almost six weeks, aren't unusual. However, a typically German problem is to actually find the time to take one's vacation. Vacation time is often carried over into the next year when hopefully it can be taken.

Commanding the Command Form

Office work entails assignments and tasks you might be given or have to give to somebody. The *command form* of the verb, the imperative, or **Imperativ** (*īm-pê-râ-teef*) in German, often comes into play in such circumstances.

The verb in the command form always goes before the personal pronoun. To avoid coming off as impolite, it's a good idea to always add "bitte" to these commands. This is how it works:

- ✔ **Bitte, kopieren Sie den Brief!** *(bî-te kô-pee-ren zee dehn breef)* (Please, copy the letter!)

- ✔ **Bitte, schicken Sie das Fax!** *(bî-te shî-ken zee dâs fâks)* (Please, send the fax!)

- ✔ **Bitte, übersetzen Sie das für mich!** *(bî-te uu-ber-zê-tsên zee dâs fuur mîH)* (Please, translate that for me!)

Talkin' the Talk

Let's listen in on a conversation between Kurt Seifert and his secretary, Ms. Remmert. Herr Seifert comes to the office earlier today because he has an important meeting.

Herr Seifert:	**Guten Morgen, Frau Remmert.** *goo-tn môrgn frow rê-mert* Good morning, Ms. Remmert.
Frau Remmert:	**Guten Morgen, Herr Seifert.** *goo-tn môr-gn, hêr zy-fêrt* Good morning, Mr. Seifert.

Herr Seifert: **Wissen Sie, ob Herr Krause heute im Hause ist?**
vî-ssen zee, ôb hêr <u>krow</u>-ze <u>hoy</u>-te îm <u>how</u>-ze îst
Do you know if Mr. Krause is in the office today?

Frau Remmert: **Ich glaube ja.**
îH <u>glow</u>-be yah
I think so.

Herr Seifert: **Ich muss dringend mit ihm sprechen.**
îH mûss <u>drîn</u>-gênd mît eem <u>shprê</u>-Hen
I urgently have to speak to him.

Frau Remmert: **In Ordnung.**
în <u>ôrd</u>-nûng
Okay.

Ach ja, Frau Hoffmann von der Firma Solag hat angerufen.
<u>ahH</u>-yah frow <u>hôf</u>-mân fôn dehr <u>fîr</u>-mâ <u>soh</u>-lâgk hât <u>ân</u>-gê-roofn
Oh yes, Mrs. Hoffman from (the company) Solag called.

Herr Seifert: **Gut, ich rufe sie gleich an.**
goot îH roofeh zee glyH <u>ân</u>
Good. I'll call her right away.

Und, bitte kopieren Sie die Unterlagen hier.
ûnt <u>bî</u>-te koh-<u>pee</u>-ren zee dee <u>ûn</u>-têr-lah-gen here
And please copy these documents here.

Frau Remmert: **Wird gemacht, Herr Seifert.**
vîrt gê-<u>mâHt</u> hêr <u>zy</u>-fêrt
I'll do that, Mr. Seifert.

Words to Know

gleich	glyH	in a moment
sofort	sô-fôrt	immediately
im Hause sein	îm how-ze zyn	to be in the building / office
in Ordnung	în ôrd-nûng	Okay
Wird gemacht!	vîrt ge-mâHt	I'll do that!

Speaking of This

Very early in your newfound friendship with German, you'll want to refer to something more specifically than you can with a normal article — **der, die, das, die** *(dehr, dee, dâs, dee)* (the). Eventually, you'll want to refer to something more specifically, using the pronoun *this*.

In German, the word for *this* can take a few different forms, depending on the gender of the noun it's attached to and how that noun is used in the sentence (the *case* of the noun, if you will). As always, you're dealing with three genders in German, which give rise to **dieser, diese, dieses** *(dee-zer, dee-ze, dee-zes)* (masculine, feminine, and neuter nominative versions of *this*) and one version for all the plurals: **diese**.

Tables 10-2 shows you how **dieser, diese,** and **dieses** behave in the various cases.

Table 10-2	Dieser, Diese, and Dieses and the Cases			
Noun's Gender	*Nominative*	*Genitive*	*Dative*	*Accusative*
Masculine (der)	dieser	dieses	diesem	diesen
Feminine (die)	diese	dieser	dieser	diese
Neuter (das)	dieses	dieses	diesem	dieses
Plural (die)	diese	dieser	diesen	diese

FUN & GAMES

Name the rooms of the house that are illustrated in the following drawing.

A.

B.

C.

D.

E.

A. _____

B. _____

C. _____

D. _____

E. _____

Answer key: A. Bad B. Schlafzimmer C. Esszimmer D. Küche E. Wohnzimmer

Part III
German on the Go

The 5th Wave   By Rich Tennant

"Let's see-'telephone number' is 'Telefonnummer', 'accelerator' is 'Gaspedal', 'telephone book' is 'Telefonbuch'... I get the feeling German is just English without the space bar."

In this part . . .

Most of the readers of this book are going to have to do some traveling in order to use German, and that's what this part of the book is all about. We cover all aspects of travel, from exchanging money to using public transportation to reserving a hotel room.

Chapter 11

Money, Money, Money

Money talks. But what language does it speak? Since you're reading this book, it speaks German, naturally. In this chapter, we show you how to talk back about money. Whether you're speaking to a patient teller or an ultraefficient, impersonal ATM machine, a pocketful of the right expressions will get you . . . well, a pocketful of cash.

Changing Currency

Obtaining local currency has never been difficult in multicurrrency Europe. Practically every bank is willing to accept your dollars and provide you with the local cash.

You will usually find a board with the current exchange rates (**Wechselkurse**) (_vêk-sel-kûr-ze_) displayed in a prominent location. Look for the column marked **Ankauf** (_ân-kowf_) (purchase / buy). Then you can make a bee-line to any teller window, **der Schalter** (_dehr shâl-ter_). The personnel at the counter either complete your transaction on the spot or send you on to the **Kasse** (_kâ-se_) (cash register).

In airports, for example, you might find businesses that specialize in currency transactions; they are called **Wechselstube** (_vêk-sel-stoo-be_) in German. With the introduction of the Euro, a pan-European currency, you will be able to visit 12 countries for the price of one currency. The Euro won't look the same everywhere, though, because each country is printing up its own version.

Regardless of where you decide to change your money, transacting your business isn't difficult. All you need are the following phrases:

- **Ich möchte . . . Dollar in Mark einwechseln / tauschen.** *(īH muoH-te . . . dô-lār în mârk ayn-vêk-seln / tow-shen)* (I would like to change . . . dollars into Marks.)

- **Wie ist der Wechselkurs?** *(vee īst dehr vêk-sel-kūrs)* (What's the exchange rate?)

- **Wie hoch sind die Gebühren?** *(vee hohH zīnt dee ge-buu-ren)* (How high are the fees?)

- **Nehmen Sie Reiseschecks?** *(neh-men zee ry-ze-shêks)* (Do you take traveler's checks?)

When you exchange money, you may be asked for your ID, so you need to have a passport (**Reisepass**) *(ry-ze-pâs)* or some other form of ID on you. The teller will ask you

> **Können Sie sich ausweisen?** *(kô-nen zee zīH ows-vy-zn)* (Do you have proof of your ID?)

After you've proven that you are who you say you are, the teller may ask you how you want the money:

> **Wie hätten Sie das Geld gern?** *(vee hê-tn zee dâs gêlt gêrn)* (How would you like the money?)

To which you can respond:

> **In Zehnern / in Zwanzigern / in Fünfzigern / in Hundertern, bitte.** *(in tseh-nern / in tsvân-zî-gern / in fuunf-tsî-gern / in hūn-der-tern, bî-te)* (In bills of 10 / 20 / 50 / 100, please.)

Talkin' the Talk

Anne, an American tourist, heads to a bank to change money.

Anne:	**Guten Tag. Ich möchte US-Dollar wechseln. Wie ist der Wechselkurs, bitte?**
	gûtn tahk. īH muoH-te oo-ês dô-lār vêk-seln. vee īst dehr vêk-sel-kûrs bî-te
	Good morning. I would like to change US dollars. What's the exchange rate, please?

Bankangestellter: **Guten Tag. Einen Moment, bitte. Für einen Dollar bekommen Sie 1,85 DM.**
gûtn tahk. ay-nen moh-ment, bî-te. fuur ay-nen dô-lâr be-kô-men zee ay-ne mârk fuunf-ûnt-âH-tsîgk
Good morning. One moment, please. For one dollar you get 1.85 Marks.

Anne: **Ich möchte bitte 200 Dollar in Reiseschecks in Mark einwechseln.**
îH muoH-te bî-te tsvy-hûn-dêrt dô-lâr în ry-ze-shêks în mârk ayn-vêk-seln
I would like to exchange 200 dollars in traveler's checks into German marks.

Bankangestellter: **Kein Problem. Können Sie sich ausweisen?**
kyn prô-blehm. kuo-nen zee zîH ows-vy-zen
No problem. Do you have an ID?

Anne: **Hier ist mein Reisepass.**
heer îsst myn ry-ze-pâs
Here is my passport.

Bankangestellter: **Für 200 Dollar bekommen Sie 370 DM. Abzüglich 2,50 DM Wechselgebühr sind das 367,50 DM.**
fuur tsvy-hûn-dert dô-lâr be-kô-men zee dry-hûn-dert-zeep-tsîgk mârk. âb-tsuug-lîH tsvy mârk fuunf-tsîgk vêk-sel-ge-buur zînt dâs dry-hûn-dert-zeebn-ûnt-zêH-tsîgk mârk fuunf-tsîgk
For 200 dollars, you get 370 marks. Minus a 2.50 mark transaction fee, that's 367.50 marks.

Anne: **Vielen Dank.**
fee-len dângk
Thanks a lot.

Eurocheque debit cards

Although Germans have become increasingly fond of credit cards, they also use **Eurochequekarten** *(oy-roh-shêk-kâr-tn)* (eurocheck debit cards) that are issued by many European banks. Currently, about 40 million of the cards are in circulation in Germany alone. **EC-Karten** *(eh-tseh-kâr-ten)*, as they are called for short, are accepted at ever-increasing numbers of retail businesses as cash equivalents. They can be used to withdraw money from ATMs, and newer cards have a chip that allows users to transfer money directly from their checking accounts to the cards. In this way, money becomes instantly available for small transactions.

Words to Know

Geld tauschen/ wechseln	gêlt tow-shen/ vêk-seln	exchange money
das Bargeld	dâs bâr-gêlt	cash
in bar	în bâr	in cash
einen Reisescheck einlösen	ay-nen ry-ze-shêk ayn-luo-zn	to redeem a traveler's check
eine Gebühr bezahlen	ay-ne ge-buur be-tsah-len	to pay a fee
der Wechselkurs	dehr vêk-sel-kûrs	exchange rate
sich ausweisen	zîH ows-vyzn	to show proof of identity
der Ankauf	dehr ân-kowf	purchase / acquisition
der Verkauf	dehr fêr-kowf	sale

Heading to the ATM

Instead of changing money at the teller window of a bank, you can also use an ATM machine, called a **Geldautomat** (*gêlt-ow-tô-maht*) in German. Just look for your card symbol on the machine to make sure that it takes your kind of card.

If you're lucky, the ATM machine will give you a choice of languages to communicate in, but just in case German is your only option, you want to be prepared. ATMs use phrases that aren't the least bit flowery — infinitives are the order of the day (see the following section for an explanation). A typical run-through of prompts might look like this:

✔ **Karte einführen** (*kâr-te ayn-fuu-ren*) (insert card)

✔ **Sprache wählen** (*shprah-He veh-len*) (choose a language)

✔ **Geheimzahl eingeben** (*ge-hym-tsahl ayn-geh-ben*) (enter PIN)

✔ **Betrag eingeben** (*be-trahgk ayn-geh-ben*) (enter amount)

✔ **Betrag bestätigen** *(be-trahgk be-shteh-tî-gen)* (confirm amount)

✔ **Karte entnehmen** *(kâr-te ênt-neh-men)* (remove card)

✔ **Geldbetrag entnehmen** *(gêlt-be-trahgk ênt-neh-men)* (take cash)

Transaction completed. You should now be flush with local currency. Unless something went wrong. The ATM machine might be out of order, in which case, you see the following message:

> **Geldautomat außer Betrieb.** *(gêlt-ow-tô-maht ow-ser be-treep)* (ATM out of service).

Or the ATM might spit out your card without parting with any of its bounty. In that case you might receive the message:

> **Die Karte ist ungültig. / Die Karte ist nicht zugelassen.** *(dee kâr-te îst ûn-guul-tîgk. / dee kâr-te îst nîHt tsû-ge-lâsn)* (The card is not valid.)

Or, worst case scenario: the ATM machine swallows your card whole, leaving you with only this message for consolation:

> **Die Karte wurde einbehalten. Bitte besuchen Sie uns am Schalter.** *(dee kâr-te vûr-de ayn-be-hâltn. bî-te be-zoo-Hn zee ûns âm shâl-ter)* (The card was confiscated. Please see a teller.)

Getting Imperative

ATMs and other machines often use terse-sounding phrases, like **Geheimzahl eingeben** *(ge-hym-tsahl ayn-geh-ben)* (enter PIN). Although these phrases may not sound very polite, they are used quite a bit as a way to save space. For example, a more polite way to say **Geheimzahl eingeben** would be

> **Bitte geben Sie Ihre Geheimzahl ein.** *(bî-te geh-ben zee ee-re ge-hym-tsahl ayn)* (Please enter your PIN.)

Grammatically speaking, the terse phrases are infinitves posing as *imperatives* (commands). You encounter these forms wherever language efficiency is more important to the writer (or speaker) than social niceties.

When entering a building, such as a bank, you might, for example, find the word **ziehen** *(tsee-hen)* (pull) on the door as you go in, and the word **drücken** *(drû-kn)* (push) as you leave. Speaking about doors, you might notice a sign asking you to close the doors behind you, **Türen schließen** *(tuu-ren shlee-ssen),* when entering a building or a train.

Talkin' the Talk

Mike has run out of cash. All he has left is a 500 Mark bill, which isn't exactly the right size for a small purchase. He goes to a bank to change his bill into smaller denominations.

Mike: **Ich möchte diesen 500-Mark-Schein in kleinere Scheine wechseln.**
îH muoH-te dee-zn fuunf-hûn-dert-mârk-shyn în kly-nere shy-ne vêk-seln
I would like to change this 500-mark bill for smaller bills.

Angestellte: **Wie hätten Sie's denn gern?**
vee hêtn zees dên gêrn
How would you like it?

Mike: **Bitte geben Sie mir zwei 50-Mark-Scheine, 10 Zwanziger und 20 Zehner.**
bî-te geh-bn zee meer tsvy fuunf-tsîgk-mârk-shy-ne, tsehn tsvân-tsee-ger ûnt tsvy tseh-ner
Please give me two 50-mark bills, ten 20-mark bills, and 20 10-mark bills.

Angestellte: **Bitte sehr. Haben Sie sonst noch einen Wunsch?**
bî-te zehr. hah-bn zee sônst nôH ay-nen vûnsh
Here you go. Do you need anything else?

Mike: **Danke. Das ist alles.**
dâng-ke. dâs îst â-les.
Thanks. That's all.

Knowing the Various Currencies

The currencies of twelve European countries are on the brink of extinction. They belong to the countries that are the member states of the European Monetary Union. In the year 2002, a dozen currencies will make room for the Euro. In the transition period, most price labels and statements of financial transactions will present prices or amounts of money in both Euros and the local currency.

The decimal point and comma in numbers

English and German present numbers differently. In German a comma (**Komma**) is used in decimals where in English there would be a decimal point. To illustrate the point, here are a few examples in both languages.

English: 20.75   490.99   3675.50

German: 20,75   490,99   3675,50

And this is how you say one of these numbers:
20,75 = **zwanzig Komma sieben fünf** *(tsvân-tsîgk kô-mâ zee-bn fuunf).*

To make matters even more different, a period is used in German to break up large numbers. One hundred thousand dollars expressed in numbers nets the following in both languages:

English: 100,000 dollars

German   100.000 Dollar

Until the Euro goes into circulation, the German currency remains, of course, **die Deutsche Mark** *(dee doy-tshe mârk)*, often shortened to **D-Mark** *(deh-mârk)* in speech, or just **Mark** *(mârk)*, and usually written **DM**. The smaller unit is called **der Pfennig** *(dehr pfê-nîgk)*. There are 100 **Pfennige** *(pfê-nî-ge)* in one **Mark**.

The Austrian currency is **der (Österreichische) Schilling** *(dehr uos-te-ry-Hî-she shî-lîng)* abbreviated **öS**, and the smaller unit is **der Groschen** *(dehr grô-shen)*. The Swiss currency is **der (Schweizer) Franken** *(dehr shvy-tser frân-kn)*, abbreviated **sFr** or **Fr**, and the smaller unit is **der Rappen** *(dehr râ-pen)*.

The currencies of other countries are as follows:

- **Belgian Francs: der belgische Franken** *(dehr bêl-gîshe Frân-kn)*
- **British Pounds: das Pfund** *(dâs pfûnt)*
- **Danish Crowns: die Krone** *(dee deh-nî-she kroh-ne)*
- **Dutch Guilders: der holländische Gulden** *(dehr hô-lên-dî-she gûl-dn)*
- **Czech Crowns: die tschechische Krone** *(dee tshê-Hî-she kroh-ne)*
- **French Francs: der französische Franken** *(dehr frân-tsuo-zî-she frân-kn)*
- **Luxembourg Francs: der luxemburgische Franken** *(dehr lûxêm-bûr-gî-she frân-kn)*
- **Polish zlotys: der polnische Zloty** *(dehr pôl-nî-she slô-tee)*
- **U.S. dollars and cents: der Dollar / der Cent** *(dehr dô-lâr / dehr sênt)*

Fun & Games

Most ATM machines are very to-the-point — no frills. Sometimes you might encounter a cash machine that is a little more verbose. The problem in this case is that some of the words got loose. Time to put them back where they belong.

Geheimzahl   Betrag   Karte   Geldbetrag   wählen   entnehmen   bestätigen

1. Bitte führen Sie die _____ ein.

2. Bitte _____ Sie eine Sprache.

3. Bitte geben Sie Ihre _____ ein.

4. Bitte geben Sie den _____ ein.

5. Bitte _____ Sie den Betrag.

6. Bitte _____ Sie die Karte.

7. Bitte entnehmen Sie den _____.]

Answer key: 1. Karte 2. wählen 3. Geheimzahl 4. Geldbetrag 5. bestätigen 6. entnehmen 7. Betrag

Fun & Games

These words are missing below. See if you can fit them in.

wechselt   Reiseschecks   Reisepass   ausweisen   Wechselkurs

1. Anna _____ 200 Franken in Dollar.

2. Wie ist der _____?

3. Ich habe kein Bargeld aber _____.

4. Können Sie sich _____?

5. Hier ist mein _____.

Answer key: 1. wechselt 2. Wechselkurs 3. Reiseschecks 4. Ausweisen 5. Reisepass

Chapter 12
Asking for Directions

• •

In This Chapter

▶ Finding the places where you want to go

▶ Heading in the right directions (north, east, west, and south)

▶ Traveling by car

▶ Going here and there

• •

*T*he key to getting around is knowing how to get where you're going. Before you hop on that bus or train, or embark on your journey by car or on foot, it's always a good idea to find out where your desired goal is located. Being able to ask where the train station, bank, or museum are located is a good start. But of course you also want to understand the directions you are given — south of the bus terminal, behind the park, next to the fountain, take the second street on the left, make a right turn at the third traffic light, and so on. If you are afraid you might be lost, this is the chapter that will get you back on the map.

Asking for Help with Directions

Luckily, it's pretty easy to ask for directions in German. The secret to finding a location is the word **wo** *(voh)* (where). The question you want to ask starts with

> **Wo ist . . .?** *(voh ïst . . .)* (Where is . . .?)

At the end of the sentence, just supply the name of the location that you're looking for, which could include any of the following:

▸ **der Bahnhof** *(dehr <u>bahn</u>-hohf)* (train station)

▸ **der Taxistand** *(dehr <u>tâxee</u>-shtânt)* (taxi stand)

▸ **die U-Bahnhaltestelle** *(dee <u>oo</u>-bahn-<u>hâl</u>-te-shtê-le)* (subway station)

▸ **die Bushaltestelle** *(dee <u>bûs</u>-hâl-te-shtê-le)* (bus stop)

▸ **der Flughafen** *(dehr <u>floogk</u>-hah-fen)* (airport)

- ✔ **der Hafen** *(dehr <u>hah</u>-fen)* (harbor)

- ✔ **die Bank** *(dee bânk)* (bank)

- ✔ **das Hotel** *(dâs hoh-<u>têl</u>)* (hotel)

- ✔ **die Kirche** *(dee <u>kîr</u>-He)* (church)

- ✔ **die Post** *(dee pôst)* (post office)

- ✔ **der Markt** *(dehr mârkt)* (market)

- ✔ **das Museum** *(dâs mû-<u>zeh</u>-ûm)* (museum)

- ✔ **der Park** *(dehr pârk)* (park)

- ✔ **das Theater** *(dâs teh-<u>ah</u>-ter)* (theater)

Of course, if you're in a town of any size at all, a very general question like "Where is the bus stop?" or "Where is the bank" may be met with a quizical look — there may be multiple bus stops or banks in the near vicinity alone. You need to make your questions as specific as possible. For example, if you know the proper name of the bus stop, bank, or church, don't forget to include that in your question. For example, your questions about specific things might sound like this:

- ✔ **Wo ist die Bushaltestelle Karlsplatz?** *(voh îst dee <u>bûs</u>-hâl-te-shtê-le kârls-plâts)* (Where is the bus stop Karlsplatz?)

- ✔ **Wo ist die Dresdner Bank?** *(voh îst dee <u>drehs</u>-dnêr bânk)* (Where is the Dresdner bank?)

- ✔ **Wo ist die Marienkirche?** *(voh îst dee mâ-<u>ree</u>-en-kîr-He)* (Where is the Church of Mary?)

If you don't know the proper name of the location you're asking about, you can ask for directions to the nearest of whatever you're looking for. Doing so involves the word **nächste** *(<u>naiH</u>-ste)* (closest). You just insert **nächste** after the article of the location you're looking for. Check out a few examples of **nächste** as it assists you in finding the closest park, bus stop, or hotel:

- ✔ **Wo ist der nächste Park?** *(voh îst dehr <u>naiH</u>-ste pârk)* (Where is the closest park?)

- ✔ **Wo ist die nächste Bushaltestelle?** *(voh îst dee <u>naiH</u>-ste <u>bûs</u>-hâl-te-shtê-le)* (Where is the closest bus stop?)

- ✔ **Wo ist das nächste Hotel?** *(voh îst dâs <u>naiH</u>-ste hoh-<u>têl</u>)* (Where is the closest hotel?)

When it comes to getting around and asking for directions, there's a helpful verb you can use to indicate that you don't know your way around a place: **auskennen** *(<u>ows</u>-kê-nen)* (to know one's way around). The expression you might want to memorize is:

Ich kenne mich hier nicht aus. *(îH kê-ne mîH heer nîHt ows)* (I don't know my way around here.)

And if you want to make your request sound a little more friendly, you say:

Entschuldigen Sie bitte, ich kenne mich hier nicht aus. *(ênt-shûl-dî-gen zee bî-te, îH kê-ne mîH heer nîHt ows)* (Excuse me, I don't know my way around here.)

Here is the full conjugation of the verb **sich auskennen,** just in case. This is both a separable verb (which you can read about in Chapter 14) and a reflexive verb (which requires the personal pronoun in the accusative case):

Conjugation	*Pronunciation*
ich kenne mich aus	îH kê-ne mîH ows
du kennst dich aus	doo kênst dîH ows
Sie kennen sich aus	zee kê-nen zîH ows
er, sie, es kennt sich aus	ehr, zee, ês kênt zîH ows
wir kennen uns aus	veer kê-nen ûns ows
ihr kennt euch aus	eer kênt oyH ows
Sie kennen sich aus	zee kê-nen zîH ows
sie kennen sich aus	zee kê-nen zîH ows

How Far Is It?

In order to decide whether you want to walk someplace or take a bus or cab, it may be helpful to find out how far away your destination is. You have a couple of options to find out if something is located in the vicinity or far away, and the key words to know are **nah** *(nah)* (close) and **weit** *(vyt)* (far).

You can ask the question

Ist . . . weit entfernt? *(îst . . . vyt ênt-fêrnt)* (Is . . . far away?)

You just fill in the name of the location you're asking about. So, for example, if you were headed to the museum, you might ask someone

Ist das Museum weit entfernt? *(îst dâs mû-zeh-ûm vyt ênt-fêrnt)* (Is the museum far away?)

Hopefully, you will get the answer

> **Nein, das Museum ist nicht weit von hier.** *(nyn, dâs mû-zeh-ûm îst nîHt vyt fôn heer)* (No, the museum isn't far from here.)

The person you're talking to may even start to give you directions to the place you are on your way to. For help in understanding directions, read the section "Describing a Position or Location" later in this chapter.

You might also approach the issue the other way around and find out how close something is by using the noun **Nähe** *(nai-he)* (vicinity). You can ask the question

> **Ist . . . in der Nähe?** *(îst . . . în dehr nai-he)* (Is . . . in the vicinity?)

Going Here and There

The words **hier** *(heer)* (hier) and **dort** *(dôrt)* (there) often play an important part in communicating directions. They make directions just a little more specific. Look at the following sample sentences to see how **hier** and **dort** work in directions:

- ✔ **Das Museum ist nicht weit von hier.** *(dâs mû-zeh-ûm îst nîHt vyt fôn heer)* (The museum isn't far from here.)
- ✔ **Der Park ist nicht weit von dort.** *(dehr pârk îst nîHt vyt fôn dôrt)* (The park isn't far from there.)

A common expression you might hear is

> **Das ist gleich hier vorne / dort drüben.** *(dâs îst glyH heer fôr-ne / dôrt druu-ben)* (That is right here / over there.)

Although "right here" and "over there" are the most common combinations, there also is

> **Das ist gleich hier drüben.** *(dâs îst glyH heer druu-ben)* (That is right over here.)

The expressions **dort drüben** and **hier drüben** are practically interchangeable.

Asking "How Do I Get There?"

When you want to ask "How do I get there?" you use the verb **kommen** *(kô-men),* which means both "to come" and, when used with a preposition, "to get to."

You conjugate **kommen** like this:

Conjugation	*Pronunciation*
ich komme	îH kô-me
du kommst	doo kômst
Sie kommen	zee kô-men
er, sie, es kommt	ehr, zee, ês kômt
wir kommen	veer kô-men
ihr kommt	eer kômt
Sie kommen	zee kô-men
sie kommen	zee kô-men

The basic form of the question "How do I get there?" is

Wie komme ich . . .? *(vee kô-me îH . . .)* (How do I get . . .?)

To finish the rest of the sentence, you need to use a preposition — to help you say "*to* the train station" or "*to* the hotel." This is where things get a wee bit tricky.

In German, you're not just dealing with one prepostion as in English, where you would simply use "to" (How do I get to . . .?). In fact, you may need to use any of a number of prepositions, all of which can mean "to." The most commonly used "to" prepositions are the following:

- **in** *(în)*
- **nach** *(nahH)*
- **zu** *(tsû)*

Using "in"

You use the preposition **in** *(în)* when you want to get to a certain part of a city, such as the center, the suburbs, or the park. For example

Wie komme ich in die Innenstadt? *(vee kô-me îH în dee în-nên-shtât)* (How do I get to the center of the city?)

When you use the preposition **in** in this way, the article that comes after **in** goes into the *accusative case,* which means that the article changes form slightly. (See Chapter 2 for a complete explanation of the accusative case.) As a reminder, here is how the articles change:

- ✔ **der** becomes **den** *(dehn)*
- ✔ **die** stays just **die** *(dee)*
- ✔ **das** stays **das** *(dâs)*

For example, the article of a masculine noun like **der Park** *(dehr pârk)* (park) changes like this:

Wie komme ich in den Park? *(vee kô-me îH în dehn pârk)* (How do I get to the park?)

The article of a feminine noun, like **die Stadt** *(dee shtât)* (city), just stays the same:

Wie komme ich in die Stadt? *(vee kô-me îH în dee shtât)* (How do I get to the city?)

The article of a neuter noun like **das Zentrum** *(dâs tsên-trûm)* (center) also stays the same, but when the preposition **in** is used with neuter nouns in the accusative case, the preposition and article contract to form the word **ins**:

in + das = ins

This contraction is almost always used, giving you phrases like

Wie komme ich ins Zentrum? *(vee kô-me îH îns tsên-trûm)* (How do I get to the city center?)

Using "nach"

The preposition **nach** only comes into play in a very specific context. If you want to get to a city or country, you use **nach** *(nahH):*

Wie komme ich nach Köln? *(vee kô-me îH nahH kuoln)* (How do I get to Cologne?)

You have no troublesome articles to bother with for once, because city names and most country names don't need articles.

Using "zu"

For all the other locations you might want to reach, **zu** *(tsū)* is a pretty safe bet.

The preposition **zu** requires the dative case, which means that the articles used right after **zu** change in the following ways:

- **der** becomes **dem** *(dehm)*
- **die** becomes **der** *(dehr)*
- **das** also becomes **dem** *(dehm)*

When the preposition **zu** is used with masculine and neuter nouns in the dative case, the preposition and article contract to form the word **zum**:

> **Wie komme ich zum Bahnhof?** *(vee kô-me îH tsūm bahn-hohf)* (How do I get to the train station?)

For a masculine noun like **der Bahnhof** *(dehr bahn-hohf)* (train station), **zu** and **dem** combine to become **zum**:

> zu + dem Bahnhof = **zum Bahnhof** *(tsūm bahn-hohf)* (to the train station)

A neuter noun, like **das Auto** *(dâs ow-toh)* (car), behaves in much the same way with **zu**:

> zu + dem Auto = **zum Auto** *(tsūm ow-toh)* (to the car)

Take a look at how a feminine noun like **die Bushaltestelle** *(dee bûs-hâl-te-shtê-le)* (bus stop) behaves with **zu**:

> zu + der Bushaltestelle = **zur Bushaltestelle** *(tsūr bûs-hâl-te-shtê-le)* (to the bus stop)

> **Wie komme ich zur Bushaltestelle?** *(vee kôm-me îH tsūr bûs-hâl-te-shtê-le)* (How do I get to the bus stop?)

Describing a Position or Location

After you ask for directions, you must be ready to understand the possible answers. It's very common for someone to express the location of a place in relation to a well-known landmark or location. There are quite a few prepositions that are used to describe locations in this way. Luckily, all of these prepositions use the dative case in this context, so any articles after the preposition behave just like they do for the use of **zu** described in the previous section.

Getting a cab

The secret to getting a cab in Germany is making a phone call. You might be used to the idea that in big cities, you can just hail a cab on the street, but this isn't common practice in Germany, even in big cities. You usually call a dispatcher, but phone books also often list individual taxi stands, so that you might find the number of the taxi stand closest to where you are located. Of course, you find taxi stands in front of airports, train stations, and major hotels.

Table 12-1 shows you some common prepositions that are used to express the location of one thing in relation to another.

Table 12-1		Prepositions that Express Locations	
Preposition	*Pronunciation*	*Meaning*	*Example*
auf	owf	on	**auf der Museumstraße** *(owf dehr mû-zeh-ûms-shtrah-se)* on Museum Street
bei	by	near / next to	**beim Bahnhof** *(bym bahn-hohf)* near to the train station
hinter	<u>hîn</u>-ter	behind	**hinter der Kirche** *(hîn-ter dehr kîr-He)* behind the church
vor	fohr	in front of	**vor der Post** *(fohr dehr pôst)* in front of the post office
neben	<u>neh</u>-bn	next to	**neben der Bank** *(neh-bn dehr bânk)* next to the bank
zwischen	<u>tsvî</u>-shen	between	**zwischen dem Theater und der Bank** *(tsvî-shen dehm teh-ah-ter ûnt dehr bânk)* between the theater and the bank
gegenüber	geh-gen-<u>uu</u>-ber	opposite	**gegenüber dem Museum** *(geh-gen-uu-ber dehm mû-zeh-ûm)* opposite the museum
an	ân	at	**an der Ecke** *(ân dehr êke)* at the corner

Talkin' the Talk

 Mike has gone on a business trip to München, a city he hasn't vis-
ited before. He wants to take a cab to get to a friend's house, and
since he needs some help finding the next taxi stand, he
approaches a woman on the street.

Mike: **Entschuldigen Sie bitte, wo ist der nächste Taxistand?**
*ênt-shûl-dî-gen zee bî-te, voh îst dehr naiH-ste tâxee-
shtant*
Excuse me, where is the closest taxi stand?

Frau: **Auf der Königsstraße.**
owf dehr kuo-nîgks-shtrah-se
On King Street.

Mike: **Ich kenne mich in München leider nicht aus. Wie
komme ich zur Königsstraße?**
*îH kê-ne mîH în muun-Hen ly-der nîHt ows. vee kô-me
îH tsûr kuo-nîgks-shtrah-se*
Unfortunately, I don't know my way around Munich.
How do I get to King Street?

Frau: **Sehen Sie die Kirche an der Ecke? Neben der Kirche
ist ein Park und direkt gegenüber ist der Taxistand.**
*zehn zee dee kîr-He ân dehr êke? neh-bn dehr kîr-He
îst ein pârk ûnt dee-rêkt geh-gen-uu-ber îst dehr
tâxee-shtânt*
Do you see the church at the corner? Next to the
church is a park and directly opposite is the taxi
stand.

Mike: **Vielen Dank!**
fee-len dângk
Thanks a lot!

Words to Know

Wo ist . . .?	voh ist	Where is . . .?
nächste	naiH-ste	next
sich auskennen	ziH ows-kê-nen	to know one's way around
weit	vyt	far
nah	nah	near
hinter	hin-ter	behind
vor	fohr	in front of
neben	neh-ben	next to
an	ân	at

Going Right, Left, North, South, East, and West

Unless you tackle the words for the various directions — such as left and right, north and south — you will forever be pulling out your map and asking people to point you on your way. Talk about embarassing and inconvenient! Help sever your dependency on maps by mastering the few simple words you need to understand (and give) the various directions.

Left and right

When it comes to asking for or giving directions, there's no way to get around the key words for defining position: left and right or, in German:

- **links** *(līnks)* (left)
- **rechts** *(rêHts)* (right)

If you want to express that something is located to the left or right of something else, you add the preposition **von** *(fôn)* (of), making the following:

✔ **links von** *(lînks fôn)* (to the left of): For example — **Das Museum ist links von der Kirche.** *(dâs mû-zeh-ûm îst lînks fôn dehr kîr-He)* (The museum is to the left of the church.)

✔ **rechts von** *(rêHts fôn)* (to the right of): For example — **Die Kirche ist rechts vom Theater.** *(dee kîr-He îst rêHts fôm teh-ah-ter)* (The museum is to the right of the theater.)

You might also hear the word for side, **die Seite** *(dee zy-te),* when talking about directions. Along with the words for left and right, **Seite** can help directions be more specific. For example:

✔ **Das Museum ist auf der linken Seite.** *(dâs mû-zeh-ûm îst owf dehr lîng-ken zy-te)* (The museum is on the left side.)

✔ **Die Kirche ist auf der rechten Seite.** *(dee kîr-He îst owf dehr rêH-ten zy-te)* (The church is on the right side.)

The cardinal points

The other key elements that come in handy when you need to define your position (or the position of something) are the cardinal points. They are:

✔ **der Norden** *(deht nôr-den)* (North)

✔ **der Süden** *(dehr zuu-den)* (South)

✔ **der Osten** *(dehr ôs-ten)* (East)

✔ **der Westen** *(dehr wês-ten)* (West)

To describe a position, you combine these with the preposition **im** *(îm).* For example:

Der Hafen liegt im Norden *(dehr hah-fen leegkt îm nôr-den)* / **Süden** *(zuu-den)* / **Osten** *(ôs-ten)* / **Westen** *(wês-ten).* (The harbor lies in the North / South / East / West).

Getting on the Move

If you've asked somebody for directions, you might very well get the answer that you should take a specific street — the second street on the left or the first street on the right, for example.

The verbs you need to be familiar with in this context are **gehen** *(gehn)* (to go) and **nehmen** *(neh-men)* (to take). In order to give directions, you use the imperative. (See the section "Getting Imperative" in Chapter 11 for more information on the imperative.) The verb goes at the beginning of the sentence. For example:

- ✔ **Nehmen Sie die zweite Straße links!** *(neh-men zee dee tsvy-te shtrah-se links)* (Take the second street on the left.)

- ✔ **Gehen Sie die erste Straße rechts!** *(gehn zee dee ers-te shtrah-se rêHts)* (Take the first street on the right.)

If you give instructions to a friend, you wouldn't use the formal but the informal form of address, and the above instructions would turn into

- ✔ **Nimm die zweite Straße links!** *(nîm dee tsvy-te shtrah-se links)* (Take the second street on the left.)

- ✔ **Geh die erste Straße rechts!** *(geh dee ers-te shtrah-se rêHts)* (Take the first street on the right.)

See the following section "The First, Second, Third, and So On" for more information on using these types of words.

If you are looking for a specific building, you might hear something like:

Es ist das dritte Haus auf der linken Seite. *(ês îst dâs drî-te hows owf dehr ling-ken zy-te)* (It is the third house on the left side.)

And if you don't have to make a left or right but simply have to go straight on, you might hear the instruction:

Gehen Sie geradeaus! *(gehn zee grah-de-ows)* (Go straight ahead.)

The First, Second, Third, and So On

Words like second, third, fourth, and so on are called *ordinal numbers*. They refer to a specific number in a series and answer the question "Which one?" For example, to the question "Which house?" you use an ordinal number to answer "The second on the left."

In German, you form the ordinal numbers by adding the suffix "te" to the cardinal numbers (one, two, three, and so on) for numbers between 1 and 19 — with two exceptions, which are:

- **eins** *(ayns)* (one) / **erste** *(êrs-te)* (first)
- **drei** *(dry)* (three) / **dritte** *(drî-te)* (third)

Table 12-2 shows you how to form the ordinal numbers of numbers 1 through 10 and one example of an ordinal number formed with a "-teen" number.

Table 12-2	Sample Ordinal Numbers by Cardinal Number
Cardinal Number	*Ordinal Number*
eins *(ayns)* (one)	der / die / das **erste** *(êrs-te)* (first)
zwei *(tsvy)* (two)	**zweite** *(tsvy-te)* (second)
drei *(dry)* (three)	**dritte** *(drî-te)* (third)
vier *(veer)* (four)	**vierte** *(feer-te)* (fourth)
fünf *(fuunf)* (five)	**fünfte** *(fuunf-te)* (fifth)
sechs *(zêks)* (six)	**sechste** *(zêks-te)* (sixth)
sieben *(zeebn)* (seven)	**siebte** *(zeeb-te)* (seventh)
acht *(âHt)* (eight)	**achte** *(âH-te)* (eighth)
neun *(noyn)* (nine)	**neunte** *(noyn-te)* (ninth)
zehn *(tsehn)* (ten)	**zehnte** *(tsehn-te)* (tenth)
siebzehn *(zeeb-tsehn)* (seventeen)	**siebzehnte** *(zeeb-tsehn-te)* (seventeenth)

You form the ordinal numbers above 19 by adding the suffix "ste" to the cardinal numbers. For example:

- **zwanzig** *(tsvân-tsîgk)* (twenty) / **zwanzigste** *(tsvân-tsîgks-te)* (twentieth)
- **dreissig** *(dry-sîgk)* (thirty) / **dreissigste** *(dry-sîgks-te)* (thirtieth)
- **vierzig** *(fîr-tsîgk)* (forty) / **vierzigste** *(fîr-tsîgks-te)* (fourtieth)

Because they are used like adjectives, the ordinal numbers take the gender and case of the noun they refer to. Table 12-3 shows you how the adjective **erste** changes in each case along with the article that comes before it.

Table 12-3:	Declining a Sample Ordinal Number: Erste _(êrs-te)_ (first)			
Noun's Gender	**Nominative**	**Genitive**	**Dative**	**Accusative**
Masculine (der)	der erste	des ersten	dem ersten	den ersten
Feminine (die)	die erste	der ersten	der ersten	die erste
Neuter (das)	das erste	des ersten	dem ersten	das erste
Plural (die)	die ersten	der ersten	den ersten	die ersten

Talkin' the Talk

 Erika wants to meet an old friend who also happens to be in town on business. She has the address of the hotel her friend is staying at, but she isn't sure where the street is located, so she has to ask for help.

Erika: **Entschuldigung?**
ênt-_shûl_-dî-gûng
Excuse me?

Mann: **Ja, bitte?**
yah, bî-te
Yes, please?

Erika : **Wie komme ich zur Beethovenstraße?**
vee _kô_-me îH tsûr _beht_-hohfên-shtrah-se
How do I get to Beethoven Street?

Mann: **Nehmen Sie die U-Bahn am Opernplatz.**
neh-men zee dee _oo_-bahn âm _oh_-pêrn-plâts
You have to take the subway at Opera Square.

Erika: **Und wo ist der Opernplatz?**
ûnt voo îst dehr _oh_-pêrn-plâts
And where is Opera Square?

Mann:	**Gehen Sie die Wodanstraße geradeaus. Dann gehen Sie links in die Reuterstraße. Rechts liegt der Bahnhof und direkt gegenüber ist der Opernplatz.** *gehn zee dee voh-dahn-shtrah-se grah-de-ows. dân gehn zee lînks în dee roy-ter-shtrah-se. rêHts leegkt dehr bahn-hohf ûnt dee-rêkt geh-gen-uu-ber îst dehr oh-pêrn-plâts* Go straight down Wodan Street. Then make a left into Reuter Way. To the right you see the train station and directly opposite is Opera Square.
Erika:	**Und welche U-Bahn nehme ich?** *ûnt vêl-He oo-bahn neh-me îH* And which subway do I take?
Mann:	**U5 bis zur Haltestelle Beethovenstraße.** *oo fuunf bîs tsûr hâl-te-shtê-le beht-hohfên-shtrah-se* Take the subway 5 to the stop Beethoven Street.
Erika:	**Vielen Dank!** *fee-len dângk* Thanks a lot!

Words to Know

links	lînks	left
rechts	rêHts	right
Wo ist . . . ?	voo îst	Where is . . . ?
Nehmen Sie . . . !	neh-men zee	Take . . . !
Gehen Sie . . . !	gehn zee	Go . . . !
die U-Bahn	dee oo-bahn	subway
die Haltestelle	dee hâl-te-shtê-le	stop (bus, subway, and so on)

Traveling by Car or Another Vehicle

In English, it doesn't make a big difference if you're going by car or on foot — distance aside, you're still going. Unfortunately, the German verb **gehen** *(gehn)* (to go) isn't that flexible. You may go on foot — **zu Fuß gehen** *(tsū fuhs gehn)* — but if you take the car, you're driving, — **fahren** *(fah-ren)* — not going.

When using **fahren** in a sentence, you need three things: the word for the type of vehicle you're using, the preposition **mit** *(mĭt)* (with), and the dative version of the vehicle's article. Here are a few examples of how you use the verb **fahren** in a sentence to say that you're taking a specific kind of transportation:

> **Ich fahre mit dem Auto.** *(ĭH <u>fah</u>-re mĭt dehm <u>ow</u>-tô)* (I'm going by car. Literally: I'm driving with the car.)

You don't need driving experience to use the following words and phrases about turning left and right. You can use them to describe turns you make on a bike, or on your skateboard!

To tell somebody to make a left or right turn, you can use your old friend, the verb **fahren.** You say

> **Fahren Sie links / rechts!** *(<u>fah</u>-ren zee lĭnks / rêHts)* (Go left / right. Literally: Drive left / right.)

You can also use the verb **abbiegen** *(<u> âp</u>-beegn)* (to make a turn) to instruct somebody to make a left or right turn

> **Biegen Sie links / rechts ab!** *(beegn zee lĭnks / rêHts âp)* (Make a left / right turn!)

If you've lost your way driving around, this is the expression to memorize:

> **Ich habe mich verfahren. Ich suche . . .** *(ĭH <u>hah</u>-be mĭH fêr-<u>fah</u>-ren. ĭH zoo-He . . .)* (I've lost my way. I'm looking for . . .)

See Chapter 14 for more information on words you need for getting around in a car.

Talkin' the Talk

Paula has rented a car to go to Frankfurt for a day trip. She's on her way to Bockenheim, a district of Frankfurt, and she stops at a gas station to ask for directions.

Paula: **Entschuldigen Sie, wie komme ich nach Bockenhelm?**
ênt-shûl-dî-gên zee, vee kô-me îH nahH bôkn-hym
Excuse me, how do I get to Bockenheim?

Tankwart: **Nehmen Sie die Ausfahrt Frankfurt-Messe! Das sind ungefähr vier Kilometer von hier.**
neh-men zee dee ows-fahrt frânk-fûrt mê-se! Dâs zînt ûn-ge-fair feer kîlô-meh-ter fôn heer
Take the exit Frankfurt-Messe! That is approximately 10 kilometers from here.

Paula: **Alles klar! Danke.**
âlês klahr! dâng-ke
Okay! Thank you.

Paula makes it to Bockenheim but then seems to have lost her way. She stops her car and asks a policeman for directions.

Paula: **Entschuldigen Sie, ich habe mich verfahren! Ich suche den Hessenplatz.**
ênt-shûl-dî-gên zee, îH hah-be mîH fêr-fah-ren. îH zoo-He dehn hê-sên-plâts
Excuse me. I've lost my way! I'm looking for Hessen Square.

Polizei: **Biegen Sie an der nächsten Kreuzung rechts ab. Dann fahren Sie geradeaus, ungefähr einen Kilometer. Der Hessenplatz liegt auf der linken Seite.**
beegn zee ân dehr naiH-sten kroy-tsûng rêHts âp. dân fah-ren zee grah-de-ows, ûn-ge-fair ay-nen kîlô-meh-ter. dehr hê-sên-plâts leegkt owf dehr lîng-ken zy-te
Make a left turn at the next intersection. Then go straight on, approximately one kilometer. Hessen Square is on the left side.

Paula: **Vielen Dank!**
fee-len dângk
Thank you!

FUN & GAMES

Match the descriptions to the pictures.

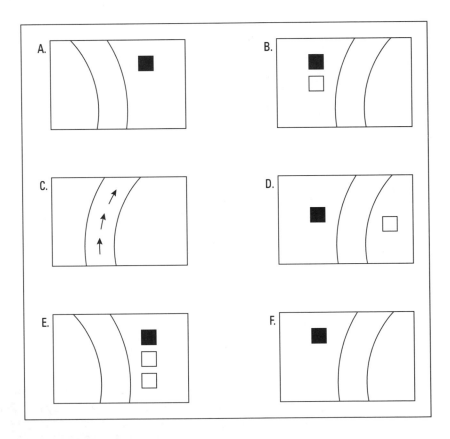

1. gegenüber

2. rechts

3. das dritte Haus auf der rechten Seite

4. geradeaus

5. links

6. das zweite Haus auf der linken Seite

Chapter 13

Staying at a Hotel

● ●

In This Chapter

▶ Finding a hotel

▶ Making reservations

▶ Checking in: names, addresses, and room numbers

▶ Checking out and paying the bill

● ●

*R*egardless of whether you are traveling for business or pleasure, comfortable accomodations are an important part of your trip. This chapter should help you with the vocabulary and phrases that you need to find a hotel, make reservations, inquire about your hotel's facilities, and check in and out.

Finding a Hotel

If you need assistance in finding a hotel, you might want to buy a hotel guide or **Hotelführer** *(hoh-tēl-fuu-rer)*, which you can get in book stores. And of course, you will also get information about all types of accomodations through the tourist information center in any town, which is called **das Fremdenverkehrsbüro** *(dās frēm-den-fēr-kehrs-buu-roh)*.

Perhaps you want to ask other people you know or meet if they can recommend a hotel. In this case, you would ask

> **Können Sie ein Hotel in . . . empfehlen?** *(kuo-nen zee ayn hoh-tēl in . . . ēm-pfeh-len)* (Can you recommend a hotel in . . .?)

The basic word for hotel in German is **das Hotel** *(dās hoh-tēl)*. You can find a wide variety of hotels in German-speaking countries which offer different atmospheres and levels of service. In rural areas and smaller towns, hotels are often labeled a little differently. For example, the following types of hotels are common:

- **das Hotel garni** *(dãs hoh-têl gâr-nee)* (A hotel that serves only breakfast)

- **der Rasthof / das Motel** *(dehr râst-hohf / dãs moh-têl)* (A roadside lodge, or motel, located just off an expressway)

- **das Gasthaus / der Gasthof** *(dãs gâst-hows / dehr gâst-hohf)* (An inn providing food and drinks and often lodging)

- **die Pension** *(dee pâng-zîohn)* (A boardinghouse offering full board — breakfast, lunch, and dinner — or half board — breakfast, lunch or dinner. Meals are usually served to houseguests only.)

- **die Jugendherberge** *(die yoo-gênt-hêr-bêr-ge)* (A youth hostel; in Austria, Germany, and Switzerland, youth hostels are quite comfortable and sometimes pretty upscale.)

- **die Ferienwohnung** *(dee feh-rî-ên-voh-nûng)* (A "vacation apartment;" a furnished apartment in holiday resorts)

Reserving Rooms

As usual, it's best to book a hotel room in advance, especially during the high season or when a special event in town may cause the hotels to fill up quickly. If you haven't made a reservation and you have difficulty finding a room, you're more likely to find a hotel outside of towns and city centers. Ask for some assistance at the **Fremdenverkehrsbüro.** (See the previous section for more information on that helpful office.)

Reservations for hotel rooms are usually made over the telephone, so you may want to read Chapter 9 before you pick up the phone to call in your order. When the hotel picks up the phone, you can say the following to announce the purpose of your call

> **Ich möchte gern ein Zimmer reservieren.** *(îH muoH-te gêrn ayn tsî-mer rê-zêr-vee-ren)* (I would like to reserve a room.)

If you would like to reserve more than one room, you just have to insert the appropriate number: **zwei** *(tsvy)* (two), **drei** *(dry)* (three) **Zimmer,** and so on.

Depending on who answers the phone, you may get to start making your reservation right away.

Saying when and how long you want to stay

It's very probable that the person taking your reservation will ask you a series of questions in order to complete your reservation. Among the first of these quesitons might be something along the lines of

> **Von wann bis wann möchten Sie ein Zimmer reservieren?** *(fôn vân bîs vân muoH-ten zee ayn tsî-mer rê-zêr-vee-ren)* (For what dates would you like to reserve a room?)

Before you call to make a reservation, make sure that you've read "Using the Calendar and Dates" in Chapter 15 so that you know how to say the dates that you need for making your reservation.

In order to specify how many nights you want to stay or for what dates you want to reserve, you could say either of the following, depending on what might fit your needs:

- ✔ **Ich möchte gern ein Zimmer für . . . Nächte reservieren.** *(îH muoH-te gêrn ayn tsî-mer fuur . . . naiH-te rê-zêr-vee-ren)* (I would like to reserve a room for . . . nights.)
- ✔ **Ich möchte gern ein Zimmer vom 11. 3. bis zum 15. 3. reservieren.** *(îH muoH-te gêrn ayn tsî-mer fôm êlf-ten drî-ten bîs tsûm fuunf-tsehn-ten drî-ten rê-zêr-vee-ren)* (I would like to reserve a room from the 11th to the 15th of March.)

Specifying the kind of room you want

The person taking your reservation will certainly ask you something like the following in order to find out what kind of room you'd like:

> **Was für ein Zimmer möchten Sie gern?** *(vâs fuur ayn tsî-mer muoH-ten zee gêrn)* (What kind of room would you like?)

You can take the initiative and state what kind of room you want with the phrase

> **Ich hätte gern . . .** *(îH ha-te gêrn . . .)* (I would like . . .)

Was für . . .? *(vâs fuur. . .)* (What kind of . . .?)

This is a very good phrase to remember. This phrase can come up any time you're speaking with all sorts of service providers, from a sales person to an assistant at the **Fremdenverkehrsbüro**. These questions help people find out exactly what it is that you want — for example:

✔ **Was für eine Ferienwohnung möchten Sie gern?** *(vâs fuur ay-ne feh-rî-ên-voh-nûng muoH-ten zee gêrn)* (What kind of vacation apartment would you like?)

✔ **Was für einen Rasthof suchen Sie?** *(vâs fuur ay-nen râst-hohf zoo-Hen zee)* (What kind of lodge are looking for?)

Remember that the question **Was für . . .?** is always used with the indefinite article in the accusative case. (See Chapter 2 for more information about the accusative case.)

At the end of the phrase, substitute any of the following (or combination of the following) to specify exactly what kind of room you'd like to put your suitcase in:

✔ **ein Einzelzimmer** *(ayn ayn-tsêl-tsî-mer)* (a single room)

✔ **ein Doppelzimmer** *(ayn dôpl-tsî-mer)* (a double room)

✔ **ein Zimmer mit . . .** *(ayn tsî-mer mît . . .)* (a room with . . .)

  • **Dusche** *(doo-she)* (shower)

  • **Bad** *(baht)* (bathtub)

  • **zwei Einzelbetten** *(tsvy ayn-tsêl-bê-ten)* (two twin beds)

  • **einem Doppelbett** *(ay-nêm dôpl-bêt)* (one double bed)

Asking about the price

You also might want to find out what the hotel room costs. These are some possible ways to ask the question, depending on whether you want to know the basic price or the price with other features included:

✔ **Was kostet das Zimmer pro Nacht?** *(vâs kôs-tet dâs tsî-mer proh nâHt)* (What does the room cost per night?)

✔ **Was kostet eine Übernachtung mit Frühstück?** *(vâs kôs-tet ay-ne uubêr-nâH-tûngk mît fruu-shtuuk)* (What does accommodation including breakfast cost?)

- **Was kostet ein Zimmer mit Vollpension?** (*vâs kôs-tet ayn tsî-mer mît fôl-pâng-zîohn*) (What does a room with full board cost?)

- **Was kostet ein Zimmer mit Halbpension?** (*vâs kôs-tet ayn tsî-mer mît hâlp-pâng-zîohn*) (What does a room with half board cost?)

Finalizing the reservation

If the room is available and you're happy with the price, you can seal the deal by saying

Können Sie das Zimmer bitte reservieren? (*kuo-nen zee dâs tsî-mer bî-te reh-zêr-vee-ren*) (Could you please reserve that room?)

Talkin' the Talk

Klaus und Ulrike Huber want to take a vacation in Österreich, and they have found a hotel in the area they are planning to visit. Klaus calls the Hotel Staiger and talks to the receptionist.

Rezeption: **Hotel Staiger, guten Tag.**
hoh-têl staiger gûtn tahgk
Hello, Hotel Staiger.

Klaus: **Guten Tag, ich möchte ein Zimmer reservieren. Vom 15. bis zum 23 Juni.**
gûtn tahgk, îH muoH-te ayn tsî-mer rê-zêr-vee-ren. fôm fuunf-tsehn-ten bîs tsûm dry-ûnt-tsvân-tsigk-sten yoo-nee
Hello. I would like to reserve a room from the 15th to the 23rd of June.

Rezeption: **Ja, das geht. Was für ein Zimmer möchten Sie?**
yah, dâs geht. vâs fuur ayn tsî-mer muoH-ten zee
Yes, that's possible. What kind of room would you like?

Klaus: **Ein Doppelzimmer mit Bad, bitte. Was kostet das Zimmer pro Nacht?**
ayn dôpl-tsî-mer mît baht bî-te. vâs kôs-tet dâs tsî-mer proh nâHtt
A double room with bathroom, please. What does the room cost per night?

Rezeption:	**1500 Schillinge für Übernachtung mit Frühstück.**
	fuunf-zehn-hûn-dêrt <u>shî</u>-lînge fuur <u>uubêr</u>-nâH-tûngk mît <u>fruu</u>-shtuuk
	1500 Shillings for accommodation including breakfast.
Klaus:	**Gut, können Sie es bitte reservieren? Mein Name ist Huber.**
	gût, <u>kuon</u>-nen zee ês <u>bî</u>-te rê-zêr-<u>vee</u>-ren? myn <u>nah</u>-me îsst <u>hoo</u>-ber
	Fine. Could you please reserve it? My name is Huber.
Rezeption:	**Geht in Ordnung, Herr Huber.**
	geht în <u>ôrt</u>-nûngk hair hoo-ber
	Okay, Mr. Huber.
Klaus:	**Vielen Dank!**
	<u>fee</u>-len dângk
	Thanks a lot!

Words to Know

das Fremdenverkehrsbüro	dâs <u>frêm</u>-den-<u>fêr</u>-kehrs-buu-<u>roh</u>	tourist information center
das Einzelzimmer	dâs <u>ayn</u>-tsêl-tsî-mer	single room
das Doppelzimmer	dâs <u>dôpl</u>-tsî-mer	double room
das Bad	dâs baht	bathtub
die Dusche	dee <u>doo</u>-she	shower
Geht in Ordnung!	geht în <u>ôrt</u>-nûngk	Okay!

Checking In: Names, Addresses, and Room Numbers

Once you arrive at your hotel, you have to check in at the **Rezeption** _(dee <u>rê</u>-tsêp-tsjohn)_ (the reception desk). To let the receptionist know that you have made reservations, you say

Ich habe ein Zimmer reserviert. *(îH hah-be ayn tsî-mer rê-zêr-veert)* (I have reserved a room.)

Of course, you also have to let the receptionist know what your name is:

Mein Name ist . . . *(myn nah-me îst . . .)* (My name is . . .)

How long are you staying?

If you haven't made a reservation, or the receptionist wants to double-check the length of your stay, you might hear the question:

Wie lange bleiben Sie? *(vee lânge bly-ben zee)* (How long are you going to stay?)

To the question about how long you want to stay, you can reply with the phrase

Ich bleibe / Wir bleiben . . . *(îH bly-be . . . / veer bly-ben . . .)* (I'm going to stay . . . / We are going to stay . . .)

Then end the phrase with any of the appropriate lenghts of time:

- ✔ **. . . nur eine Nacht.** *(. . . noor ay-ne nâHt)* (. . . just one night.)
- ✔ **. . . drei Tage.** *(. . . dry tah-ge)* (. . . three days.)
- ✔ **. . . eine Woche.** *(. . . ay-ne vô-He)* (. . . one week.)

Filling out the registration form

At some hotels, you might have to fill in a form, **das Formular** *(dâs fôr-mû-lahr)*, at the reception desk as part of the registration process. The receptionist will hand you the form, saying something like the following:

Bitte füllen Sie dieses Formular aus. *(bî-te fuu-ln zee dee-zês fôr-mû-lahr ows)* (Please fill in this form.)

The information the form asks you for varies; in most cases, your name and address are sufficient, but you might also be asked for any of the following information:

- ✔ **Name / Vorname** *(nah-me / fohr-nah-me)* (Surname / First Name)
- ✔ **Straße / Nummer (Nr.)** *(shtrah-se / nû-mer)* (Street / Number)
- ✔ **Postleitzahl / Wohnort** *(pôst-lyt-tsahl / vohn-ôrt)* (Zip Code / City)

- ✔ **Geburtsdatum / Geburtsort** *(gê-bûrts-dah-tûm / gê-bûrts-ôrt)* (Birth Date / Place of Birth)

- ✔ **Nationalität** *(nâ-tsjoh-nah-lî-tait)* (Nationality)

- ✔ **Beruf** *(bê-roof)* (Occupation)

- ✔ **Passnummer** *(pâss-nû-mer)* (Passport Number)

- ✔ **Kraftfahrzeugkennzeichen** *(krâft-fahr-tsoygk-kên-tsy-Hen)* (License Plate Number)

- ✔ **Ort / Datum** *(ôrt / dah-tûm)* (Place / Date)

- ✔ **Unterschrift** *(ûn-ter-shrîft)* (Signature)

Understanding the key game

Once you've checked in, the receptionist lets you know what your room number is:

> **Sie haben Zimmer Nummer 203.** *(zee hah-bn tsî-mer nû-mer tsvy-hûn-dêrt-dry)* (You have room number 203.)

Your room number is usually conveniently written on the key, just as it is in most American hotels.

In some hotels, usually in smaller towns, you might have to leave your key at the reception desk instead of taking it with you when you're going out. When you arrive back at the hotel and need the key to your room, you can use either of the following phrases to request your key:

- ✔ **Können Sie mir bitte den Schlüssel für Zimmer . . . geben?** *(kuon-nen zee meer bî-te dehn shluu-sêl fuur tsî-mer nû-mer . . . geh-ben)* (Could you give me the key for room number . . .?)

- ✔ **Den Schlüssel für Zimmer . . . bitte.** *(dehn shluu-sêl fuur tsî-mer . . . bî-te)* (The key for room number . . . please.)

Getting your luggage in hand

In all likelihood, you'll travel with some kind of luggage, **das Gepäck** *(dâs ge-pêk)*. Your luggage could be **der Koffer** *(dehr kô-fer)* (suitcase) or maybe even **die Koffer** *(dee kô-fer)* (suitcases).

No that's not a mistake — the only difference between the singular and plural for "suitcase" is the article.

Hotel breakfast

Most big hotels offer a breakfast buffet, from which you can choose anything ranging from cereals, eggs, a variety of breads and juices, jam, cheese, and so on. In smaller towns or hotels, however, you still might get what used to be the typical German breakfast: rolls and bread, jam, soft-boiled eggs, and a choice of cold cuts and cheeses. So if you can't do without your scrambled eggs in the morning, you might have to put in a special order! (See Chapter 5 for help on how to do that.)

Asking about amenities and facilities

You might also want to find out what kind of services and facilities the hotel offers — does your room have a phone or a mini bar? Does the hotel have a laundry service?

Your room

When you want to ask about specific features of your room, start with the phrase

> **Hat das Zimmer . . .?** *(hât dâs ͟tsî-mer . . .)* (Does the room have . . .?)

Then end the phrase with any of the following items you might want to ask about:

- ✔ **. . . Kabelfernsehen?** *(. . . ͟kah-bel-fêrn-zehn)* (. . . cable TV?)
- ✔ **. . . Satellitenfernsehen** *(. . . zâtê-͟lee-ten- fêrn-zehn)* (. . . satellite TV?)
- ✔ **. . . ein Telefon?** *(. . . ayn ͟tê-le-fohn)* (. . . a phone?)
- ✔ **. . . eine Minibar?** *(. . . ͟ay-ne mînî-bahr)* (. . . a minibar?)

When all you want to do is get to your room and rest, you can make sure that no service personnel disturb you by hanging a sign with the following message on your door (you should find this sign somewhere in your room):

> **Bitte nicht stören!** *(͟bî-te nîHt ͟shtuo-rên)* (Please don't disturb!)

The hotel

The hotel may offer a number of services. Usually these services are outlined in a pamphlet or menu that you find in your room. However, if you don't find any written clues about services waiting for your in your room, you can call up the reception desk and ask:

Hat das Hotel . . .? *(hât dâs hoh-__têl__ . . .)* (Does the hotel have . . .?)

You can then ask about any of the following services by ending the preceding phrase with:

- ✔ **. . . eine Sauna?** *(. . . __ay__-ne __zow__-nah)* (. . . a sauna?)

- ✔ **. . . ein Schwimmbad?** *(. . . ayn __shvîm__-baht)* (. . . a swimming pool?)

- ✔ **. . . einen Faxdienst?** *(. . . __ay__-nen __fâks__-deenst)* (. . . a fax machine?)

- ✔ **. . . einen Wäschedienst?** *(. . . __ay__-nen __vai__-she-deenst)* (. . . laundry service?)

- ✔ **. . . eine Klimaanlage?** *(. . . __ay__-ne __klee__-mah-ân-__lah__-ge)* (. . . air conditioning?)

- ✔ **. . . eine Hotelgarage?** *(. . . __ay__-ne hoh-__têl__-gâ-__rah__-ge)* (. . . hotel garage?)

- ✔ **. . . einen Parkplatz?** *(. . . ay-nen __pârk__-plâts)* (. . . parking house?)

And here are the questions that allow you to inquire about breakfast and room service:

- ✔ **Wann wird das Frühstück serviert?** *(vân vîrt dâs __fruu__-shtuuk zêr-__veert__)* (At what time is breakfast served?)

- ✔ **Gibt es Zimmerservice?** *(gîpt ês __tsî__-mer-ser-vîs)* (Is there room service?)

An important part of making your life easier while staying at a hotel is to be able to check if you received any calls. The question to ask is:

Hat jemand eine Nachricht für mich hinterlassen? *(hât __yeh__-mânt ay-ne __nahH__-rîHt fuur mîH hîn-ter-__lâsn__)* (Did somebody leave a message for me?)

Talkin' the Talk

Klaus und Ulrike Huber arrive safely at their hotel in Österreich. They park their car in front of the entrance and then go to the reception desk to check in.

Klaus:	**Guten Abend! Mein Name ist Huber. Wir haben ein Zimmer reserviert.**
	gûtn ah-bnt! myn nah-me îst hoo-ber. veer hah-bn ayn tsî-mer rê-zêr-veert
	Good evening! My name is Huber. We have reserved a room.
Rezeption:	**Ja richtig, ein Doppelzimmer mit Bad. Bitte füllen Sie dieses Formular aus.**
	yah, rîH-tîgk, ayn dôpl-tsî-mer mît baht. bî-te fuu-ln zee dee-zês fôr-mû-lahr ows
	Yes right, a double room with bath. Please fill in this form.
Klaus:	**Haben Sie eine Garage oder einen Parkplatz?**
	hah-bn zee ay-ne gâ-rah-ge oh-der ay-nen pârk-plâts
	Do you have a garage or a parking lot?
Rezeption:	**Der Parkplatz ist hinter dem Hotel. Und hier ist Ihr Zimmerschlüssel, Nummer 203.**
	dehr pârk-plâts îst hîn-ter dehm hoh-têl. ûnt heer îst eer tsî-mer-shluu-sêl, nû-mer tsvy-hûn-dêrt-dry
	The parking lot is behind the hotel. And here is your key, room number 203.
Ulrike:	**Wann servieren Sie Frühstück?**
	vân zêr-vee-ren zee fruu-shtuuk
	When do you serve breakfast?
Rezeption:	**Von sieben bis zehn Uhr.**
	fôn zeebn bîs tsehn oor
	From 7 to 10 o'clock.
Ulrike:	**Vielen Dank.**
	fee-len dângk
	Thanks a lot.

Words to Know

bleiben	bly-ben	to stay
das Formular	dâs fôr-mû-lahr	form
ausfüllen	ows- fuu-ln	to fill out
der Schlüssel	dehr shluu-sêl	key
Bitte nicht stören!	bî-te nîHt shtuo-rên	Please don't disturb!
der Zimmerservice	dehr tsî-mer-ser-vîs	room service
der Parkplatz	dehr pârk-plâts	parking lot

Checking Out and Paying the Bill

Once your stay is over, you have to make arrangements for checking out and paying your bill.

The German language has no exact equivalent for the convenient English term "to check out." The German term you use for checking out of your room is **das Zimmer räumen** *(dâs tsî-mêr roy-men),* which literally translates into "to clear out the room." If you want to inquire at what time you have to leave your room, you ask:

> **Bis wann müssen wir das Zimmer räumen?** *(bîs vân muusn veer dâs tsî-mêr roy-men)* (At what time do we have to check out of our room?)

Asking for your bill

When it comes to checking out of the hotel, the word commonly used is **abreisen** *(âp-ry-zên),* which means "to leave" or, literally, "to travel on." When you want to travel on, take your key to the reception desk and announce your intention to leave by saying

> **Ich reise ab. / Wir reisen ab.** *(îH ry-ze âp / veer ry-zên âp)* (I'm leaving / We are leaving.)

Tipping at a hotel

Although service charges are usually included in the price for your hotel room, there might be occasions where you want to give a tip — **das Trinkgeld** *(dâs trîngk-gêlt)* — to the porter who brings up your luggage. In this case, 1 or 2 DM are a reasonable amount. On rare occasions, you also might see a little envelope in your room where you can leave money for the cleaning personnel. Depending on the hotel and service, you could give a tip of 5 to 10 DM per week.

The preceding phrase will probably be enough to get the reception desk busy preparing your bill. However, if you need to drive home the point that you'd like to have your bill, you can say

> **Kann ich bitte die Rechnung haben?** *(kân îH bî-te dee rêH-nûngk hah-bn)* (Can I please get the bill?)

Chapter 5 tells you all about dealing with bills, paying with a credit card, and asking for a receipt.

Asking about special charges

Of course, you have to pay extra for any special services that you've used. You might want to know how high your phone bill is or let the receptionist know that you have taken something from the minibar. Here's how you do it:

- ✔ **Können Sie mir sagen, wie hoch meine Telefonrechnung war?** *(kuo-nen zee meer zah-gen vee hohH my-ne tê-le-fohn-rêH-nûngk vahr)* (Can you please tell me how high my telephone bill was?)

- ✔ **Ich habe . . . aus der Minibar genommen.** *(îH hah-be . . . ows dehr mînî-bahr gê-nômn)* (I've taken . . . from the minibar.)

Parting shots at the hotel

If you have to check out of the hotel before you actually want to continue your travels, you might want to leave your luggage for a couple of hours (most hotels will allow you to do this):

> **Können wir unser / Kann ich mein Gepäck bis . . . Uhr hier lassen?** *(kuo-nen veer ûn-zer / kân îH myn ge-pêk bîs . . . oor heer lâssn)* (Can we leave our / Can I leave my luggage here until . . . o'clock?)

Once you return to pick up your luggage, you could say

> **Können wir / Kann ich bitte unser / mein Gepäck haben?** *(kuo-nen veer / kân îH bî-te ûn-zer / myn ge-pêk hah-ben)* (Can we / Can I get our / my luggage, please?)

Ready to go to the airport or train station? If you want the receptionist to call you a cab, you ask

> **Können Sie mir bitte ein Taxi bestellen?** *(kuon-nen zee meer bî-te ayn tâxee be-shtêl-len)* (Can you call a cab for me?)

The receptionist will need to know where you intend to go before he or she places the call to order your taxi. Make sure that you know the name of the place where you want to go before you approach the receptionist. The receptionist might ask you:

> **Wo möchten Sie hin?** *(voh muoH-ten zee hin)* (Where would you like to go?)

Talkin' the Talk

Klaus and Ulrike Huber are ready to move on and explore other parts of the country. They go to the reception to check out.

Klaus: **Guten Morgen! Wir reisen heute ab. Kann ich bitte die Rechnung haben?**
gûtn môr-gn! veer ry-zên hoy-te âp. kân îH bî-te dee rêH-nûngk hah-bn
Good morning! We are leaving today. Can I please get the bill?

Rezeption: **Sicher, einen Moment bitte. Haben Sie gestern abend noch etwas aus der Minibar genommen?**
zî-Her, ay-nen moh-mênt bî-te. hah-bn zee gês-têrn ah-bnt nôH êt-vâs ows dehr mînî-bahr ge-nômn
Sure, one moment please. Did you take anything from the minibar last night?

Klaus: **Ja, zwei Bier. Können Sie mir sagen, wie hoch meine Telefonrechnung war?**
yah, tsvy beer. kuon-nen zee meer zah-gen vee hohH my-ne tê-le-fohn-rêH-nûngk vahr
Yes, two beers. Could you tell me how high my phone bill was?

Rezeption: **Ja, 50 Schillinge.**
yah, fuunf-tsîgk <u>shî</u>-lînge
Yes, 50 Schillings.

Klaus: **Kann ich mit Kreditkarte bezahlen?**
kân îH mît kreh-<u>dît</u>-kâr-te be-<u>tsah</u>-len
Can I pay with a credit card?

Rezeption: **Selbstverständlich. Unterschreiben Sie bitte hier.**
zêlpst-fêr-<u>shtaint</u>-lîH. ûn-tershry-ben zee <u>bî</u>-te heer
Of course. Please sign here.

Klaus: **Vielen Dank und auf Wiedersehen!**
<u>fee</u>-len dângk ûnt owf <u>vee</u>-der-zehn
Thanks a lot and good-bye!

Rezeption: **Gute Reise!**
<u>gû</u>-te <u>ry</u>-ze
Have a good trip!

Words to Know

abreisen	âp-ry-zên	to leave
das Gepäck	dâs ge-pêk	luggage
selbstverständlich	zêlpst-fêr-shtaint-lîH	of course
Gute Reise!	gû-te ry-ze	Have a good trip!

Fun & Games

Use the correct words to complete the questions:

Wo   Was für   Wie   Wann   Was

1. _____ kostet das Zimmer ? (How much is the room?)
2. _____ lange bleiben Sie? (How long are you going to stay?)
3. _____ wird das Frühstück serviert? (At what time is breakfast served?)
4. _____ möchten Sie hin? (Where would you like to go?)
5. _____ ein Zimmer möchten Sie? (What kind of room would you like?)

Answer key: 1. Was 2. Wie 3. Wann 4. Wo 5. Was für

Chapter 14

Getting Around: Planes, Trains, Taxis, and Buses

• •

In This Chapter

▶ Departing from the airport

▶ Renting a car

▶ Reading maps and roadsigns

▶ Traveling from the train station

▶ Navigating buses, subways, and taxis

• •

*I*n this chapter, you're on the move on planes, trains, cars, and buses. We tell you what you need to know to deal with ticket agents, customs officials, a car-rental staff, and train and bus personnel. We also show you how to ask the occasional bystander for help, all the while keeping a cool head, smiling, and being polite.

At the Airport

The shortest distance between two points is a straight line.The trick is figuring out which line to get in — especially in an airport. There are lines for just about everything you need to do, from picking up your ticket to checking your luggage. With so many long lines to choose from, don't waste your time standing in the wrong one. We'll get you in the right line and tell you what to say when you are finally being helped.

Most airline personnel speak several languages, so they will usually be able to assist you in English. Just to make sure you know what you're holding in your hand, **das Flugticket / der Flugschein** *(dâs floogk-tîket / dehr floogk-shyn),* is your airplane ticket. It's probably a **Rückflugticket** *(ruuk-floogk-tî-ket)* (a roundtrip ticket). When you're checking in, you will be handed **die Bordkarte** *(dee bôrd-kâr-te)* (boarding pass).

Picking up your ticket

Unless you had your ticket mailed to you ahead of time, you need to pick up your ticket. First you have to find the appropriate airline counter. If the signs in the airport can't help you (and sometimes they can't), stop an attendant and ask for directions to your airline's ticket counter:

> **Wo ist der . . .-Schalter?** *(vô îst dehr . . . -shâl-ter)* (Where is the . . . counter?)

When you arrive at the ticket counter, just say the following to inquire about your ticket

> **Ich möchte mein Ticket abholen.** *(îH muoH-te myn tî-ket âp-hoh-len)* (I would like to pick up my ticket.)

After you pick up your ticket, you may want to ask **Wann muss ich einchecken?** *(vân mûs îH ayn-chê-kn)* (When do I have to check in?) just to make sure that you know when to report to the gate for boarding. You should also ask **Wie viele Gepäckstücke kann ich mitnehmen?** *(vee fee-le ge-pêk-stuu-ke kân îH mît-neh-men)* (How many pieces of luggage can I take along?) to confirm just how much luggage you will be allowed to take on the plane.

Checking in

When you check in, the attendant will ask you a few questions to prepare you for boarding the plane:

> ✔ **Haben Sie Gepäck?** *(hah-bn zee ge-pêk)* (Do you have luggage?)
>
> ✔ **Wo möchten Sie sitzen, am Fenster oder am Gang?** *(vô muoH-ten zee zîtsn, âm fêns-ter oh-der âm gâng)* (Where would you like to sit, by the window or by the aisle?)

In reponse to the question about where you want to sit, you can respond simply **am Fenster / am Gang** *(âm fêns-ter / âm gâng)* (by a window / on the aisle), according to your preference.

You may also want to ask the following to get some details about the flight:

> ✔ **Wie lange dauert der Flug?** *(vee lân-ge dow-êrt dehr floogk)* (How long is the flight?)
>
> ✔ **Wann fliegt die Maschine ab?** *(vân fleekt dee mâ-shee-ne âp)* (When does the plane leave?)

If you're at the airport to meet somebody who is arriving on another plane, you can ask

Wann kommt die Maschine aus . . . an? *(vân kômt dee mâ-shee-ne ows . . . ân)* (When does the plane from . . . arrive?)

Words to Know

das Flugticket / der Flugschein	dâs floogk-tîket / dehr floogk-shyn	airplane ticket
das Rückflugticket	dâs ruuk-floogk-tî-ket	roundtrip ticket
die Bordkarte	dee bôrd-kâr-te	boarding pass
das Gepäck / Handgepäck	dâs ge-pêk / hând-ge-pêk	luggage / hand luggage
das Flugzeug / die Maschine	das floogk-tsoyg / dee mâ-shee-ne	airplane
der Flug	dehr floogk	flight
abholen	âp-hoh-len	to pick up
dauern	dow-ern	to last

Talkin' the Talk

Frau Schöller is flying to London on short notice. At the airport she's heading straight to the Lufthansa counter to pick up her ticket.

Frau Schöller: **Guten Morgen. Ich möchte mein Ticket abholen.**
gûtn môr-gn. îH muoH-te myn tî-ket âp-hoh-len
Good morning. I would like to pick up my ticket.

Angestellter: **Ihr Name bitte.**
eer nah-me bî-te
Your name please.

Frau Schöller: **Schöller.**
shuo-ler.

Angestellter: **Hier, Frau Schöller. Ein Rückflugticket nach London. Flug LH 83.**
heer frow shuo-ler. ayn ruuk-floogk-tî-ket nâH lôn-dôn. floogk êl-hah âHt-dry
Here it is. A return ticket to London. Flight number LH 83.

Frau Schöller: **Wann fliegt die Maschine ab?**
vân fleekt dee mâ-shee-ne âp
When does the plane leave?

Angestellter: **Pünktlich um 11.15 Uhr. Wo möchten Sie sitzen, am Fenster oder am Gang?**
puunkt-lîH ûm êlf oor fuunf-tsehn. vô muoH-ten zee zîtsn, âm fêns-ter oh-der âm gâng
On time at 11:15. am. Where would you like to sit, by the window or by the aisle?

Frau Schöller: **Am Fenster, bitte.**
âm fêns-ter, bî-te
By the window, please.

Angestellter: **Sie haben Platz 15A, einen Fensterplatz. Hier ist Ihre Bordekarte. Haben Sie Gepäck?**
zee hah-bn plâts fuunf-tsehn ah, ay-nen fêns-ter-plâts. heer îst ee-re bôrt-kârt-te. hah-bn zee ge-pêk
You have seat 15A, a window seat. Here is your boarding pass. Do you have any luggage?

Frau Schöller: **Meine kleine Reisetasche heir nehme ich als Handgepäck.**
my-ne kly-ne ry-ze-tâ-she heer neh-me îH âls hând-ge-pêk
I'll take my small carrying bag here as hand luggage.

Angestellter: **Dann können Sie direkt zum Flugsteig gehen.**
dân kuo-nen zee dî-rêkt tsûm floogk-shtyk gehn
Then you can go straight to the gate.

Frau Schöller: **Danke.**
dâng-keh
Thank you.

Words to Know

der Abflug	dehr âp-floogk	departure
die Ankunft	dee ân-kûnft	arrival
der Flugsteig	dehr floogk-shtyk	gate
mitnehmen	mît-neh-men	to take along
einchecken	ayn-tshê-ken	to check in
fliegen	flee-gen	to fly
abfliegen	âp-flee-gen	to leave (on a plane)
ankommen	ân-kô-men	to arrive
pünktlich	puunkt-lîH	on time
verspätet	fêr-shpeh-tet	delayed

Going through immigration

When you're getting off a transatlantic flight, you will usually be directed straight to passport control, **die Passkontrolle** *(dee pâs-kôn-trô-le)*. Make sure that you have your passport handy.

Most of the time you get to choose between two lines: one is for **EU-Bürger** *(eh-oo-buur-ger)* (citizens of countries within the European Union) and the other is for **Nicht-EU-Bürger** *(nîHt-eh-oo-buur-ger)* (citizens of countries outside the EU). After passing through passport control, you claim your baggage and go through customs, **der Zoll** *(dehr tsôl),* where you may have to open your luggage for inspection.

Matters are slightly different when you're driving around Europe in a car or riding aboard a train and happen to cross one of the internal borders of the European Union, **die europäische Union** *(dee oy-roh-pê-îshe ûn-yohn)*. With the introduction of the Single European Market, the currently 15 countries belonging to the EU did away with passport controls at their internal borders and lifted import restrictions within the EU. So when driving from Germany to France, for example, you might not even notice that you're leaving one country and entering another until all of a sudden all the signs along the road are in French. And you can import virtually unlimited quantities of goods bought from one EU country into another.

Rattled from a long flight, all you want to do is leave the airport. But you have two more stops to make. To help you in your travel-weary confusion, these are the words you may need to wield when you go through passport control:

- **der Reisepass / der Pass** *(dehr ry-ze-pâs/ dehr pâs)* (passport)
- **EU-Bürger** *(eh-oo-buur-ger)* (citizen of a country of the European Union)
- **Nicht-EU-Bürger** *(nĩHt-eh-oo-buur-ger)* citizen of a country outside the EU)
- **Ich bin im Urlaub hier.** *(ĩH bĩn ĩm ũr-lowp heer)* (I'm here on vacation.)
- **Ich bin geschäftlich hier.** *(ĩH bĩn ge-shêft-lĩH heer)* (I'm here on business.)
- **Ich bin auf der Durchreise nach . . .** *(ĩH bĩn owf dehr dũrH-ry-ze nâH . . .)* (I am on my way to . . .)

Going through customs

You passed the first hurdle and are on your way to customs. Are you one of those people who feels guilty even when you haven't done anything wrong? Customs officers can make you feel that way. It pays to know how to answer their questions quickly and succinctly so that you can get past them as quickly as possible.

At customs, **der Zoll** *(dehr tzôl)*, you usually get to choose between two options. Either you pick the line for people who have to declare goods — **anmeldepflichtige Waren** *(ân-mêl-de-pflĩH-tee-ge vah-ren)* — or you get in the line for those who carry only things they don't need to declare. Those goodies are called **anmeldefreie Waren** *(ân-mêl-de-fry-e vah-ren)*.

So far, so good. Customs officers might, of course, choose to ask you personally if you have anything to declare. A customs officer may ask you:

Haben Sie etwas zu verzollen? *(hah-bn zee êt-vâs tsũ fêr-tsô-len)* (Do you have anything to declare?)

or

Haben Sie etwas anzumelden? *(hah-bn zee êt-vâs ân-tsũ-mêl-den)* (Do you have anything to declare?)

To this question, you would respond with either of the following:

> ✔ **Ich möchte . . . anmelden.** *(īH muoH-te . . . ân-mêl-den)* (I would like to declare . . .)
>
> ✔ **Ich habe nichts zu verzollen.** *(īH hah-be nīHts tsū fêr-tsô-len)* (I have nothing to declare.)

Despite your most engaging smile, the customs officer might ask to have a look at your not-so-suspicious looking stuff and say:

> **Bitte öffnen Sie diesen Koffer / diese Tasche.** *(bî-te uof-nen zee dee-zn kô-fer / dee-ze tâ-she)* (Please open this suitcase / bag.)

And when the customs officer asks what you're planning to do with a purchase you may answer:

> ✔ **Es ist für meinen persönlichen Gebrauch.** *(ês īst fuur my-nen pêr-suon-līHen ge-browH)* (It's for my personal use.)
>
> ✔ **Es ist ein Geschenk.** *(ês īst ayn ge-shênk)* (It's a gift.)

Traveling in a Car

Before setting out on a European road trip in a rental car, it's probably best to acquire an international driver's license, **internationaler Führerschein** *(īn-têr-nâ-tyoh-nâ-ler fuu-rer-shyn)*. Then you're all set to discover new territory.

The roads you are most likely to travel are called **Autobahn** *(ow-tô-bahn)* (freeway, four to six lanes), **Bundesstraße** *(bûn-des-shtrah-se)* (two- to four-lane highway), or **Nationalstrasse** *(nâ-tyoh-nahl-shtrah-se)* in Switzerland, and **Landstraße** *(lânt-shtrah-se)* (two-lane highway).

Renting a car

If you've decided to rent a car, you need to make your way to the **Autovermietung** *(ow-tô-fêr-mee-tûng)* (car rental agency). When you arrive at the car rental agency, you can start out by saying

> **Ich möchte ein Auto mieten.** *(īH muoH-te ayn ow-tô mee-tn)* (I would like to rent a car.)

The attendant will ask you questions about what kind of car you want by saying something like

> **Was für ein Auto möchten Sie?** *(vâs fuur ayn ow̱-tô muoH̲-ten zee)* (What kind of car would you like?)

To which you can respond with any of the following:

- ✔ **ein zweitüriges / viertüriges Auto** *(ayn tsv̱y-tuu-rî-ges / feer-tuu-rî-ges ow̱-tô)* (a two-door / four-door car)
- ✔ **einen Kombi** *(ay-nen ḵôm-bî)* (station wagon)
- ✔ **einen Automatikwagen** *(ay-nen ow-tô-m̱ah-tîk-vah-gen)* (car with automatic transmission)
- ✔ **einen Schaltwagen** *(ay-nen sẖâlt-vah-gen)* (car with stick shift)

You might also be asked:

- ✔ **Für wie lange möchten Sie den Wagen mieten?** *(fuur vee ḻân-ge muoH̲-ten zee dehn vaẖ-gen meetn)* (For how long would you like to rent the car?)
- ✔ **Ab wann möchten Sie den Wagen mieten?** *(âp vân m̱uoH-ten zee dehn vaẖ-gen mee-ten)* (Starting when would you like to rent the car?)
- ✔ **Bis wann möchten Sie den Wagen mieten?** *(bîs vân m̱uoH-ten zee dehn vaẖ-gen mee-ten)* (Until when would you like to rent the car?)
- ✔ **Wann / Wo möchten Sie den Wagen zurückgeben?** *(vân / vô m̱uoH-ten zee dehn vaẖ-gen tsû-ruuk̲-geh-ben)* (Where / When would you like to return the car?)

To which you can answer:

- ✔ **Ich brauche den Wagen für . . .** *(îH brow̱-He dehn vaẖ-gen fuur . . .)* (I need the car for . . .)
- ✔ **Ich möchte den Wagen ab dem . . . mieten.** *(îH m̱uoH-te dehn vaẖ-gen âp dehm . . . mee̱-ten)* (I would like to rent the car starting . . .)
- ✔ **Ich möchte den Wagen bis zum . . . mieten.** *(îH m̱uoH-te dehn vaẖ-gen bîs tsûm . . . mee̱-ten)* (I would like to rent the car until the . . .)
- ✔ **Ich möchte den Wagen am . . . zurückgeben.** *(îH m̱uoH-te dehn vaẖ-gen âm . . . tsû-ruuk̲-geh-ben)* (I would like to return the car on the . . .)
- ✔ **Ich möchte den Wagen in . . . zurückgeben.** *(îH m̱uoH-te dehn vaẖ-gen în . . . tsû-ruuk̲-geh-ben)* (I would like to return the car in . . .)

During the rental process, you will hear the following words spoken:

✔ **die Vollkaskoversicherung** (*dee f̲ô̲l̲-kâs-kô-fêr-z̲î̲-He-rûng*) (full insurance)

✔ **inbegriffen** (*î̲n̲-be-grîfn*) (included)

✔ **der Führerschein** (*dehr f̲u̲u̲-rer-shyn*) (driver's licence)

✔ **ohne Kilometerbegrenzung** (*o̲h̲-ne kî-lô-m̲e̲h̲-ter-be-g̲r̲ê̲n̲-tsûng*) (unlimited mileage)

Talkin' the Talk

Anke just arrived in Frankfurt. After going through customs, she is visiting a car rental agency. She is talking to an emplyee.

Anke:	**Guten Morgen. Ich möchte ein Auto mieten.**
	gûtn m̲ô̲r̲-gn. îH m̲u̲o̲H̲-te ayn o̲w̲-tô m̲ee-ten
	Good morning. I would like to rent a car.
Angestellter:	**Was für ein Auto möchten Sie?**
	vâs fuur ayn o̲w̲-tô m̲o̲u̲H̲-ten zee
	What kind of car would you like?
Anke:	**Einen Kombi.**
	ay-nen k̲ô̲m̲-bî
	A station wagon.
Angestellter:	**Möchten Sie einen Schaltwagen oder einen Automatikwagen?**
	m̲u̲o̲H̲-ten zee a̲y̲-nen s̲h̲â̲l̲t̲-vah-gen o̲h̲-der a̲y̲-nen ow-tô-m̲a̲h̲-tîk-v̲a̲h̲-gen
	Would you like a car with stick shift or a car with automatic transmission?
Anke:	**Ein Automatikwagen.**
	ayn ow-tô-m̲a̲h̲-tîk-v̲a̲h̲-gen
	An automatic.
Angestellter:	**Für wie lange möchten Sie den Wagen mieten?**
	fuur vee l̲â̲n̲-ge m̲u̲o̲H̲-ten zee dehn v̲a̲h̲-gen meetn
	For how long would you like to rent the car?
Anke:	**Für eine Woche.**
	fuur a̲y̲-ne v̲ô̲-He
	For one week.

Angestellter: **Ein Kombi kostet für eine Woche ohne
Kilometerbregrenzung 689 Mark Versicherung.**
*ayn kôm-bî kôs-tet fuur ay-ne vô-He oh-ne kî-lô-meh-
ter-be-grên-tsûng sêks-hûn-dêrt-noyn-ûnt–âHt-sîgk
mârk în-klû-zee-ve fêr-zî-He-rûng*
A station wagon costs for one week with unlimited
mileage 689 marks including insurance.

Anke: **Ja, heir bitte.**
yah, heer bî-te
Yes, here you are.

Reading maps and road signs

Lines, especially long ones, may not be fun, but they are better than circles —
that is, driving around in circles. We want to point you in the right direction
and get you where you want to go. You'll need a trusty road map and a working knowledge of German road signs.

Maps

A good map tells you where you are, where things are, how to get there, and
how far you have to go — that's a vast amount of information on just one
sheet of paper. The best thing about maps is that they are primarily visual, so
you don't need to know too much of the language in order to read one.
However, you might like to know the following words for different kinds of
maps, in case you need to ask for one:

- **die Landkarte** *(dee lânt-kâr-te)* (map)
- **die Straßenkarte** *(dee shtrah-sn-kâr-te)* (road map)
- **der Stadtplan** *(dehr shtât-plahn)* (map of a city)

On a map written in German, you might see the following words:

- **die Autobahn** *(dee ow-tô-bahn)* (freeway)
- **die Ausfahrt** *(dee ows-fahrt)* (exit ramp)
- **die Auffahrt** *(dee owf-fahrt)* (entrance ramp)
- **das Autobahnkreuz** *(dâs ow-tô-bahn-kroyts)* (two-freeway junction)
- **das Autobahndreieck** *(dâs ow-tô-bahn-dry-êk)* (three-freeway junction)
- **die Altstadt** *(dee âlt-shtât)* (old town)

> ✔ **die Fußgängerzone** *(dee foos-gên-ger-tsoh-ne)* (pedestrian zone)

> ✔ **das Theater** *(dâs teh-ah-ter)* (theater)

> ✔ **die Kirche** *(dee kîr-He)* (church)

> ✔ **der Parkplatz** *(dehr pârk-plâts)* (parking area)

Road signs

You don't want to get stopped for speeding down a one-way street going in the wrong direction on a slippery road. Here are some of the most common road signs that you encounter in German-speaking counties:

> ✔ **Anlieger frei** *(ân-lee-ger fry)* (access only; no exit)

> ✔ **Einbahnstraße** *(ayn-bahn-shtrah-se)* (one-way street)

> ✔ **Einordnen** *(ayn-ôrd-nen)* (merge)

> ✔ **Gesperrt** *(ge-shpêrt)* (closed)

> ✔ **Licht an / aus** *(lîHt ân / ows)* (lights on / off)

> ✔ **Umleitung** *(ûm-ly-tûng)* (detour)

> ✔ **Vorsicht Glätte** *(fohr-zîHt glê-te)* (slippery when wet)

> ✔ **50 bei Nebel** *(fuunf-tsîgk by neh-bel)* (50 km/h when foggy)

> ✔ **Baustelle** *(bow-shtê-le)* (construction site)

At the Train Station

Traveling by rail is a very comfortable way of visiting Europe. No matter if you'd like to whiz from one city to another on the **Intercity Express (ICE)** *(în-têr-sî-tee-êks-prês / ee-tseh-eh)* or are headed to a smaller town and are riding aboard the slower **Interregio (IR)** *(în-têr-reh-ghee-oh / ee-êr)*, you can get practically anywhere by train.

Rail travel is very popular with Europeans, so it's advisable to make a reservation during peak traveling times, for example at the beginning and end of school vacations or during the major holidays. If you're covering a lot of ground in a short time, it might be worth enquiring about the availability of prepaid rail passes before you leave home.

Reading train schedules

Every train station displays schedules for all the trains that run through that particular station. However, since one schedule contains running times for several or all the different trains, you might find it difficult to obtain the information about the specific train that you want to catch. The following expressions should provide some guidance for demystifying train schedules:

✔ **der Fahrplan** *(dehr fahr-plahn)* (train schedule)

✔ **die Abfahrt** *(dee ap-fahrt)* (departure)

✔ **die Ankunft** *(dee an-kûnft)* (arrival)

✔ **über** *(uu-ber)* (via)

✔ **werktags** *(verk-tāks)* (workdays)

✔ **sonn- und feiertags** *(zôn ûnt fy-êr-tāhks)* (Sundays and holidays)

Getting information

When you have questions about a train you want to take, head to the information counter, **die Auskunft** *(dee ows-kûnft)*. There, you may need to ask any of the following questions:

✔ **Von welchem Gleis fährt der Zug nach . . . ab?** *(fôn vel-Hem glys fehrt dehr tsoog nahH . . . ap)* (Which track does the train to . . . leave from?)

✔ **Auf welchem Gleis kommt der Zug aus . . . an?** *(fôn vel-Hem glys kômt dehr tsoog ows . . . ân)* (Which track does the train from . . . arrive on?)

✔ **Hat der Zug Verspätung?** *(hât dehr tsoog fêr-shpeh-tûng)* (Is the train delayed?)

✔ **Gibt es einen direkten Zug von . . . nach . . .?** *(gîpt ês ay-nen dî-rêk-ten tsoog fôn . . . nahh)* (Is there a direct train from . . . to . . .?)

The answer to most of these questions will be straightforward — the attendant will tell you the number of the platform you need to go to, for example. However, for the last question in the preceding list, you may hear that no direct trains are available:

Nein, Sie müssen in . . . umsteigen. *(nyn, zee muu-sn în . . . ûm-shty-gen)* (No. You have to change trains in . . .)

Words to Know

der Bahnsteig	dehr <u>bahn</u>-shtyk	platform
das Gleis	dâs glys	track
die Verspätung	dee fêr-<u>shpeh</u>-tûng	delay
einsteigen	<u>ayn</u>-shty-gen	get on
aussteigen	<u>ows</u>-shty-gen	get off
umsteigen	<u>ûm</u>-shty-gen	change (trains, buses, and so on)
abfahren	<u>âp</u>-fah-ren	leave
ankommen	<u>ân</u>-kô-men	arrive
fahren	<u>fah</u>-ren	go by

Buying tickets

For tickets, you need to go to the ticket booth, **der Fahrkartenschalter** *(dehr <u>fahr</u>-kâr-ten-<u>shâl</u>-ter)*. With the help of these words you should be able to pro-cure yourself passage to virtually anywhere German, Austrian, and Swiss Rail may take you.

The basics

When it's your turn to talk to the ticket person, just say the following to get yourself a ticket:

> **Eine Fahrkarte nach . . ., bitte.** *(<u>ay</u>-ne <u>fahr</u>-kâr-te nahH . . ., <u>bî</u>-te)* (A train ticket to . . . please.)

Because it's always possible to get a one-way or a round-trip ticket, the atten-dant will certainly ask you

> **Einfach oder hin und zurück?** *(<u>ayn</u>-fâH oh-der hîn ûnt tsû-<u>ruuk</u>)* (One-way or round-trip?)

If you're especially concerned about the price, you can ask

- ✔ **Was kostet eine Rückfahrkarte nach . . .?** *(vâs kôs-tet ay-ne ruuk-fahr-kâr-te nahH . . .)* (How much does a round-trip ticket to . . . cost?)

- ✔ **Was kostet eine einfache Fahrt nach . . .?** *(vâs kôs-tet ay-ne ayn-fâ-He fahrt nahH . . .)* (How much does a one-way ticket to . . . cost?)

- ✔ **Erster oder zweiter Klasse?** *(ehrs-ter oh-der tsvy-ter klâ-se?)* (In first or second class?)

On especially busy trains, you may be better off making a reservation for a seat in advance. To do so, simply ask

> **Ich möchte gern eine Platzkarte für den . . . von . . . nach . . .** *(îH muoH-te gêrn ay-ne plâts-kâr-te fuur dehn . . . fôn . . . naH . . .)* (I would like to reserve a seat on the . . . from . . . to . . .)

Because you're talking about a train trip that you might make later in the future, the attendant may ask you:

- ✔ **Fahren Sie heute?** *(fah-ren zee hoy-te)* (Are you traveling today?)

- ✔ **Wann fahren Sie?** *(vân fah-ren zee)* (When are you traveling?)

You have to pay extra for that

How much you're paying for a ticket depends on how many miles you're traveling. There is a set base price per kilometer for first and second class. In addition, you have to pay a surcharge, **der Zuschlag** *(dehr tsû-shlahg),* for trains marked **ICE** (Intercity Express), **IC** (Intercity), or **EC** (Eurocity). These are very fast trains connecting large cities.

The word **Zuschlag** usually appears on the board displaying departures. If you're not sure, check with the information desk or at the ticket counter. If you haven't made up your mind about which train to take or are in a hurry, you can pay for the surchange aboard the train — for a small additional surcharge.

To find out for sure if the train you want to board requires a **Zuschlag,** you can ask

> **Muss ich für den Zug um 11.45 Uhr nach . . . einen Zuschlag bezahlen?** *(mûs îH fuur dehn tsoog ûm êlf oor fuunf-ûntfîr-tsîgk naH . . . ay-nen tsû-shlâk be-tsah-len)* (Do I have to pay a surchange for the train to . . . at 11:45 a.m.?)

To this question, the attendant may respond

> **Das ist ein Intercity. Sie brauchen einen IC-Zuschlag.** *(dâs îst ayn în-têr-sî-tee. zee brow-Hen ay-nen ee-tseh-tsû-shlahk)* (It's an Intercity. You need the ICE surcharge.)

Words to Know

die Fahrkarte	dee <u>fahr</u>-kâr-te	train ticket
die erste Klasse	dee êrs-te klâ-se	first class
die zweite Klasse	dee <u>tsvy</u>-te klâ-se	second class
der Zuschlag	dehr <u>tsû</u>-shlâk	surcharge
die Rückfahrkarte	dee <u>ruuk</u>-fahr-kâr-te	round-trip ticket
die Platzkarte	dee <u>plâts</u>-kâr-te	reserved seat
hin und zurück	hîn ûnt tsû-<u>ruuk</u>	round-trip
einfach	<u>ayn</u>-fâH	one-way

Knowing When to Separate Your Verbs

Many German verbs, including many of the verbs that we show you in this chapter, share a peculiar trait. They all have prefixes that are actual words in their own right (like the prepositions **ab, an, um, ein,** and **aus**). These prefixes are detachable from the body of the verb, its stem. When used in the present tense in a sentence, the verb stem and prefix of these verbs separate. The verb stem takes its expected verb ending and assumes its usual place in the sentence, while the prefix jumps to the very end of the sentence.

Take a look at this phenomenon in action, using the verb **ankommen** (*ân-kô-men)* (to arrive). Notice how the prefix always goes to the end of the sentence, no matter how many words come between it and the verb:

- **Der Zug kommt an.** *(dehr tsoog kômt ân)* (The train arrives.)

- **Der Zug kommt um 18.15 Uhr an.** *(dehr tsoog kômt ûm <u>âHt</u>-tsehn oor <u>fuunf</u>-tsehn ân)* (The train arrives at 6:15 p.m.)

- **Der Zug kommt um 18.15 Uhr in Dessau an.** *(dehr tsoog kômt ûm <u>âHt</u>-tsehn oor <u>fuunf</u>-tsehn în <u>dê</u>-ssow ân)* (The train arrives at 6:15 p.m. in Dessau.)

How do you know if a verb is separable? Two things can guide you:

- The verb needs to have a preposition serving as a prefix.

- The infinitive is emphasized on the first syllable.

Here are a few verbs that follow this pattern. You encounter several more separable verbs throughout this book:

- **anfangen** (*ân-fân-gen*) (to start)
- **aufhören** (*owf-huo-ren*) (to end)
- **aufmachen** (*owf-mâ-Hen*) (to open)
- **zumachen** (*tsû-mâ-hen*) (to close)
- **abfahren** (*âp-fah-ten*) (to depart [train])
- **abfliegen** (*âp-flee-gen*) (to depart [plane])
- **ankommen** (*ân-kô-mem*) (to arrive)
- **einsteigen** (*ayn-shty-gen*) (to get on)
- **aussteigen** (*ows-shty-gen*) (to get off)
- **aufstehen** (*owf-shteh-en*) (to get up)
- **zuhören** (*tsû-huo-ren*) (to listen)

When using separable verbs, the main verb stem with the appropriate ending goes in its usual place. The prefix is the last word in the sentence. This rule works for present tense and simple past.

Navigating Buses, Subways, and Taxis

German cities and towns usually have a well-oiled public transportation system. A combination of **Bus** (*bûs*) (bus), **U-Bahn** (*oo-bahn*) (subway), **Straßenbahn** (*shtrah-sn-bahn*) (streetcar), and **S-Bahn** (*ês-bahn*) (local trains to suburbia) should get you safely where you want to go.

Catching the bus

If you need help finding the right bus or train to take, you might ask the **Fahrkartenschalter** (*fahr-kârtn-shâl-ter*) (ticket window), or any busdriver **(der Busfahrer)** (*dehr bûs-fah-rer*) any of the following questions:

- **Welche Buslinie fährt ins Stadtzentrum?** (*vêl-He bûs-lîn-ye fehrt îns shtât-tsên-trûm*) (Which bus line goes to the city center?)
- **Ist das die richtige Straßenbahn zum Stadion?** (*îst dâs dee rîH-tee-ge shtrah-sn-bahn tsûm shtah-dî-on*) (Is this the right streetcar to the stadium?)
- **Muss ich umsteigen?** (*mûs îH ûm-shty-gen*) (Do I have to switch buses?)
- **Hält diese U-Bahn am Hauptbahnhof?** (*hêlt dee-ze oo-bahn âm howpt-bahn-hohf*) (Does this subway stop at the main train station?)

The honor system

When entering a subway station in a German-speaking country you will notice the absence of turnstiles. So how do people pay for the ride? They buy tickets at a station or at a newspaper stand ahead of time and validate them with a date and time stamp at machines set out in the station or aboard trains. The same goes for buses. So, when purchasing tickets you should remember that in many instances, it is necessary to validate a ticket before getting on a subway or bus. Plainclothes ticket inspectors make frequent checks, and anyone caught without a valid ticket can count on a hefty on-the-spot fine. To avoid any kind of hassles, it's a good idea to find out how the system works in a particular city or town before hopping on a train or bus.

Words to Know

der Bus	dehr bûs	bus
die U-bahn	dee oo-bahn	subway
die S-Bahn	dee ês-bahn	local train
die Straßenbahn	dee shtrah-sn-bahn	streetcar
die Buslinie / U-Bahnlinie	dee bûs-leen-ye / oo-bahn-leen-ye	bus line / subway line
die Haltestelle	dee hâl-te-shtê-le	station, stop
halten	hâl-ten	to stop
die U-Bahnstation	dee oo-bahn-shtâts-yohn	subway station
das Taxi	dâs tâxee	taxi
der Taxistand	dehr tâxee-shtânt	taxi stand
der Fahrscheinautomat	dehr fahr-shyn-ow-tô-maht	ticket vending machine

Talkin' the Talk

Ben wants to take the bus, but he is not quite sure which bus he should take. That's why he approaches a teenager who is standing next to him at the bus stop.

Ben:	**Entschuldigen Sie bitte, hält hier die Buslinie 9?** *ênt-shûl-dee-gen zee bî-te, hêlt heer dee bûs-leen-ye noyn* Excuse me please. Does the bus number 9 stop here?
Teenager:	**Nein, hier hält nur die Linie 8. Wohin wollen Sie denn?** *nyn, heer hêlt noor dee leen-ye âHt. vô-hîn vô-len zee dên* No, only number 8 stops here. Where do you want to go?
Ben:	**Zum Rathaus.** *tsûm raht-hows* To the town hall.
Teenager:	**Fahren Sie mit der Linie 8 bis zum Goetheplatz, und dort steigen Sie in die Linie 9 um.** *fah-ren zee mît dehr leen-ye âHt bîs tsûm guo-te-plâts, ûnt dôrt shty-gen zee în dee leen-ye noyn ûm* Take this bus to Goethe Square and switch there to number 9.
Ben:	**Wie viele Haltestellen sind es bis zum Goetheplatz?** *vee fee-le hâl-te-shtê-len zînt ês bîs tsûm guo-te-plâts* How many stops are there to Goethe Square?
Teenager:	**Es sind vier Haltestellen von hier.** *ês zînt feer hâl-te-shtê-len fôn heer* It's four stops from here.
Ben:	**Vielen Dank für die Auskunft.** *fee-len dângk fuur dee ows-kûnft* Thank you very much for the information.

Getting a taxi

Taking a taxi isn't hard. Just make your way over to the nearest **Taxistand** *(tâxee-shtânt)* (taxi stand) and go straight up to the first car in the line. When you get in the taxidriver (**Taxifahrer**) *(tâxee-fah-rer)* will turn on the meter, and you pay the price indicated on the meter when you reach your destination.

To ask for the nearest taxi stand, just say the following

> **Wo ist der nächste Taxistand?** *(vô îst dehr naiH-ste tâxee-shtânt)* (Where is the closest taxi stand?)

Once you're in the cab, the driver might ask:

> **Wohin möchten Sie?** *(vô-hîn muoH-ten zee)* (Where would you like to go?)

FUN & GAMES

Find the perfect match. We give you the questions in German and English, but the answers only in German. Watch out: There's one answer too many!

1. Wohin möchten Sie? (Where do you want to go?)

2. Wo hält die Linie 8? (Where does bus number 8 stop?)

3. Wie viele Haltestellen sind es bis zum Rathaus? (How many stops are there to city hall?)

4. Welcher Bus fährt zum Bahnhof? (Which bus goes to the train station?)

5. Für wie lange möchten Sie das Auto mieten? (For how long do you want to rent the car?)

6. Wann fliegt die Maschine nach Paris ab? (When does the plane to Paris leave?)

A. Die Linie 20.

B. Am Goetheplatz.

C. Zum Flughafen.

D. Inklusiv Versicherung.

E. Von hier, vier.

F. Pünktlich um 18 Uhr.

G. Für zwei Wochen.

Answer key: 1-C; 2-B; 3-E; 4-A; 5-G; 6-F.

Chapter 15

Planning a Trip

· ·

In This Chapter

▶ Visiting a travel agency

▶ Working with the calendar and dates

▶ Passports, visas, and other travel necessities

· ·

Would you like to go hiking in the mountains, visit the countryside, or head to the sea? No matter what destination you decide on, every trip requires some preparation. You need to take a look at the calendar and set the dates, make sure your passport is in good order, talk to your travel agent, and so on. Then it's time to secure a valid visa (if necessary), and off you go.

Getting Help from a Travel Agency

Travel agents are a nice way to let someone else do your planning, but you have to help them out a little by telling them what kind of planning you want them to do. After all, you don't want to spend the night in a tree house with a bunch of noisy crows.

When you arrive at the travel agency, **das Reisebüro** *(dāss <u>ry</u>-ze-buu-roh),* tell the employee the following:

> **Ich möchte gern . . .** *(īH <u>muoH</u>-te gêrn . . .)* (I would like to . . .)

At the end of this phrase, you can say any of the following to specify what it is that you want the agency to do for you:

✔ **einen Flug nach . . . buchen.** *(<u>ay</u>-nen floogk nahH . . . <u>boo</u>-Hen)* (book a flight to . . .)

✔ **am . . . abfliegen.** *(âm . . . <u>âp</u>-flee-gen)* (depart [fly] on the. . .)

✔ **am . . . zurückfliegen.** *(âm . . . tsû-<u>ruuk</u>-flee-gen)* (return [fly back] on the . . .)

> ✔ **ein Hotelzimmer reservieren.** *(ayn hoh-têl-tsî-mer reh-zêr-vee-ren)* (reserve a hotel room.)

> ✔ **ein Hotel buchen.** *(ayn hoh-têl boo-Hen)* (book a hotel.)

You may also want to ask the travel agent about the weather in the area that you plan to travel to, if you expect it to be different from the weather where you are:

Wie ist das Wetter in . . . im Frühjahr / Herbst / Winter / Sommer / zu dieser Jahreszeit? *(vee îst dâs vê-ter în . . . îm fruu-yahr / hêrpst / vîn-têr / sô-mêr / tsû dee-zer yah-rês-tsyt)* (How is the weather in . . . in the spring / fall / winter / summer / at this time of year?)

Talkin' the Talk

Frau Burger does a lot of business travel. Next week, she'll fly to Wien for a meeting. She calls a travel agency to book her trip.

Angestellter: **Reisebüro Kunze, guten Tag!**
ry-ze-buu-roh kûn-tse, gûtn tahgk
Travel agency Kunze, good day.

Frau Burger: **Tag, hier spricht Claudia Burger von der Firma Transwelt.**
tahk, heer shprîht klow-dî-ah bûr-ger fôn dehr fîr-mâ trânts-vêlt
Hi! This is Claudia Burger from (the company) Transwelt.

Angestellter: **Hallo Frau Burger. Was kann ich für Sie tun?**
hâ-lô frow bûr-ger. vâs kân îH fuur zee toon
Hi, Ms. Burger. What can I do for you?

Frau Burger: **Ich muss nächsten Montag nach Wien fliegen.**
îcH mûs naiH-sten mohn-tahk nahH veen flee-gen
I have to fly to Vienna next Monday.

Angestellter: **Moment, das ist der 15. In der Maschine um 10 Uhr ist noch etwas frei.**
moh-mênt, dâs îst dehr fuunf-tsehn-te. în dehr mâ-shee-ne ûm tsehn oor îst nôH êt-vâs fry
One moment, that's the 15th. In the plane at 10:00 there is still room.

Frau Burger: **10 Uhr passt ausgezeichnet. Und wann kann ich zurückfliegen? Ich werde bis Mittwoch bleiben.**
tsehn oor pâst ows-ge-tsyH-net. ûnt vân kân îcH tsoo-ruuk-flee-gen? îcH ver-de bîs mît-vôH bly-ben
10:00 is excellent. And when can I fly back? I will stay until Wednesday.

Angestellter: **Das ist der 17. 10. Die letzte Maschine fliegt um 21.20 Uhr ab.**
dâs îst dehr zeep-sehn-te tsehn-te. dee lêts-te mâ-shee-ne fleegt ûm ayn-ûnt-tsvân-tsîgk oor tsvân-tsîgk âp
That's the 17th of October. The last flight departs at 9:20 p.m.

Frau Burger: **21.20 Uhr? Das geht.**
ayn-und-zwan-tsig oohr? Dahs geht
9:20. That's okay.

Angestellter: **Sehr gut. Ich buche den Flug für Sie.**
zehr goot. îH boo-He dehn floogk fuur zee
Very good. I'll book the flight for you.

Frau Burger: **Danke.**
dâng-keh
Thank you.

Words to Know

die Reise	dee ry-ze	trip
reisen	ry-zen	to travel
buchen	boo-Hen	to book
das Reisebüro	dâs ry-ze-buu-roh	travel agency
die Übernachtung	dee uu-ber-nâH-tûng	accommodation

Planning Ahead: Using the Future Tense

When talking about things that are going to take place in the future, you use the *future tense*. Some examples of the future tense in English are:

- ✔ I will buy a pair of hiking boots tomorrow.
- ✔ We will not go skiing in the summertime.
- ✔ You will need some help planning that trip to Antarctica.

See how the future tense is formed in English? The verb "will" signals that you're talking about the future.

Forming the future tense in German is pretty similar to English. You take the appropriate form of the verb **werden** (*vehr-den*) and add an infinitive verb. The conjugated form of **werden** goes into the usual place for the verb, and the infinitive goes to the very end of the sentence. In this case, **werden** is used as an auxiliary verb meaning "will" (when used on its own, the verb **werden** means "to become").

Table 15-1 shows you the proper conjugation of the verb werden.

Table 15-1	Conjugating the Verb werden	
Conjugation	*Pronunciation*	*Translation*
ich werde	îH vehr-de	I will
du wirst	dû vîrst	you will
Sie werden	zee vehr-den	you will
er, sie, es wird	ehr, zee, ês vîrt	he, she, it will
wir werden	veer vehr-den	we will
ihr werdet	eer vehr-det	you will
Sie werden	zee vehr-den	you will
sie werden	zee vehr-den	they will

The following sentences show you some good examples of the future tense. Take note of how the infinitives always go to the end of the sentences:

- ✔ **Ich werde anrufen.** (*îH vehr-de ân-roo-fen*) (I will call.)
- ✔ **Wir werden morgen kommen.** (*veer vehr-dn môr-gn kô-men*) (We will come tomorrow.)

- ✔ **Wirst du nächstes Jahr nach Österreich fahren?** *(vîrst dû naiH-stes yahr nahH uo-ste-ryH fah-ren)* (Will you go to Austria next year?)

- ✔ **Frau Meier wird nächste Woche ins Reisebüro gehen.** *(frow my-er vîrt naiH-ste vô-He îns ry-ze-buu-roh geh-en)* (Ms. Meier will go to the travel agency next week.)

German speakers are pretty lackadaisical about the future tense; they don't use it all the time. Very often, they prefer to talk about the future using the present tense. Expressions like **morgen** *(môr-gn)* (tomorrow) or **nächstes Jahr** *(naiH-stes yahr)* (next year) serve to indicate future meaning. The following statements all have future meaning, although the verb in each one of them is in the present tense:

- ✔ **Morgen gehe ich wandern.** *(môr-gn geh-e îH vân-dêrn)* (Tomorrow I'll go hiking.)

- ✔ **Fährst du nächstes Jahr wieder zu den Festspielen?** *(fehrst dû naiH-stes yahr vee-der tsû dehn fêst-shpee-len)* (Are you going to go to the festival next year?)

- ✔ **Susanne geht übermorgen zum Konsulat.** *(sû-zâ-ne geht uu-ber-môr-gn tsûm kôn-zû-laht)* (Susanne will go to the consulate the day after tomorrow.)

- ✔ **Fahrt ihr am nächsten Wochenende weg?** *(fahrt eer âm naiH-sten vô-Hen-ên-de vêk)* (Are you going to go away next weekend?)

Using the Calendar and Dates

Thirty days has September, April, June, and November. You should be happy to know that this little rhyme translates easily into German. But don't get overly confident yet — you still have to learn the years, too.

Learning the units of the calendar

The following sentences show you how to build the calendar, **der Kalender** *(dehr kâ-lên-der),* in German:

- ✔ **Ein Jahr hat 12 Monate.** *(ayn yahr hât tsvuolf moh-nâ-te)* (A year has 12 months.)

- ✔ **Ein Monat hat 30 oder 31 Tage.** *(ayn moh-nât hât dry-sîgk oh-der ayn-ûnt-dry-sîgk tah-ge)* (A month has 30 or 31 days.)

- ✔ **Der Februar hat 28 oder 29 Tage.** *(dehr feh-brû-ahr hât âHt-ûn-tsvân-tsîgk oh-der noyn-ûn-tsvân-tsîgk tahge)* (February has 28 or 29 days.)

- ✔ **Eine Woche hat 7 Tage.** *(ay-ne vô-He hât zee-bn tah-ge)* (A week has 7 days.)

The basic names of the months

The following list shows you all the names of the months. All the months'
names are masculine, meaning that their article is **der**:

- **Januar** (_yâ-nû-ahr_) (January)
- **Februar** (_feh-brû-ahr_) (February)
- **März** (_mêrts_) (March)
- **April** (_ah-prîl_) (April)
- **Mai** (_my_) (May)
- **Juni** (_yoo-nee_) (June)
- **Juli** (_yoo-lee_) (July)
- **August** (_ow-gûst_) (August)
- **September** (_zêp-têm-ber_) (September)
- **Oktober** (_ôk-toh-ber_) (October)
- **November** (_nô-vêm-ber_) (November)
- **Dezember** (_deh-tsêm-ber_) (December)

Describing events in specific months

If something takes place in a particular month, you combine the name of the
month with the preposition **im**:

- **Ich fliege im Januar ab.** (_îH flee-ge îm yâ-nû-ahr âp_) (I'm flying off in
  January.)
- **Ich fliege im Februar zurück.** (_îH flee-ge îm feh-brû-ahr tsû-ruuk_) (I'm
  flying back in February.)
- **Im März werde ich zu Hause sein.** (_îm mêrts vehr-de îH tsû how-ze zyn_)
  (In March, I'll be home.)

Naming specific times in the months

If you need to be somewhat specific about the time of the month, the following phrases help narrow down the field:

- **Anfang Januar** (_ân-fâng yâ-nû-ahr_) (in the beginnig of January)
- **Mitte Februar** (_mî-te feh-brû-ahr_) (in the middle of February)
- **Ende März** (_ên-de mêrts_) (at the end of March)

Of course, you can substitute any month name after **Anfang, Mitte,** and **Ende:**

> ✔ **Anfang April fliegen wir nach Berlin.** *(ân-fâng â-prîl flee-gn veer nahh bêr-leen)* (In the beginning of April we'll fly to Berlin.)
>
> ✔ **Ich werde Ende Mai verreisen.** *(îH vêr-de ên-de my fêr-ry-zen)* (I'll go traveling at the end of May.)
>
> ✔ **Herr Behr wird Mitte Februar in Skiurlaub fahren.** *(hêr behr vîrt mî-te feh-brû-ahr în shee-ûr-lowp fah-ren)* (Mr. Behr will go on a skiing trip in the middle of February.)

Dates

When talking about the date, **das Datum** *(dâs dah-tûm)*, you need to adjust your way of thinking a little bit. In German, the day always comes first, and the month comes second (see Table 15-2). Note the period after the numeral identifying it as an ordinal number. (Please see Chapter 12 for the lowdown on ordinal numbers.)

Table 15-2	German Dates, Long Version	
Write	*Say*	*Pronunciation*
1. Januar 2000	erster Januar Zweitausend	êrs-ter yâ-nû-ahr tsvy-tow-zênt
10. Juni 1999	zehnter Juni Neunzehnhundertneunundneunzig	tsehn-ter yoo-nee noyn-tsehn-hûn-dêrt-noyn-ûnt-noyn-tsîgk
20. März 1888	zwanzigster März Achtzehnhundertachtundachtzig	tsvân-tsîgk-ster mêrts âH-tsehn-hûn-dêrt âHt-ûnt-âH-tsîgk

As you can see from the last example in Table 15-2, going back in time to another century is not hard.

That was the long version. And now for the short version, which is popular for both the spoken and the written languages (see Table 15-3). The day still goes first, and the month goes second. Again, note the periods after the numerals (both the day and month are ordinals).

Table 15-3	German Dates, Short Version	
Write	*Say*	*Pronunciation*
1. 1. 2000	erster erster Zweitausend	<u>êrs</u>-ter <u>êrs</u>-ter tsvy-<u>tow</u>-zênt
2. 4. 1999	zweiter vierter Neunzehnhundertneunundneunzig	tsvy-ter <u>feer</u>-ter <u>noyn</u>-tsehn-hûn-dêrt-<u>noyn</u>-ûnt-noyn-tsîgk
3. 5. 1617	dritter fünfter Sechzehnhundertsiebzehn	<u>drî</u>-ter <u>fuunf</u>-ter <u>sêH</u>-tsehn-hûn-dêrt-<u>zeep</u>-tsehn

If you want to find out what today's date is you ask:

> **Den Wievielten haben wir heute?** *(dehn <u>vee</u>-feel-ten <u>hah</u>-ben veer <u>hoy</u>-te)* (What's today's date?)

The answer will be one of the following:

- ✔ **Heute haben wir den . . .** *(<u>hoy</u>-te <u>hah</u>-ben veer dehn)* (Today we have the . . .)

- ✔ **Heute ist der . . .** *(<u>hoy</u>-te îst dehr)* (Today is the . . .)

You may hear the name of a year integrated into a sentence in one of two ways. The first, longer way uses the preposition **im** to create the phrase **"im Jahr . . .",** and the second, shorter way doesn't. The following sentences show you examples of both ways of doing things:

- ✔ **Im Jahr 2000 fährt Herr Diebold in die USA.** *(îm yahr tsvy-<u>tow</u>-zênt fehrt hêr <u>dee</u>-bôlt în dee oo-ês-<u>ah</u>)* (In the year 2000, Mr. Diebold is going to the United States.)

- ✔ **1999 war er in Kanada.** *(<u>noyn</u>-tsehn-hûn-dêrt-<u>noyn</u>-ûnt-noyn-tsîgk vâr ehr în <u>kâ</u>-nâ-dâ)* (In 1999 he was in Canada.)

Words to Know

das Jahr	dâs yahr	year
das Vierteljahr	dâs fîr-têl-yahr	quarter
der Monat	dehr moh-nât	month
die Woche	dee vô-He	week
der Tag	dehr tahk	day
das Datum	dâs dah-tûm	date
der Kalender	dehr kâ-lên-der	calendar

Dealing with Passports and Visas

Although the world is getting smaller through telecommunications and virtual travel, we still need paperwork to go places. You know — that small little booklet with the embarrassing picture, the one you always seem to misplace or let expire just before you are about to leave on vacation. And then there is the issue of visas!

Your passport

Before you leave on a trip, you want to check to make sure that your passport is valid for the entire length of your stay. After all, you don't want to spend your time away from home trying to find an American consulate in order to renew your passport. If you forget to take care of this very important chore, you will hear the following when you show your passport at the border:

Ihr Pass ist abgelaufen! *(eer pâs îst âp-ge-low-fn)* (Your passport has expired!)

At that point, you will be directed to the nearest American consulate, **das amerikanische Konsulat** *(dâs â-mê-ree-kah-nî-she kôn-zû-laht)*, in order to take care of the nesessary paperwork.

In the event that you notice your passport is missing, head straight to the American consulate to report it. If necessary, you can stop a policeman or file a report at a police station and say the following in order to get help:

Ich habe meinen Pass verloren. *(îH hah-be my-nen pâs fêr-loh-ren)* (I lost my passport.)

Inquiring about visas

You don't need a visa if you're traveling to Europe on vacation and are planning to stay a few short weeks or months. But just in case you like it so much that you want to stay longer or continue on to a place where you are required to have a visa, the following phrases will come in handy when you apply for a visa:

- **Braucht man ein Visum für Reisen nach . . .?** *(browHt mân ayn vee-zûm fuur ry-zn nahH . . .)* (Does one need a visa for trips to . . .?)

- **Wie lange ist das Visum gültig?** *(vee lân-ge îst dâs vee-zûm guul-tîg)* (For how long is the visa valid?)

- **Wer stellt das Visum aus?** *(vehr shtêlt dâs vee-zûm ows)* (Who issues the visa?)

- **Ich möchte ein Visum beantragen.** *(îH muoH-te ayn vee-zûm bê-ân-trah-gen)* (I would like to apply for a visa.)

Talkin' the Talk

George Beck, an American living in Germany, wants to go on a skiing trip to Davos in Switzerland. After making all the necessary arrangements at the travel agency, he talks to the agent about entry.

George: **Brauche ich ein Visum für die Schweiz?**
brow-He îH ayn vee-zûm fuur dee shvyts
Do I need a visa for Switzerland?

Angestellte: **Nein, für die Schweiz nicht.**
nyn fuur dee shvyts nîHt
No, not for Switzerland.

George: **Gut. Aber ich brauche meinen Reisepass, stimmts?**
goot ah-ber îH brow-He my-nen ry-ze-pâss, shtîmts
Good. But I need my passport, right?

Angestellte: **Ja, den Pass brauchen Sie. Ist er noch gültig?**

> *yah, dehn pâss <u>brow</u>-Hen zee. Îst ehr noH <u>guul</u>-tîg*
> Yes, you'll need your passport. Is it still valid?

George: **Ich glaube ja.**
ÎH <u>glow</u>-bêh yah
I think so.

Angestellte: **Prima! Noch irgendwelche Fragen, Herr Beck?**
pr<u>ee</u>-mah nohH <u>eer</u>-ghent-vell-shê <u>frah</u>-ghen herr beck
Great. Any other questions, Mr. Beck?

George: **Nein, das war's. Vielen Dank.**
nyn dâs vahrs. <u>fee</u>-len dângk
No, that was it. Thank you very much.

Angestellte: **Gern geschehen. Und, Gute Reise!**
gêrn gêh-shehn. Ûnt <u>goo</u>-teh <u>ry</u>-seh
You're welcome. And, have a nice trip!

Words to Know

der Reisepass	dehr <u>ry</u>-ze-pâs	passport
das Visum	dâs <u>vee</u>-zûm	visa
beantragen	bê-<u>ân</u>-trah-gen	to apply for
gültig / ungültig	<u>guul</u>-tîg / <u>ûn</u>-guul-tîg	valid / invalid
verlängern	fêr-<u>lêng</u>-êrn	to renew, to extend
ablaufen	<u>âp</u>-low-fen	to expire
das Konsulat	dâs kôn-zû-<u>laht</u>	consulate
die Botschaft	dee <u>boht</u>-shâft	embassy

Fun & Games

• •

The following statements all take place in the future. It's your job to put the verb **werden** into the appropriate form.

1. Wir _____ ans Meer fahren.

2. _____ du mit deinen Eltern in die USA fliegen?

3. Ich _____ meinen Urlaub im Reisebüro buchen.

4. _____ ihr mit dem Bus nach Dänemark fahren?

5. Kai _____ ein Visum für Kanada bantragen.

6. Claudia und Bärbel _____ dieses Jahr nach Polen reisen.

Answer key: 1. werden; 2. Wirst; 3. werde; 4. Werdet; 5. wird; 6. werden.

• •

Match the expressions on the right to the ones on the left.

A. _____ zwölf Monate   a. eine Stunde

B. _____ 30 Tage   b. eine Woche

C. _____ 7 Tage   c. ein Tag

D. _____ 24 Stunden   d. ein Jahr

E. _____ 60 Minuten   e. ein Monat

Answer key: A=D; B=E; C=D; D=C; E=A

Chapter 16

Handling Emergencies

. . . .

In This Chapter
▶ Asking for help
▶ Going to the doctor or hospital
▶ Talking to the police

. . . .

Hopefully, you will never need to use the vocabulary and information in this chapter, but it still may be helpful for you to read it. Aside from dealing with accidents and talking to the police, there might be other kinds of emergencies you need to handle — what if you suddenly come down with a bad case of the flu? This chapter assists you in dealing with all kinds of emergency situations, from going to the doctor to reporting a theft.

Asking for Help with Accidents and Emergencies

The hardest part of handling emergencies is keeping your cool so that you can clearly communicate to somebody — be it a police officer, emergency medical technician, or a doctor — what the problem is. So don't panic if you have to put these unpleasantries into German. Should you really get tongue-tied, at the very least, you need to know how to ask for someone who speaks English.

Shouting for help

The following expressions come in handy if you need to call for help in emergency situations:

> ✔ **Hilfe!** (*hĭl-fe*) (Help!)
>
> ✔ **Rufen Sie die Polizei!** (*roo-fn zee dee pô-lī-tsy*) (Call the police!)

- **Rufen Sie einen Krankenwagen!** (_roo_-fn zee _ay_-nen _krânkn_-vahgn) (Call an ambulance.)

- **Rufen Sie die Feuerwehr!** (_roo_-fn zee dee _foy_-er-vehr) (Call the fire department!)

- **Holen Sie einen Arzt!** (_hoh_-ln zee _ay_-nen ârtst) (Get a doctor!)

- **Feuer!** (_foy_-êr) (Fire!)

Reporting a problem

If you need to report an accident or have to let people know that you or other people are hurt, this basic vocabulary should help:

- **Ich möchte einen Unfall melden.** (îH _muoH_-te ay-nen _ûn_-fâl mêldn) (I want to report an accident.)

- **Ich möchte einen Unfall auf der Autobahn melden.** (îH _muoH_-te _ay_-nen _ûn_-fâl owf dehr _ow_-tô-bahn mêldn) (I want to report an accident on the freeway.)

- **Ich bin verletzt.** (îH bîn fêr-_lêtst_) (I am hurt.)

- **Es gibt Verletzte.** (ês gîpt fêr-_lêtste_) (There are injured people.)

Accidents aside, there are other emergencies you have to be prepared for, such as robbery or theft:

- **Ich möchte einen Diebstahl / Raubüberfall melden.** (îH _muoH_-te _ay_-nen _deep_-shtahl / _rowp_-uu-bêr-fâl mêldn) (I want to report a theft / robbery.)

- **Haltet den Dieb!** (_hâl_-tet dehn deep) (Catch the thief!)

Asking for English-speaking help

If you find that you can't get the help that you need by speaking German, this is what you say to find out if there's somebody around who speaks English:

Spricht hier jemand Englisch? (shprîHt heer _yeh_-mânt _êng_-lîsh) (Does anybody here speak English?)

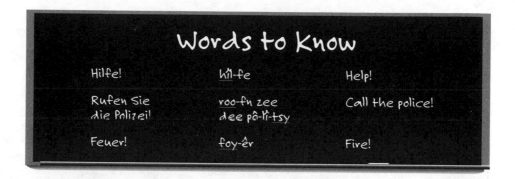

Going to the Doctor or Hospital

Open your mouth. Yes, a little wider. Good. Say ahhhhhh. Now breathe. Rest. Breathe again. Great! Now you should be relaxed enough to learn how to explain what ails you. And if you are a bit of a hypochondriac, this part of the book is exactly what the doctor ordered.

Here are a few words you'll need when you start to feel like things aren't the way that they should be:

- **der Arzt / die Ärztin** *(dehr ârtst / dee ērts-tīn)* (doctor)
- **der Doktor** *(dehr dôk-tohr)* (doctor)
- **das Krankenhaus** *(dâs krânkn-hows)* (hospital)
- **die Notaufnahme** *(dee noht-owf-nah-me)* (emergency room)
- **die Arztpraxis** *(dee ârtst-prâ-xîs)* (doctor's office)

If you are in need of medical help, you can ask for a doctor, or inquire where the next doctor's office or hospital is located by saying:

- **Ich brauche einen Arzt.** *(îH brow-He ay-nen ârtst)* (I need a doctor.)
- **Wo ist die nächste Arztpraxis / das nächste Krankenhaus?** *(voh îst dee naiH-ste ârtst-prâ-xîs / dâs naiH-ste krânkn-hows)* (Where is the next doctor's office / the next hospital?)

Emergency calls

In case of emergencies, it's always good to have the right phone numbers handy. If you find yourself in an emergency situation while you're in Germany, dialing 911 won't get you far, so here are the crucial numbers you may want to memorize or keep in your wallet:

- **Polizei** *(pô-lî-tsy)* (police): 110 (Germany); 133 (Austria); 117 (Switzerland)

- **Feuerwehr** *(foy-êr-vehr)* (fire department): 112 (Germany); 122 (Austria); 118 (Switzerland)

You also find these numbers on the first page of the phone book.

In the age of cell phones and car phones, it has become much easier to call for help if you have to report an accident. However, the German highway system has been pretty well prepared for this kind of emergency for quite some time. On the Autobahn, you will find **Notrufsäulen** *(noht-roof-zoy-len)* (motorist aid call boxes) at regular intervals. There also are signs that tell you how far you are from the next emergency phone.

Describing what ails you

Stomach aching? Feeling feverish? Shooting pains up your neck? Consumed by nausea? Great, you've come to the right place. This is what you say if you want to express that you aren't feeling well and where it hurts:

- **Ich fühle mich nicht wohl.** *(îH fuu-le mîH nîHt vohl)* (I'm not feeling well.)

- **Ich bin krank.** *(îH bîn krânk)* (I am sick.)

- **Ich habe Fieber.** *(îH hah-be fee-ber)* (I have a fever.)

- **Mir tut der Hals / Bauch / Rücken weh.** *(meer tût dehr hâlts / bowh / ruu-kn veh)* (My neck / stomach / back hurts.)

- **Ich habe Schmerzen im Arm / Bauch.** *(îH hah-be shmêr-tsn îm ârm / bowH)* (I feel pain in the arm / stomach.)

- **Ich habe (starke) Bauchschmerzen / Kopfschmerzen / Zahnschmerzen.** *(îH hah-be shtâr-ke bowH-shmêr-tsn / kôpf-shmêr-tsn / tsahn-shmêr-tsn)* (I have (a severe) stomachache / headache / toothache.)

- **Ich habe Halsschmerzen / Rückenschmerzen.** *(îH hah-be hâlts-shmêr-tsn / ruu-kn-shmêr-tsn)* (I have a sore throat / backpain.)

Announcing any special conditions

An important part of getting treatment is to let the doctor know if you are allergic to something or if you have any medical conditions. To do so, start out by saying

Ich bin . . . *(îh bîn . . .)* (I am . . .)

Then finish the sentence with any of the following:

- **allergisch gegen . . .** *(â-<u>lêr</u>-gîsh geh-gn . . .)* (allergic to . . .)
- **behindert** *(bê-<u>hîn</u>-dêrt)* (handicapped)
- **schwanger** *(<u>shvâng</u>-er)* (pregnant)
- **Diabetiker** *(dîa-<u>beh</u>-tî-ker)* (a diabetic)
- **Epileptiker** *(eh-pî-<u>lêp</u>-tî-ker)* (an epileptic)

A few specific conditions may require that you begin with:

Ich habe . . . *(îH <u>hah</u>-be . . .)* (I have . . .)

You can end this phrase with any of the following:

- **ein Herzleiden** *(ayn <u>hêrts</u>-ly-dn)* (a heart condition)
- **zu hohen / niedrigen Blutdruck** *(tsû <u>hoh</u>-en / <u>nee</u>-drî-gen <u>bloot</u>-drûk)* (high / low blood pressure)

Getting an examination

After you make it into the examination room, you want to make sure you understand the doctor's questions and instructions and leave with the right remedy, so you can go on to some more pleasant conversation. Here are some of the questions you might hear in the examination room:

- **Was haben Sie für Beschwerden?** *(vâs <u>hah</u>-bn zee fuur be-<u>shvehr</u>-dn)* (What complaints do you have?)
- **Haben Sie Schmerzen?** *(<u>hah</u>-bn zee <u>shmêr</u>-tsn)* (Are you in pain?)
- **Wo tut es weh?** *(voh toot ês veh)* (Where does it hurt?)
- **Tut es hier weh?** *(toot ês heer veh)* (Does it hurt here?)
- **Wie lange fühlen Sie sich schon so?** *(vee <u>lân</u>-ge <u>fuu</u>-len zee zîH shohn zoh)* (How long have you been feeling this way?)
- **Sind Sie gegen irgendetwas allergisch?** *(zînt zee <u>geh</u>-gen <u>îr</u>-gênt-êt-vâs ah-<u>lêr</u>-gîsh)* (Are you allergic to something?)

Here are some fun instructions you might get from the doctor:

- **Bitte streifen Sie den Ärmel hoch.** (_bî-te shtry-fn zee dehn êr-mel hoH_) (Please pull up your sleeve.)

- **Bitte machen Sie den Oberkörper frei.** (_bî-te mâ-Hen zee dehn oh-bêr-kuor-per fry_) (Please take off your shirt.)

- **Bitte legen Sie sich hin.** (_bî-te leh-gn zee zîH hîn_) (Please lie down.)

- **Machen Sie bitte den Mund auf.** (_mâ-Hn zee bî-te dehn mûnt owf_) (Please open your mouth.)

- **Atmen Sie bitte tief durch.** (_aht-men zee bî-te teef dûrH_) (Please take a deep breath.)

- **Husten Sie bitte.** (_hoos-tn zee bî-te_) (Please cough.)

Specifying parts of the body

To the question **Wo tut es weh?** (_voh toot ês veh_) (Where does it hurt?), you can answer any of the following:

- **der Arm** (_dehr ârm_) (arm)

- **das Auge** (_dâs ow-ge_) (eye)

- **der Bauch** (_dehr bowH_) (stomach)

- **das Bein** (_dâs byn_) (leg)

- **die Brust** (_dee brûst_) (chest)

- **der Daumen** (_dehr dow-men_) (thumb)

- **der Finger** (_dehr fîng-er_) (finger)

- **der Fuß** (_dehr foos_) (foot)

- **der Hals** (_dehr hâlts_) (neck)

- **die Hand** (_dee hânt_) (hand)

- **das Herz** (_dâs hêrts_) (heart)

- **der Kiefer** (_dehr kee-fr_) (jaw)

- **das Knie** (_dâs knee_) (knee)

- **der Fußknöchel** (_dehr foos-knuoHl_) (ankle)

- **der Magen** (_dehr mah-gn_) (stomach)

- **der Mund** (_dehr mûnt_) (mouth)

- ✔ **der Muskel** *(dehr mûs-kl)* (muscle)
- ✔ **die Nase** *(dee nah-ze)* (nose)
- ✔ **das Ohr** *(dâs ohr)* (ear)
- ✔ **der Rücken** *(dehr ruu-kn)* (back)
- ✔ **die Schulter** *(dee shûl-tr)* (shoulder)
- ✔ **der Zeh** *(dehr tseh)* (toe)
- ✔ **die Zunge** *(dee tsûn-ge)* (tongue)

You may also need to identify the following parts of the body:

- ✔ **das Gesicht** *(dâs ge-zîHt)* (face)
- ✔ **das Haar** *(dâs hahr)* (hair)
- ✔ **der Kopf** *(dehr kôpf)* (head)
- ✔ **die Lippe** *(dee lî-pe)* (lip)

Getting the diagnosis

On to the next step: understanding what the doctor thinks might be wrong with you. Here are some very useful phrases so that you are not left in the dark:

- ✔ **die Diagnose** *(dee dî-âg-noh-ze)* (diagnosis)
- ✔ **Sie haben . . .** *(zee hah-bn . . .)* (You have . . .)
- ✔ **eine Erkältung** *(ay-ne êr-kêl-tûng)* (a cold)
- ✔ **eine Grippe** *(ay-ne grî-pe)* (the flu)
- ✔ **eine Entzündung** *(ay-ne ênt-tsuun-dûng)* (an inflammation)
- ✔ **Blinddarmentzündung / Lungenentzündung / Mandelentzündung** *(blînt-dârm-ênt-tsuun-dûng / lûngn-ênt-tsuun-dûng / mân-del-ênt-tsuun-dûng)* (appendicitis / pneumonia / tonsillitis)
- ✔ **Wir müssen eine Röntgenaufnahme machen.** *(veer muu-sn ay-ne ruont-gên-owf-nah-me mâ-Hn)* (We have to take an X ray.)
- ✔ **Sie müssen geröntgt werden.** *(zee muu-sn ge-ruonHt vêr-dn)* (You have to get an X ray.)
- ✔ **Ihr Knöchel ist gebrochen / verstaucht / verrenkt.** *(eer knuo-Hêl îst ge-brôHn / fêr-shtowHt / fêr-rênkt)* (Your ankle is broken / sprained / dislocated.)

Talkin' the Talk

Ulrich Lempert hasn't been feeling well for a couple of days and has made an appointment with his doctor, Dr. Grewen.

Dr. Grewen:	**Guten Morgen, Herr Lempert. Was haben Sie für Beschwerden?**
	gûtn môr-gn, hêr <u>lêm</u>-pêrt. vâs <u>hah</u>-bn zee fuur be-<u>shvehr</u>-dn
	Good morning, Mr. Lempert. What complaints do you have?

Ulrich:	**Ich fühle mich seit ein paar Tagen nicht wohl.**
	îH <u>fuu</u>-le mîH zyt ayn pahr <u>tah</u>-gn nîHt vohl
	I haven't been feeling well for a couple of days.

Dr. Grewen:	**Haben Sie Schmerzen?**
	hah-bn zee <u>shmêr</u>-tsn
	Are you in pain?

Ulrich:	**Ja, ich habe starke Kopf- und Magenschmerzen.**
	yah, îH <u>hah</u>-be <u>stâr</u>-ke kôpf ûnt <u>mah</u>-gn-shmêr-tsn
	Yes, I have a severe headache and stomachache.

Dr. Grewen:	**Bitte setzen Sie sich hier hin und machen Sie den Oberkörper frei.**
	bî-te zêtsn zee zîH heer hîn ûnt <u>mâ</u>-Hn zee dehn <u>oh</u>-bêr-kuor-pêr fry
	Please sit down here and take off your shirt.

Dr. Grewen starts examining Ulrich.

Dr. Grewen:	**Machen Sie bitte den Mund auf, danke. Atmen Sie bitte tief durch. Husten Sie bitte.**
	mâ-Hn zee bî-te dehn mûnt owf, <u>dâng</u>-ke. <u>aht</u>-mên zee bî-te teef dûrH. <u>hoo</u>-stn zee bî-te
	Please open your mouth — thank you. Take a deep breath, please. Please cough.

Ulrich:	**Und, was stimmt nicht mit mir?**
	ûnt vâs shtîmt nîHt mît meer
	And, what's wrong with me?

Dr. Grewen: **Sie haben eine Grippe. Ich gebe Ihnen ein Rezept. Und bleiben Sie die nächsten Tage im Bett!**
zee hah-bn ay-ne grî-pe. îH geh-be ee-nen ayn rê-tsêpt ûnt bly-bn zee dee naiH-stn tah-ge îm bêt
You have the flu. I'm giving you a prescription. And stay in bed for the next few days.

Words to Know

Ich brauche einen Arzt.	îH brow-He ay-nen ârtst	I need a doctor.
Ich bin krank.	îH bîn krânk	I am sick.
Wo tut es weh?	voh toot ês veh	Where does it hurt?
Haben Sie Schmerzen?	hah-bn zee shmêr-tsn	Are you in pain?

Getting treatment

After the doctor tells you what the problem is, he or she will advise you what you should do about it. The doctor may ask you one final question before deciding on what treatment would be best for you:

> **Nehmen Sie noch andere Medikamente?** *(neh-mn zee nôH ân-de-re meh-dee-kâ-mên-te)* (Are you taking any other medication?)

This is what the doctor might prescribe:

- **Ich gebe Ihnen . . . / Ich verschreibe Ihnen . . .** *(îH geh-be ee-nen . . . / îH fêr-shry-be ee-nen . . .)* (I'll give you . . . / I'll prescribe for you . . .)
- **ein Schmerzmittel** *(ayn shmêrts-mîtl)* (a painkiller)
- **Antibiotika** *(ân-tee-byoh-tî-kâ)* (antibiotics)
- **Tabletten** *(tâ-blêtn)* (pills)
- **das Medikament / die Medikamente** (pl) *(dâs meh-dee-kâ-mênt / dee meh-dee-kâ-mên-te)* (medication)

Getting your medication

You might be used to getting most of your medication at a drugstore, which usually has a counter for prescription medication. In Germany, however, it works a little differently. The German equivalent of the drugstore is the **Drogerie** *(droh-ge-ree)*, where you get everything from toothpaste to laundry detergent and nail polish, as well as non-prescription drugs, such as aspirin and cough syrup. For every prescription drug, however, you have to go to the so-called **Apotheke** *(âpoh-teh-ke)* (pharmacy). You will find that the people working there are very skilled and often as knowledgeable as a doctor. When it comes to prescriptions, the German laws are very strict: You may notice that a lot of the medication (such as allergy medication) that you can buy over the counter in the United States requires a prescription in Germany (and thus, a trip to the doctor).

The doctor will give you a prescription, **das Rezept** *(dâs rê-tsêpt)*, that you will take to a pharmacy, called **die Apotheke** *(dee âpô-teh-ke)*, to be filled.

The following vocabulary will help you to understand when and how often you are supposed to take your medication:

- ✔ **Bitte, nehmen Sie . . . Tabletten / Teelöffel . . .** *(bî-te neh-men zee . . . tah-blêtn / teh-luof . . .)* (Please take . . . pills / teaspoons . . .)

- ✔ **dreimal am Tag / täglich** *(dry-mahl âm tahgk / taig-lîH)* (three times a day / daily)

- ✔ **alle . . . Stunden** *(â-le . . . shtûn-dn)* (every . . . hours)

- ✔ **vor / nach dem Essen** *(fohr / naH dehm êssn)* (before / after meals)

Finally, the doctor may wish to see you again, saying:

Kommen Sie in . . . Tagen / einer Woche wieder. *(kô-mn zee în . . . tah-gn / ay-ner vô-He vee-der)* (Come back in . . . days / one week.)

Talkin' the Talk

After Ulrich gets his diagnosis, he takes the prescription to his neighborhood pharmacy and talks to the pharmacist.

Ulrich:	**Guten Morgen. Meine Ärztin hat mir dieses Medikament verschrieben.** *gûtn <u>môr</u>-gn. <u>my</u>-ne <u>êrts</u>-tîn hât meer <u>dee</u>-zes mê-dî-kâ-<u>mênt</u> fêr-<u>shree</u>-bn* Good morning. My doctor has precribed this medication for me.
Apothekerin:	**Einen Moment.** <u>ay</u>-nen moh-<u>ment</u> Just a moment.

The pharmascist goes to the back, gets Ulrich's medicine, and returns.

	So, Herr Lempert. Bitte, nehmen Sie dreimal am Tag zwei von diesen Tabletten. *zoh hêr <u>lêm</u>-pêrt. <u>bî</u>-te <u>neh</u>-men zee <u>dry</u>-mahl âm tahg tsvy fôn <u>dee</u>-zn tâ-<u>blêtn</u>* Okay, Mr. Lempert. Please take two of these pills three times a day.
Ulrich:	**Vor oder nach dem Essen?** *fohr <u>oh</u>-der nahH dehm êssn* Before or after meals?
Apothekerin:	**Nach dem Essen.** *nahH dehm êssn* After meals.
Ulrich:	**Wird gemacht.** *vîrt ge-<u>mâHt</u>* I'll do that.
Apothekerin:	**Gute Besserung, Herr Lempert!** <u>goo</u>-te <u>bê</u>-se-<u>rûng</u>, hêr <u>lêm</u>-pêrt Feel better, Mr. Lempert.

Talking to the Police

You have just discovered that your hotel room has been robbed. They've gotten away with a lot, but fortuntely, they left *German For Dummies* behind. A stroke of good luck, don't you think?

Here are some helpful expressions for handling the situation:

- ✔ **Wo ist die nächste Polizeiwache?** *(voh ĩsst dee naiH-ste pô-lĩ-tsy-vâ-he)* (Where is the closest police station?)

- ✔ **Ich möchte einen Diebstahl melden.** *(ĩH muoH-te ay-nen deep-shtahl mêl-dn)* (I would like to report a theft.)

Describing what was stolen

To describe a theft, you start out by saying

Man hat mir . . . gestohlen. *(mân hât meer . . . ge-shtoh-len)* (Someone has stolen . . .)

You can then finish the sentence by inserting any of the following:

- ✔ **meine Brieftasche / mein Portemonnaie** *(my-ne breef-tâ-she / myn pôr-te-moh-neh)* (my wallet)

- ✔ **meine Tasche** *(my-ne tâ-she)* (my bag)

- ✔ **mein Geld** *(myn gêlt)* (my money)

- ✔ **meinen Pass** *(my-nen pâs)* (my passport)

- ✔ **mein Auto** *(myn ow-toh)* (my car)

If you want to express that someone has broken into your house or office, you use the verb **einbrechen** *(ayn-brê-Hen)* (break into):

Man hat bei mir eingebrochen. *(mân hât by meer ayn-ge-brôHn)* (Someone has broken into my room.)

If you are talking about your car, however, you use a similar but slightly different verb, **aufbrechen** *(owf-brê-Hen),* which literally means "to break open":

Man hat mein Auto aufgebrochen. *(mân hât myn ow-tô owf-ge-brôHn)* (Someone has broken into my car.)

The indefinite pronoun **man** *(mân),* which means one, that is, people in general, comes in handy — and better yet: it's easy to use, because it never changes its ending. For example:

- ✔ **Man hat seine Tasche gestohlen.** *(mân hât zy-ne tâ-she ge-shtoh-len)* (Someone has stolen his bag.)

- ✔ **Man hat ihre Tasche gestohlen.** *(mân hât ee-re tâ-she ge-shtoh-len)* (Someone has stolen her bag.)

Answering questions from the police

So you got a good look at the fiend. Was he or she tall or short, skinny or fat, hairy or bald? The police will want to know all. And once you have learned how to describe people, you will also be ready for the personal pages of the newspaper.

The police will ask you

Können Sie die Person beschreiben? *(kuo-nen zee dee pêr-zohn be-shrybn)* (Can you describe that person?)

Your answer to this question can begin

Die Person hatte . . . *(dee per-zohn hâ-te . . .)* (The person had . . .)

Then finish the sentence with any of the following (You can combine traits by saying "und" between any of the following answers):

- **blonde / schwarze / rote / graue Haare** *(blôn-de / shvâr-tse / roh-te / grâû-e hah-re)* (blond / black / red / gray hair)
- **einen Bart / keinen Bart** *(ay-nen bahrt / ky-nen bahrt)* (a beard / no beard)
- **eine Glatze** *(ay-ne glâ-tse)* (a bald head)
- **eine Brille** *(ay-ne brî-le)* (glasses)

Or your answer can begin **Die Person war . . .** *(dee pêr-zohn vahr . . .)* (The person was . . .) and end with any of the following:

- **groß / klein** *(grohs / klyn)* (tall / short)
- **ungefähr . . . Meter . . . groß** *(ûn-ge-fair . . . meh-ter . . . grohs)* (approximately . . . meters tall)
- **ungefähr . . . Jahre alt** *(ûn-ge-fair . . . yah-re âlt)* (approximately . . . years old)

The police may also ask you the following questions:

- **Wann ist das passiert?** *(vân îst dâs pâ-seert)* (When did it happen?)
- **Wo waren Sie in dem Moment?** *(voh vah-ren zee în dehm moh-mênt)* (Where were you at that moment?)

Protecting your rights abroad

Had enough for the day? If you are really not up to conversing with the law on your own, here are two very important phrases that you should know:

- ✔ **Ich brauche einen Anwalt.** (*îH brow-he ay-nen ân-vâlt*) (I need a lawyer.)

- ✔ **Ich möchte das Konsulat anrufen.** (*îH muoH-te dâs kôn-zoo-laht ân-roofn*) (I would like to call the consulate.)

Talkin' the Talk

Erika Berger has to drop off some documents at one of her client's offices. She parks her car in front of the office building and visits her client. When she returns half an hour later, she realizes that somebody broke into her car and her bag is missing. Luckily, the next police station is right around the corner.

Erika: **Guten Tag. Ich möchte einen Diebstahl melden.**
goo-tn tahgk. îH muoH-te ay-nen deep-shtahl mêl-dn
Good day. I would like to report a theft.

Man hat mein Auto aufgebrochen und meine Tasche gestohlen.
mân hât myn ow-tô owf-ge-brô-Hen ûnt my-ne tâ-she ge-shtoh-len
Someone has broken into my car and stolen my bag.

Polizist: **Wann ist das passiert?**
vân îst dâs pâ-seert
When did it happen?

Erika: **Zwischen elf und halb zwölf.**
tsvî-shen êlf ûnt hâlp tsvuolf
Between 11:00 and 11:30.

Polizist: **Und wo?**
ûnt voh
And where?

Erika: **Gleich hier auf der Rotestraße.**
glyH heer owf dehr roh-te-shtrah-sse
Right here on Rotestreet.

Polizist:	**Was war in Ihrer Tasche?** *vâs vahr în <u>ee</u>-rer <u>tâ</u>-she* What was in your bag?
Erika:	**Meine Brieftasche mit ungefähr hundert Mark, meine Kreditkarten und mein Führerschein!** *<u>my</u>-ne <u>breef</u>-tâ-she mît <u>hûn</u>-dêrt mârk, my-ne krê-<u>deet</u>-kâr-tn ûnt myn <u>fuu</u>-rer-shyn* My wallet with approximately 100 Marks in it, my credit cards, and my driver's license.
Polizist:	**Bitte, warten Sie einen Moment, und wir erstatten sofort Anzeige.** *<u>bî</u>-te vârtn zee <u>ay</u>-nen mô-<u>mênt</u> ûnt veer êr-<u>shtâtn</u> zoh-<u>fôrt</u> <u>ân</u>-tsy-ge* Please wait one moment, and we will immediately file a report.

FUN & GAMES

Identify the body parts (using German, of course) in the following drawing.

Head: _____   Shoulder: _____

Hair: _____   Arm: _____

Ear: _____   Chest: _____

Eye: _____   Hand: _____

Face: _____   Knee: _____

Mouth: _____   Leg: _____

Neck: _____   Foot: _____

Part IV

The Part of Tens

The 5th Wave   By Rich Tennant

"...and remember, no more German tongue twisters until you know the language better."

In this part . . .

Every *For Dummies* book ends with top-ten lists, and this book has some good ones. In addition to offering tips on how to learn German quickly, we provide you with German phrases you should avoid, German expressions you shouldn't hesitate to use, German holidays, and more.

Chapter 17

Ten Ways to Pick Up German Quickly

● ●

*W*hether you had years of German in high school or in college and neglected it subsequently, or you came to be interested in this language later in life, you may want to get ready for a visit or get yourself psyched for it. Here are a few tips on how you can do just that.

Looking Things Up in the Dictionary

If you are interested in picking up quantities of everyday words fast, cut up a bunch of paper into small pieces (or use sticky notes), get out your English / German dictionary, or use the dictionary at the end of this book, and do the following: look up the German word for everything you can touch in your home, such as the window (**das Fenster**) *(dâs fêns-ter),* the door (**die Tür**) *(dee tuur),* the fridge (**der Kühlschrank**) *(dehr kuul-shrânk),* or a cup (**eine Tasse**) *(ay-ne tâ-se).* Write each word on one of those pieces of paper and attach it to whatever it describes. You can't help but master these words quickly!

Compiling Lists of Words that Go Together

If you want to memorize words within a certain context, compile lists of expressions or entire sentences that all have to do with the topic you're interested in. As you go through a chapter in this book, write down vocabulary that you would like to pick up quickly. For example, write down the phrases you find most important for asking directions (How do I get to . . .? How far is it?) or the things you need to know when you want to exchange money at a bank (What is the exchange rate? I would like to change money.). Limit the list to 10 or 12 entries.

Then look for one or more convenient spots around the house to post your list; for example, next to the mirror in the bathroom works well. Mount a nice-sized paperclip on the wall at eye level and attach one sheet of notes. Every time you brush your teeth, you can casually review the compiled list. And before you know it, you will remember all those nifty expressions. Then it's time to put up a new list.

Writing Shopping Lists

Here is another thing you can do at home: make out your shopping lists in German. Write the English equivalents after the German, though, just so you won't get annoyed in the store when you can't remember what you meant. For example, write **Birnen** (_bîr-nen_)(pears) or **Zwiebeln** (_tsvee-beln_) (onions) on your list the next time you need those items.

Celebrating German Day!

You can also organize "German days" at home. Designate a day when you will try to phrase in German the little things you do as you go along, such as "I am going to the kitchen." (**Ich gehe in die Küche.**) (_îH geh-e în dee kuu-He_) or "I am making coffee." (**Ich mache Kaffee.**) (_îH mâ-He kâ-feh_).

Using Language Tapes and CDs

On your way to and from work, you can always listen to language tapes and CDs. Just listening to the German voices over and over again can do wonders to help you retain words and phrases.

Listening to German Radio and Watching German Television

The government-funded German radio and television station **Deutsche Welle** broadcasts its programs around the globe in many languages, including German and English. These broadcasts are an excellent source of information about what's going on in Germany politically, culturally, or socially. Go to the Deutsche Welle Web site (www.dwelle.de), select the language of your choice, and you're on your way.

Trying a CD-ROM

If you have a computer, there are excellent German CD-ROM courses on the market. You can listen to the way words are pronounced, see their correct spellings, record your own voice, and actually get feedback from the program.

Watching German Movies

Another fun way to pick up expressions, the accent, cultural habits, and the like is by renting a subtitled German movie on video and watching it several times. What a treat!

Reading German Publications

Buy German magazines or have someone bring you back some from traveling in a German-speaking country and then start by reading the ads. Checking out the ads and reading short articles is a guaranteed eye-opener! On international flights, you will often find bilingual in-flight magazines with German on one side and English on the other. Take one. Airline magazines are full of interesting ads and articles.

Surfing the Net

The Internet has many opportunities for you to find out more about German. Get your search engine going — Altavista, Yahoo!, Hotbot, Excite, whatever your favorite is — type *German language, learning German, German resources,* or *Germany* (or any other German-speaking country) into the search engine and then select whatever interests you.

Browse around in English or in German and pick out words you know. You can also visit a German chat room, just to listen, if you like. You may be surprised how much you can pick up by listening to informal conversations.

Chapter 18

Ten Things Never to Say

● ●

*T*his is the chapter aimed at saving you from embarassment. You probably have heard foreign visitors saying things that made you want to crack up or hold your breath. Well, it happens to the best of us linguists, but here are some pointers to help you avoid the worst pitfalls!

Knowing When to Use the Formal or Informal

If you've read Chapter 3, you already know that you have to be careful about using the familiar form of address, **du** *(dū)* (you). Never use it when speaking to anyone you don't know well who is older than 16 if you don't want to be insulting or sound uneducated. You want to use the formal **Sie** *(zee)* and say **Möchten Sie ins Kino gehen?** *(muoH-tên zee îns kee-nô-oh gehn)* (Do you want to go to the movies?) and not **Möchtest du ins Kino gehen?**

In most situations, it will be obvious to you which form you should use. If you arrive at a party and everybody addresses you with the familiar form **du**, you should just go with it. And of course, you may be offered the familiar form: **Wir können uns duzen** *(veer kuon-nen ûns doo-tsen)* (We can use the familiar form). It would be equally impolite to turn the offer down.

Addressing Service People Correctly

When you want to address a waitress or female salesperson, don't call her **Fräulein,** which used to be the German version of "Miss." **Fräulein** literally means "little woman," since the syllable "lein" is a diminutive form. Most women find this form of address offensive or will at least suspect that you aren't familiar enough with the German language to know about the word's connotations. There is no real substitute for it, so you have to rely on **Entschuldigen Sie bitte** *(ênt-shûl-dî-gen zee, bî-te)* (Excuse me, please) or eye contact to get attention.

The same goes for addressing a waiter in a restaurant: don't call him **Kellner** (_kêl-ner_). The waiters don't like it, and it's considered patronizing and condescending. Again, eye contact and gestures or a simple **Entschuldigen Sie bitte** (_ênt-shûl-dî-gen zee, bî-te_) are the best way to get attention.

Hot or Cold?

If you would like to express that you are hot or cold, be sure not to say **Ich bin heiß** (I am hot) or **Ich bin kalt** (I am cold). What you are saying here is that you're in heat or have a cold personality! In all likelihood, this is not what you want people to think about you. What you want to say is **Mir ist heiß** (_meer îst hys_) or **Mir ist kalt** (_meer îst kâlt_), both of which use the personal pronoun **mir** (_meer_) (me).

I'm Not Loaded

If someone asks you at dinner or lunch if you would like another helping and you are really full, you certainly don't want to translate the word "full" into German. Saying **Ich bin voll** (I am full) means that you are totally drunk — it is, in fact, the colloquial expression for "I'm loaded." Unless you want to let the person who's asking know that you already had too many drinks, you should say **Ich bin satt** (_îH bîn zât_) (I am full).

Speaking of the Law with Respect

Don't call a policeperson **Bulle**. Though you may hear a lot of people using this word, it is a slang expression that means "bull." The German word for a policeman or a policewoman is **der Polizist** (_dehr pô-lî-tsîst_) (m) or **die Polizistin** (_dee pô-lî-tsîs-tîn_) (f), respectively.

The Gymnasium Is for School, Not Sports

If you are trying to tell a German person that you are going to the gym by saying **Ich gehe zum Gymnasium** (_îH geh-e tsûm guum-nah-zî-um_), you will cause some serious confusion. A "Gymnasium" is not a place to work out but a high school. There actually are three types of secondary schools in Germany, and the "Gymnasium" is the highest level. The German word you want to use for "gym" is **Sportzentrum** (_shpôrt-tsên-trûm_) (sports center) or **Fitnesscenter** (pronounced just like in English).

Knowing the Appropriate Form of Know

In English, you can use the versatile verb "to know" to express that you know a person, locality, a fact, and the answer to a question. The German verb you use when it comes to people and places is **kennen** (*kê-nen*) (to know / to be acquainted with); for example, you would say **Ich kenne ihn** (*îH kê-ne eehn*) (I know him). But if someone asks you what time it is and you don't know the answer, don't say "Ich kenne nicht" — no one would understand what you're trying to say and it's not even translatable into English.

When it comes to knowledge of facts, you have to use the verb **wissen** (*vî-sen),* which is usually used with a subordinate clause. So, in German you would say **Ich weiss nicht, wie viel Uhr es ist.** (*îH vys nîHt, vee feel oor ês îst*) (I don't know what time it is.).

Going to the Right Closet

Don't mistake the German word **Klosett** for the English "closet." If you want to find out where the closet is, don't ask **Wo ist das Klosett?** *(voh îsst dâs kloh-zêt?),* since people will give you a confused look and then let you know where the bathroom is located. **Klosett** is the old-fashioned term for toilet bowl, and the right word for closet is **der Einbauschrank** *(dehr ayn-bow-shrânk).*

Using Bekommen Properly

You might conclude that the German verb **bekommen** (*be-kô-men)* corresponds to the English "to become" — a mistake commonly made by English speakers learning the German language and vice versa. Don't try to tell someone that you're going to be a doctor by saying **Ich bekomme einen Arzt.** What you are expressing here is "I get a doctor," meaning you're getting him like you would get a birthday present. The German word for "to become" is **werden** (*vehr-den),* so you have to say **Ich werde Arzt.** (*îH vehr-de artst*) or **Sie werden Freunde** (*zee vehr-den froyn-de*) (They become friends.).

Using the Right Eating Verb

In Germany, you might hear someone say **Die Kuh frisst Gras.** *(dee koo frîst grahs)* (The cow eats grass.) But please don't conclude that **fressen** *(frêsn)* just means "to eat" and say something such as **Ich fresse Kuchen.** (I eat cake.) It would mean that you're disgustingly overindulging or have bad table manners. The verb "fressen" is reserved for animals, and you should use **essen** *(êsn)* (to eat) if you're referring to human beings. In connection with human beings, "fressen" is only used in a derogatory sense, so you should say **Ich esse Kuchen** *(îH êse koo-Hen)*.

Chapter 19

Ten Favorite German Expressions

● ●

*O*nce you get tuned into German a little, you may suddenly hear people use these German expressions that seem to just slip out at any given moment. You may even have heard some of these already; now it's time to casually use them yourself.

Alles klar!

(â-les klahr)

The literal translation is: "Everything clear." You can use it to signal understanding when somebody explains something to you or to signal your agreement when someone has gone over the details of a plan. In this context, the expression means "Got it!"

Geht in Ordnung.

(geht în ôrd-nûng)

You use this phrase to indicate that you'll take care of something. It translates into "I'll do it."

Kein Problem.

(kayn proh-blehm)

This translates literally into "no problem." Use it to let somebody know that you will take care of something. You can also agree to a change in plans with this phrase.

Guten Appetit!

(gootn â-pê-teet)

This phrase literally means "Good appetite!" However, it certainly is not meant as a comment on anyone's good or bad appetite. It's what you wish each other when you begin to eat or when you see someone eating, much like the English "Enjoy!", except that German speakers wish each other "Guten Appetit" much more freely.

Deine Sorgen möchte ich haben!

(dy-ne zôr-gn muoH-te îH hah-bn)

This phrase translates: "I would like to have your worries." It is often used facetiously, when a situation seems terrible to one party, but not half as awful to the other.

Das darf doch wohl nicht wahr sein!

(dâs dârf dôH vohl nîHt vahr zâyn)

This expression translates: "This just can't be true!" and what it implies is rendered with one word in English: "Unbelievable."

Mir reicht's!

(meer ryHt's)

This phrase means "It's enough for me" or, to put it into more idiomatic English, "I've had it" or "I've had enough."

Wie schön!

(vee shuon)

The literal translation of this phrase is "How nice!" It can mean that, but sometimes it's used sarcastically, and then it's a way to vent annoyance or exasperation.

Genau.

(ge-now)

This phrase means "exactly," and it is used to show that you agree with the things someone is saying.

Stimmt's?

(shtīmts)

This translates as "Isn't it true? or "Don't you agree?" It is used when someone wants your confirmation of something just said. It is usually answered with **Stimmt!** *(stīmt)* meaning "I agree."

Chapter 20

Ten Holidays to Remember

Some of the following holidays may not be familiar to you, or at least you may not be familiar with the ways that people in Germany (or German-speaking countries) celebrate them. There are many more holidays than those listed in this chapter, many of which are celebrated regionally.

Heilige Drei Könige

January 6 is **der Heiligedreikönigstag** (*dehr hy-lî-ge-dry-kuo-nîgks-tahgk*) or **Heilige Drei Könige** (*hy-lee-ge dry kuo-nî-ge*), also known as **Epiphanias** (*eh-pî-fah-nî-ias*) (Feast of the Three Kings or Epiphany). It is not necessarily celebrated in any particular way, but there are certain "rituals" that are observed regionally. In some regions, people dressed as the Three Kings — Kaspar, Melchior, and Balthasar — walk the streets of their parish, put their initials on the doors of peoples' houses with chalk, and collect money for their church. In Switzerland, you eat a special cake with a small treasure hidden somewhere inside, usually a coin. The coin symbolizes a gift of a king. Whoever finds the coin becomes the queen or the king for the day and gets to wear a crown.

Karneval / Fastnacht / Fasching

Karneval (*câr-ne-vâl*) (carnival) or **Fastnacht** (*fâst-nâHt*), the Mardi Gras of the German-speaking countries, is celebrated at the end of February or in early March. In some regions and cities, such as Mainz, Cologne, Düsseldorf, and Munich — where the carnival is called **Fasching** (*fâ-shîng*) — or Basel in Switzerland, it is a very big event. The celebrations take place on **Rosenmontag** (*roh-zên-mohn-tahgk*) (Rose Monday) with big parades and parties where people dress up in fancy costumes. Things quiet down a little the next day, **Veilchendienstag** (*fyl-Hên-deens-tahgk*) (Shrove Tuesday), and **Aschermittwoch** (*âsher-mît-vôH*) (Ash Wednesday) marks the end of carnival and the beginning of the **Fastenzeit** (*fâs-ten-tsyt*) (Lent), the period of 40 days before Easter.

Ostern

In Germany, Easter always means a nice long weekend. It starts with **Karfreitag** *(kahr-fry-tahgk)* (Good Friday), and both **Ostersonntag** *(ohs-ter-zôn-tahgk)* (Easter Sunday) and **Ostermontag** *(ohs-ter-mohn-tahgk)* (Easter Monday) are official holidays. Easter eggs are quite popular in Germany: egg-coloring kits are sold everywhere, and children go on Easter egg hunts on Easter Sunday.

Erster April

April 1, **erster April** *(ehrs-ter â-prîl)*, is April Fool's Day. This holiday is the day for practical jokers, who like to play tricks, commonly known as **Aprilscherze** *(â-prîl-shêr-tse)*. When you fool someone successfully, you call out **April, April!** *(â-prîl, â-prîl)*.

Tag der Arbeit

May 1 is **der Tag der Arbeit** *(dehr tahgk dehr âr-byt)* (Labor Day). On this official holiday, the trade unions organize rallies, and participants wear a red carnation in their buttonhole. Union representatives and politicians make speeches.

Traditionally the evening before Labor Day is devoted to parties with dancing to live music called **Tanz in den Mai** *(tânts în dehn my)* (literally: the dance into May), and the merrymaking usually continues into the wee hours. In the countryside, people put up a **Maibaum** *(my-bâûm)* (May tree) and dance around it.

Himmelfahrt

Forty days after Easter, **Himmelfahrt** *(hî-mel-fahrt)* (Ascension Day) is celebrated. It always falls on a Thursday and is a very popular day for people to band together in groups and get out into nature.

Pfingsten

Ten days after Ascension Day, **Pfingsten** *(pfīngs-tn)* (Pentecost) is celebrated.

Monday is an official holiday (**Pfingstmontag**) *(pfīngkst-mohn-tahgk),* and many people take Friday off as well and go away for a long weekend (**ein langes Wochenende**) *(ayn lān-ges vō-Hen-ên-de).* You want to be aware of that weekend when you make your travel plans: traffic gets heavy, and it can be difficult to make hotel reservations in popular areas.

Der Tag der Deutschen Einheit

October 3 is **der Tag der Deutschen Einheit** *(dehr tahgk dehr doyt-shn ayn-hyt)* (Day of German Unity: The German national holiday). This holiday marks the day in 1990 when East and West Germany united into one country. It is not celebrated in any particular way among the population itself, but there are a lot of official government events.

Austria's national holiday is celebrated on October 26, and Switzerland's, which is called **Nationalfeiertag** *(nā-tsīoh-nahl-fyêr-tahgk)* (national holiday) or sometimes **Bundesfeier** *(būn-dês-fyr)* (Federal Celebration), is on August 1.

Nikolaustag

December 6 is **Nikolaustag** *(nī-kō-lows-tahgk)* (The feast of Saint Nicholas).

This holiday is another neat family affair. Children place a shoe or boot by a window or door, and during the night **der Nikolaus** *(dehr nī-cō-lows)* drops by and fills it with gingerbread, **Pfeffernüsse** *(pfê-fer-nuu-sse)* (gingerbread cookies), marzipan, other seasonal goodies, and maybe a small gift.

Weihnachten

There isn't a big difference between the way **Weihnachten** *(vy-nāH-ten)* (Christmas) is celebrated in Germany and the United States, except that it is one of those long holidays. Presents, however, are traditionally exchanged on Christmas Eve, and both the first and second day of Christmas are official holidays. This is very much a family celebration and one of the big travel dates of the year.

Chapter 21

Ten Phrases That Make You Sound German

This chapter provides you with some typical German expressions that almost everyone who speaks German knows and uses. The phrases in this chapter are so very German that you may even pass for a native German speaker when you use them.

Das ist ja toll!

(dâs îst yah tôl)

(This is great!) This is the most common German way to express your excitement about something and get it across.

Ruf mich an! / Rufen Sie mich an!

(roof mîH an / roofn zee mîH an)

(Call me! informal / formal) If you want to keep in touch with somebody, this is the way to do it.

Was ist los?

(vâs îst lohs)

(What's happening?) This question is most commonly used in the sense of "What's wrong?"

Keine Ahnung.

(ky-ne ah-nûng)

(No idea.) This is the short version of **Ich habe keine Ahnung.** *(îH hah-be ky-ne ah-nûng)* (I have no idea.) and is frequently used to express that you know nothing about the matter in question.

Gehen wir!

(gehn veer)

(Let's go!) This is the phrase to use if you want to get going!

Nicht zu fassen!

(nîHt tzoo fâ-sen)

(I can't believe it!) If you want to express disbelief, concern, or agitation, use this typically German phrase.

Du hast Recht! / Sie haben Recht!

(doo hâst rêHt / zee hah-bn rêHt)

(You're right! informal / formal) This is the most typical way of expressing agreement in German.

Auf keinen Fall!

(owf ky-nen fâl)

(No way!) Literally, this expression means "In no case!" and it's the one you should use if you want to make your disagreement very clear.

Nicht schlecht!

(nīHt shlēHt)

(Not bad!) As in English, this phrase not only means that something is not too bad — it's also a reserved way of expressing appreciation and approval.

Das ist mir (völlig) egal.

(dâs īst meer [vuo-līg] ê-gahl)

(I don't mind. / I don't care.) You can use this phrase to express that you don't mind if it's one way or another, or that you couldn't care less.

Part V

Appendixes

The 5th Wave   By Rich Tennant

"I'd ask for directions in German, but I don't know how to form a question into the shape of an apology."

In this part . . .

Last but not least, we give you the appendixes, which you will no doubt find quite useful. In addition to verb tables that show you how to conjugate regular and irregular verbs, we provide a pretty comprehensive mini-dictionary and a guide to the audio CD that's attached to the back of the book. We also provide you with answer keys for some of the puzzles that appear throughout the book.

Appendix A
Verb Tables

German Verbs

Regular Verbs (e.g. *bezahlen* to pay)
Past Participle: *bezahlt* (paid)
Example: Linda bezahlt die Rechnung. (Linda pays the bill.)

	Present	Past	Future
ich (I)	bezahle	habe bezahlt	werde bezahlen
du (you, sing. inf.)	bezahlst	hast bezahlt	wirst bezahlen
er/sie/es (he/she/it)	bezahlt	hat bezahlt	wird bezahlen
wir (we)	bezahlen	haben bezahlt	werden bezahlen
ihr (you, inf.)	bezahlt	habt bezahlt	werdet bezahlen
sie/Sie (they/you, form.)	bezahlen	haben bezahlt	werden bezahlen

Separable Verbs (e.g. *anrufen* to call)
Past Participle: *angerufen* (called)
Example: Wir rufen immer an. (We always call.)

	Present	Past	Future
ich (I)	rufe an	habe angerufen	werde anrufen
du (you, sing. inf.)	rufst an	hast angerufen	wirst anrufen
er/sie/es (he/she/it)	ruft an	hat angerufen	wird anrufen
wir (we)	rufen an	haben angerufen	werden anrufen
ihr (you, inf.)	ruft an	habt angerufen	werdet anrufen
sie/Sie (they/you, form.)	rufen an	haben angerufen	werden anrufen

Reflexive Verbs Dative (e.g. *sich etwas kaufen* to buy oneself something)
Example: Ich kaufe mir ein Hemd. (I buy myself a shirt.)

	Present	Past	Future
ich (I)	kaufe mir	habe mir gekauft	werde mir kaufen
du (you, sing. inf.)	kaufst dir	hast dir gekauft	wirst dir kaufen
er/sie/es (he/she/it)	kauft sich	hat sich gekauft	wird sich kaufen
wir (we)	kaufen uns	haben uns gekauft	werden uns kaufen
ihr (you, inf.)	kauft euch	habt euch gekauft	werdet euch kaufen
sie/Sie (they/you, form.)	kaufen sich	haben sich gekauft	werden sich kaufen

Reflexive Verbs Accusative, (e.g. *sich freuen* to be happy)
Example: Jim freut sich über das Geschenk. (Jim is happy about the gift.)

	Present	Past	Future
ich (I)	freue mich	habe mich gefreut	werde mich freuen
du (you, sing. inf.)	freust dich	hast dich gefreut	wirst dich freuen
er/sie/es (he/she/it)	freut sich	hat sich gefreut	wird sich freuen
wir (we)	freuen uns	haben uns gefreut	werden uns freuen
ihr (you, inf.)	freut euch	habt euch gefreut	werdet euch freuen
sie/Sie (they/you, form.)	freuen sich	haben sich gefreut	werden sich freuen

Verb *haben* (to have)
Past Participle: *gehabt* (had)
Example: Wir haben keine Zeit. (We have no time.)

	Present	Past	Future
ich (I)	habe	habe gehabt	werde haben
du (you, sing. inf.)	hast	hast gehabt	wirst haben
er/sie/es (he/she/it)	hat	hat gehabt	wird haben
wir (we)	haben	haben gehabt	werden haben
ihr (you, inf.)	habt	habt gehabt	werdet haben
sie/Sie (they/you, form.)	haben	haben gehabt	werden haben

Verb *sein* (to be)
Past Participle: *gewesen* (been)
Example: Hansens sind im Urlaub. (The Hansens are on vacation.)

	Present	Past	Future
ich (I)	bin	bin gewesen	werde sein
du (you, sing. inf.)	bist	bist gewesen	wirst sein
er/sie/es (he/she/it)	ist	ist gewesen	wird sein
wir (we)	sind	sind gewesen	werden sein
ihr (you, inf.)	seid	seid gewesen	werdet sein
sie/Sie (they/you, form.)	sind	sind gewesen	werden sein

Irregular German Verbs

		Present	Past Participle
abfahren to leave	ich	fahre ab	
	du	fährst ab	
	er/sie/es	fährt ab	abgefahren
	wir	fahren ab	(w/sein)
	ihr	fahrt ab	
	sie/Sie	fahren ab	
anfangen to start	ich	fange an	
	du	fängst an	
	er/sie/es	fängt an	angefangen
	wir	fangen an	(w/haben)
	ihr	fangt an	
	sie/Sie	fangen an	
beginnen to begin	ich	beginne	
	du	beginnst	
	er/sie/es	beginnt	begonnen
	wir	beginnen	(w/haben)
	ihr	beginnt	
	sie/Sie	beginnen	
bleiben to stay, remain	ich	bleibe	
	du	bleibst	
	er/sie/es	bleibt	geblieben
	wir	bleiben	(w/sein)
	ihr	bleibt	
	sie/Sie	bleiben	

		Present	**Past Participle**
bringen to bring	ich du er/sie/es wir ihr sie/Sie	bringe bringst bringt bringen bringt bringen	gebracht (w/haben)
denken to think	ich du er/sie/es wir ihr sie/Sie	denke denkst denkt denken denkt denken	gedacht (w/haben)
dürfen may, to be allowed to	ich du er/sie/es wir ihr sie/Sie	darf darfst darf dürfen dürft dürfen	gedurft (w/haben)
einladen to invite	ich du er/sie/es wir ihr sie/Sie	lade ein lädst ein lädt ein laden ein ladet ein laden ein	eingeladen (w/haben)
essen to eat	ich du er/sie/es wir ihr sie/Sie	esse isst isst essen esst essen	gegessen (w/haben)

		Present	Past Participle
fahren to drive	ich	fahre	
	du	fährst	
	er/sie/es	fährt	gefahren
	wir	fahren	(w/sein)
	ihr	fahrt	
	sie/Sie	fahren	
finden to find	ich	finde	
	du	findest	
	er/sie/es	findet	gefunden
	wir	finden	(w/haben)
	ihr	findet	
	sie/Sie	finden	
fliegen to fly	ich	fliege	
	du	fliegst	
	er/sie/es	fliegt	geflogen
	wir	fliegen	(w/sein)
	ihr	fliegt	
	sie/Sie	fliegen	
geben to give	ich	gebe	
	du	gibst	
	er/sie/es	gibt	gegeben
	wir	geben	(w/haben)
	ihr	gebt	
	sie/Sie	geben	
gehen to go	ich	gehe	
	du	gehst	
	er/sie/es	geht	gegangen
	wir	gehen	(w/sein)
	ihr	geht	
	sie/Sie	gehen	

		Present	**Past Participle**
halten to hold	ich	halte	
	du	hälst	
	er/sie/es	hält	gehalten
	wir	halten	(w/haben)
	ihr	haltet	
	sie/Sie	halten	
kennen to know	ich	kenne	
	du	kennst	
	er/sie/es	kennt	gekannt
	wir	kennen	(w/haben)
	ihr	kennt	
	sie/Sie	kennen	
kommen to come	ich	komme	
	du	kommst	
	er/sie/es	kommt	gekommen
	wir	kommen	(w/sein)
	ihr	kommt	
	sie/Sie	kommen	
können can, to be able to	ich	kann	
	du	kannst	
	er/sie/es	kann	gekonnt
	wir	können	(w/haben)
	ihr	könnt	
	sie/Sie	können	
lesen to read	ich	lese	
	du	liest	
	er/sie/es	liest	gelesen
	wir	lesen	(w/haben)
	ihr	lest	
	sie/Sie	lesen	

		Present	**Past Participle**
liegen to lie, rest	ich du er/sie/es wir ihr sie/Sie	liege liegst liegt liegen liegt liegen	 gelegen (w/haben)
mögen to like	ich du er/sie/es wir ihr sie	mag magst mag mögen mögt mögen	 gemocht (w/haben)
müssen to have to, must	ich du er/sie/es wir ihr sie/Sie	muss musst muss müssen müsst müssen	 gemusst (w/haben)
nehmen to take	ich du er/sie/es wir ihr sie/Sie	nehme nimmst nimmt nehmen nehmt nehmen	 genommen (w/haben)
schreiben to write	ich du er/sie/es wir ihr sie/Sie	schreibe schreibst schreibt schreiben schreibt schreiben	 geschrieben (w/haben)

		Present	**Past Participle**
sehen to see	ich du er/sie/es wir ihr sie/Sie	sehe siehst sieht sehen seht sehen	 gesehen (w/haben)
sitzen to sit	ich du er/sie/es wir ihr sie/Sie	sitze sitzt sitzt sitzen sitzt sitzen	 gesessen (w/haben)
sollen shall, to be supposed to	ich du er/sie/es wir ihr sie/Sie	soll sollst soll sollen sollt sollen	 gesollt (w/haben)
sprechen to speak	ich du er/sie/es wir ihr sie/Sie	spreche sprichst spricht sprechen sprecht sprechen	 gesprochen (w/haben)
stehen to stand	ich du er/sie/es wir ihr sie/Sie	stehen stehst steht stehen steht stehen	 gestanden (w/haben)

		Present	Past Participle
tragen to carry, wear	ich	trage	
	du	trägst	
	er/sie/es	trägt	getragen
	wir	tragen	(w/haben)
	ihr	tragt	
	sie/Sie	tragen	
treffen to meet	ich	treffe	
	du	triffst	
	er/sie/es	trifft	getroffen
	wir	treffen	(w/haben)
	ihr	trefft	
	sie/Sie	treffen	
trinken to drink	ich	trinke	
	du	trinkst	
	er/sie/es	trinkt	getrunken
	wir	trinken	(w/haben)
	ihr	trinkt	
	sie/Sie	trinken	
verlieren to lose	ich	verliere	
	du	verlierst	
	er/sie/es	verliert	verloren
	wir	verlieren	(w/haben)
	ihr	verliert	
	sie/Sie	verlieren	
wissen to know	ich	weiß	
	du	weißt	
	er/sie/es	weiß	gewusst
	wir	wissen	(w/haben)
	ihr	wisst	
	sie/Sie	wissen	

		Present	Past Participle
wollen to want	ich	will	
	du	willst	
	er/sie/es	will	gewollt
	wir	wollen	(w/haben)
	ihr	wollt	
	sie/Sie	wollen	

German-English Mini Dictionary

A

abbiegen/*ăp-beegn*/to make a turn
Abend/m/*ah-bnt*/evening
Abendessen/n/*ah-bnt-êsn*/dinner
aber/*ah-ber*/but
abfliegen/*ăp-flee-gen*/to depart
Abflug/m/*ăp-floogk*/departure
abreisen/*ăp-ry-zên*/to leave
alles/*ă-les*/all
Ampel/f/*ăm-pel*/traffic light
an/*ăn*/at
Anfang/m/*ăn-făng*/beginning
Ankauf/m/*ăn-kowf*/purchase
Ankunft/f/*ăn-kŭnft*/arrival
Anrufbeantworter/m/*ăn-roof-be-ănt-vôrtr*/answering machine
anrufen/*ăn-roo-fen*/to call
Antiquitäten/pl/*ăn-tî-kvî-teh-ten*/antiques
Anwalt/m/*ăn-vălt*/lawyer
April/m/*ah-prîl*/April
Arzt/m/*ărtst*/doctor
Arztpraxis/f/*ărtst-prā-xîs*/doctor's office
auch/*owH*/also
auf/*owf*/on
Auf Wiedersehen/*owf vee-der-zehn*/ Good-bye
August/m/*ow-gŭst*/August

Ausfahrt/f/*ows-fahrt*/exit
ausfüllen/*ows-fuu-ln*/to fill out
ausgezeichnet/*ows-ge-tsyH-net*/excellent
Ausstellung/f/*ows-shtê-lŭng*/exhibition
Auto/n/*ow-tô*/car

B

Bad/n/*baht*/bathtub
Bahnhof/m/*bahn-hohf*/train station
Bank/f/*bānk*/bank
bar/*bār*/cash
Bart/m/*bahrt*/beard
Basketball/m/*bahs-ket-bāl*/basketball
Bauernhof/m/*bow-êrn-hohf*/farm
Baum/m/*bowm*/tree
bei/*by*/by
beim/*bym*/near
Berg/m/*bêrg*/mountain
Beruf/m/*bê-roof*/occupation
beschreiben/*be-shrybn*/to describe
besetzt/*be-zêtst*/busy
Besprechung/f/*be-shprê-Hŭng*/meeting
Betrag/m/*be-trahgk*/amount
bezahlen/*be-tsah-len*/to pay
Bier/n/*beer*/beer
bisschen/*bîs-Hen*/little
bitte/*bî-te*/please
bleiben/*bly-ben*/to stay

Bordkarte/f/_bôrd_-kâr-te/boarding pass
Botschaft/f/_boht_-shâft/embassy
Brief/m/_breef_/letter
Briefkasten/m/_breef_-kâstn/mailbox
Briefmarke/f/_breef_-mâr-ke/stamp
Brieftasche/f/_breef_-tâ-she/wallet
bringen/_brîng_-en/to bring
Brot/n/_broht_/bread
Brötchen/n/_bruoht_-Hên/roll
buchen/_boo_-Hen/to book
Bus/m/_bûs_/bus
Bushaltestelle/f/_bûs_-hâl-te-shtê-le/bus stop
Butter/f/_bû_-têr/butter

C

Cerealien/pl/tseh-rê-_ah_-lî-en/cereals

D

Danke/_dâng_-ke/Thanks
Datum/n/_dah_-tûm/date
dauern/_dow_-ern/to last
deutsch/doytsh/German
Deutsche Mark/f/doy-tshe mârk/German mark
Dezember/m/deh-_tsêm_-ber/December
Dienstag/m/_deens_-tahgk/Tuesday
Donnerstag/m/_dônrs_-tahgk/Thursday
Doppelzimmer/n/_dôpl_-tsî-mer/double room
Dorf/n/_dôrf_/village
dort/_dôrt_/there
drücken/_drû_-kn/to push
durstig/_dûrstîg_/thirsty
Dusche/f/_doo_-she/shower

E

einfach/_ayn_-fâH/easy
einladen/_ayn_-lah-den/to invite
Einladung/f/_ayn_-lah-dûng/invitation
einverstanden/_ayn_-fêr-shtân-den/agreed
Einzelzimmer/n/_ayn_-tsêl-tsî-mer/single room
E-mail/f/_ee-mail_/e-mail
empfehlen/êm-_pfeh_-len/to recommend
Ende/n/_ên_-de/end
Entschuldigung/ênt-_shûl_-dî-gûng/ Excuse me
Erkältung/f/êr-_kêl_-tûng/cold
essen/_êsn_/to eat
etwas/_êt_-vâs/something

F

fahren/_fah_-ren/to drive
Fahrrad/n/_fah_-rât/bicycle
faxen/_fâ_-ksen/to fax
Februar/m/_feh_-brû-ahr/February
Fenster/n/_fêns_-ter/window
Feuerwehr/f/_foy_-er-vehr/fire department
Fieber/n/_fee_-ber/fever
Firma/f/_fîr_-mâ/company
fliegen/_flee_-gen/to fly
Flug/m/_floogk_/flight
Flughafen/m/_floogk_-hah-fen/airport
Flugsteig/m/_floogk_-shtyk/airport gate
Flugticket/n/_floogk_-tîket/airplane ticket
Flugzeug/n/_floogk_-tsoyg/airplane
Fluss/m/_flûs_/river
Formular/n/fôr-mû-_lahr_/form
fragen/_frah_-gen/to ask

Freitag/m/*fry-tāgk*/Friday

Fremdenverkehrsbüro/n/*frēm-den-fēr-kehrs-buu-roh*/tourist information office

Freund/m/*froynt*/friend (masculine)

Freundin/f/*froyn-dīn*/friend

früh/*fruu*/early

Frühstück/n/*fruu-shtuuk*/breakfast

für/*fuor*/for

Fußball/*m*/*foos-bāl*/soccer

G

Gabel/f/*gah-bl*/fork

Gang/m/*gāng*/aisle

ganz/*gānts*/all

Gebirge/n/*ge-bîr-ge*/mountains

Gebühr/f/*ge-buu-r*/fee

Gegend/f/*geh-*gent/area

gegenüber/*geh-gen-uu-ber*/opposite

Geheimzahl/f/*ge-hym-tsahl*/Personal Identification Number (PIN)

gehen/*geh-en*/to go

Geld/n/*gēlt*/money

Geldautomat/m/*gēlt-ow-tô-maht*/ATM

geöffnet/*ge-ūof-net*/open

Gepäck/n/*ge-pēk*/luggage

geradeaus/*grah-de-ows*/straight ahead

geschlossen/*ge-shlôsn*/closed

gestern/*gēs-tern*/yesterday

getrennt/*ge-trēnt*/separate

gewinnen/*gē-vî-nen*/to win

Glas/n/*glahs*/glass

Gleis/n/*glys*/track

Golf/n/*gôlf*/golf

groß/*grohs*/tall, big

gültig/*guul-tîg*/valid

gut/*gūt*/good

Gute Nacht/*gū-te nāHt*/Good night

Gute Reise/*gū-te ry-ze*/Have a good trip

Guten Abend/*gūtn ah-bnt*/Good evening

Guten Morgen/*gūtn môr-gn*/Good morning

Guten Tag/*gūtn tahgk*/Good day

H

Haar/n/*hah-r*/hair

Halbpension/f/*hālp-pāng-zîohn*/room with half board

Hallo/*hā-lo*/Hello

halten/*hāl-ten*/to stop

Haltestelle/f/*hāl-te-stê-le*/station, stop

Handball/m/*hānt-bāl*/handball

Hauptspeise/f/*howpt-shpy-ze*/main dish

heissen/*hy-sen*/to be called

helfen/*hêl-fen*/to help

heute/*hoy-te*/today

hier/*heer*/here

Hilfe/f/*hîl-fe*/help

hinter/*hîn-ter*/behind

Hobby/n/*hô-bee*/hobby

hören/*huo-ren*/to hear

Hotel/n/*hoh-têl*/hotel

Hügel/m/*huu-gel*/hill

hungrig/*hūngrîg*/hungry

I

interessant/*în-te-re-ssānt*/interesting

Internet/n/*în-ter-nêt*/Internet

J

ja/*yah*/yes
Jahr/n/*yahr*/year
Januar/m/*yâ-nû-ahr*/January
jemand/*yeh-mânt*/somebody
joggen/*jô-gen*/to jog
Jugendherberge/f/*yoo-gênt-hêr-bêr-ge*/youth hostel
Juli/m/*yoo-lee*/July
Juni/m/*yoo-nee*/June

K

Kaffee/m/*kâ-fê*/coffee
Kalender/m/*kâ-lên-der*/calendar
Karte/f/*kâr-te*/map, ticket
Kasse/f/*kâ-se*/cash register
kaufen/*kow-fen*/to buy
Kellner/m/*kêl-nêr*/waiter
kennenlernen/*kên-nen-lêr-nen*/to become acquainted with
Kino/n/*kee-nô*/movie house
Kirche/f/*kîr-He*/church
klatschen/*klât-shen*/to clap
klein/*klyn*/short, small
Klimaanlage/f/*klee-mah-ân-lah-ge*/air conditioning
Kneipe/f/*kny-pe*/bar, pub
Koffer/m/*kô-fer*/suitcase
kommen/*kô-men*/to come
Konsulat/n/*kôn-zû-laht*/consulate
Konzert/n/*kôn-tsert*/concert
krank/*krânk*/sick
Krankenhaus/n/*krânkn-hows*/hospital

Krankenschwester/f/*krânkn-shvês-ter*/nurse
Krankenwagen/m/*krânkn-vah-gn*/ambulance
Kreuzung/f/*kroy-tsûng*/intersection
Kuchen/m/*koo-Hen*/cake
Kuh/f/*koo*/cow
Küste/f/*kuus-te*/coast

L

lachen/*lâ-Hen*/to laugh
Land/n/*lânt*/country
langweilig/*lâng-vy-lîg*/boring
legen/*leh-gen*/to lay
leider/*ly-der*/unfortunately
Leitung/f/*ly-tûng*/line
lesen/*leh-zen*/to read
links/*lînks*/left
Liter/n/*lîtr*/liter
Löffel/m/*luofl*/spoon
Luftpost/f/*lûft-pôst*/air mail

M

machen/*mâ-Hen*/to do
Macht nichts/*mâHt nîHts*/Never mind
Mai/m/*my*/May
Mannschaft/f/*mân-shâft*/team
Markt/m/*mârkt*/market
März/m/*mêrts*/March
Meer/n/*mehr*/sea, ocean
mein/*myn*/my
Messer/n/*mê-ser*/knife
Milch/f/*mîlH*/milk
Minute/f/*mî-noo-te*/minute

mit/*mĭt*/with
Mittag/m/*mĭ-tahgk*/noon
Mittagessen/n/*mĭ-tahgk-êsn*/lunch
Mitte/f/*mĭ-te*/middle
Mittwoch/m/*mĭt-vôH*/Wednesday
Monat/m/*moh-nât*/month
Montag/m/*mohn-tahgk*/Monday
Morgen/m/*môr-gn*/morning
morgen/*môr-gn*/tomorrow
Museum/n/*mû-zeh-ûm*/museum

N

nach/*nahH*/to
Nachmittag/m/*nāH-mĭ-tahgk*/afternoon
Nachricht/f/*nahH-rĭHt*/message
Nacht/f/*nâHt*/night
Nachtisch/m/*naH-tĭsh*/dessert
nah/*nah*/close, near
Name/m/*nah-me*/name
Nationalität/f/*nā-tsjoh-nah-lĭ-tait*/
   nationality
natürlich/*nā-tuur-lĭH*/naturally
Naturschutzgebiet/n/*nā-toor-shûts-ge-beet*/nature preserve
neben/*neh-bn*/next to
nehmen/*neh-men*/to take
nein/*nyn*/no
nie/*nee*/never
Norden/m/*nôr-den*/North
Notaufnahme/f/*noht-owf-nah-me*/emergency room
November/m/*nô-vêm-ber*/November
nur/*noor*/just, only

O

öffnen/*uof-nen*/to open
Oktober/m/*ôk-toh-ber*/October
Oper/f/*oh-per*/opera
Osten/m/*ô-sten*/east

P

Paket/n/*pâ-keht*/package
Park/m/*pârk*/park
Parkplatz/m/*pârk-plâts*/parking lot
Pferd/n/*pfêrt*/horse
phantastisch/*fân-tâs-tĭsh*/fantastic
Polizei/f/*pô-lĭ-tsy*/police
Portier/m/*pôr-tjeh*/doorman
Post/f/*pôst*/post office, mail
Postamt/n/*pôst-âmt*/post office
Postkarte/f/*pôst-kâr-te*/postcard
Postleitzahl/f/*pôst-lyt-tsahl*/zip code
pro/*proh*/per
pünktlich/*puunkt-lĭH*/on time

Q

Quittung/f/*kvĭ-tûngk*/receipt

R

Rechnung/f/*rêH-nûng*/check, bill
rechts/*rêHts*/right
reden/*reh-den*/to talk
Reh/n/*reh*/deer
Reisebüro/n/*ry-ze-buu-roh*/travel agency
reisen/*ry-zen*/to travel

Reisepass/m/_ry-ze-pás_/passport

Reisescheck/m/_ry-ze-shêk_/traveler's check

reservieren/_reh_-zêr-_vee_-ren/to reserve

Restaurant/n/_rês_-toh-_rong_/restaurant

Rezeption/f/_rê_-tsêp-tsjohn/reception desk

Rückflugticket/n/_ruuk_-floogk-tî-_ket_/roundtrip ticket

S

Saft/m/_zâft_/juice

sagen/_zah_-gn/to say

Samstag/m/_zâmss_-tahgk/Saturday

Sänger/m/_zên_-ger/singer

Sängerin/f/_zên_-ge-rîn/singer

S-Bahn/f/_ês_-bahn/local train

Schaf/n/_shaf_/sheep

Schalter/m/_shâl_-ter/teller window, counter

Schauspieler/m/_show_-shpee-ler/actor

Schauspielerin/f/_show_-spee-le-rîn/actress

Scheck/m/_shêk_/check

Schein/m/_shyn_/bill

schicken/_shî_-ken/to send

Schlüssel/m/_shluu_-sêl/key

Schmerz/m/_shmêr_-ts/pain

schön/_shuon_/pretty

Schule/f/_shoo_-le/school

Schwimmbad/n/_shvîm_-baht/swimming pool

schwimmen/_shvî_-men/to swim

See/f/_zeh_/lake

segeln/_zeh_-geln/to sail

sehen/_zeh_-en/to see

sehr/_zehr_/very

sein/_zyn_/to be

Sekunde/f/_sê_-_kûn_-de/second

selbstverständlich/_zêlpst_-fêr-_shtant_-lîH/of course, certainly

September/m/_zêp_-_têm_-ber/September

sich auskennen/_zîH ows_-kê-nen/to know one's way around

sich erinnern/_zîH_ êr-_în_-ern/to remember

sich freuen/_zîH froy_-en/to be happy

sich freuen auf/_zîH froy_-en owf/to look forward to

sich freuen über/_zîH froy_-en _uu_-ber/to be glad about

sich interessieren für/_zîH_ în-te-rê-_see_-ren fuur/to be interested in

sich setzen/_zîH zê_-tsen/to sit down

sich unterhalten/_zîH_ ûn-têr-_hâl_-ten/to talk, to enjoy oneself

sich vorstellen/_zîh fohr_-shtê-len/to introduce oneself, to imagine

singen/_zîn_-gen/to sing

Sonnabend/m/_zôn_-ah-bênt/Saturday

Sonntag/m/_zôn_-tahgk/Sunday

spannend/_shpâ_-nênt/suspenseful

spazieren gehen/_shpâ_-_tsee_-ren gehn/to take a walk

Speisekarte/f/_shpy_-ze-kâr-tê/menu

Spiel/n/_shpeel_/game

spielen/_shpee_-len/to play

sprechen/_shprê_-Hen/to speak

Stadt/f/_shtât_/city

Straße/f/_shtrah_-se/street

Straßenbahn/f/_shtrah_-sn-bahn/streetcar

Stunde/f/_shtûn_-de/hour

Süden/m/_zuu_-den/South

Suppe/f/_zû_-pe/soup

Suppenteller/m/_zû_-pen-têl-ler/soup bowl

T

Tag/m/*tahgk*/day

Tal/n/*tahl*/valley

tanzen/*tân-tsen*/to dance

Tasche/f/*tâ shc*/bag

Tasse/f/*tâ-se*/cup

Taxi/n/*tâxee*/taxi

Taxistand/m/*tâxee-shtânt*/taxi stand

Tee/m/*the*/tea

teilnehmen/*tyl-neh-men*/ to participate

Telefon/n/*tê-le-fohn*/phone

Telefonbuch/n/*tê-le-fohn-booH*/phone book

telefonieren/*tê-le-foh-nee-ren*/to make a call

Telefonkarte/f/*tê-le-fohn-kâr-te*/phone cards

Telefonnummer/f/*tê-le-fohn-nû-mer*/phone number

Telefonzelle/f/*tê-le-fohn-tsê-le*/phone booth

Teller/m/*tê-ler*/plate

Tennis/n/*tê-nîs*/tennis

Termin/m/*têr-meen*/appointment

Theater/n/*teh-ah-ter*/theater

Toast/m/*tohst*/toast

trinken/*trînkn*/to drink

Trinkgeld/n/*trîngk-gêlt*/tip

Trödel/m/*truo-dl*/bric-a-brac

Tschüs/*tshuus*/Bye (informal)

Tür/f/*tuur*/door

U

U-Bahnhaltestelle/f/*oo-bahn-hâl-te-shtê-le*/subway station

U-Bahnstation/f/*oo-bahn-shtâts-yohn*/subway station

Übernachtung/f/*uu-ber-nâH-tûng*/accommodation

Uhr/f/*oor*/clock, watch

und/*ûnt*/and

Unfall/m/*ûn-fâl*/accident

ungefähr/*ûn-ge-fair*/approximately

ungültig/*ûn-guul-tigk*/invalid

Unterschrift/f/*ûn-ter-shrîft*/Signature

Urlaub/m/*oor-lowp*/vacation

V

Verkauf/m/*fêr-kowf*/sale

verletzt/*fêr-lêtst*/hurt

verreisen/*fêr-ry-zen*/to travel

verspätet/*fêr-shpeh-tet*/delayed

Verspätung/f/*fêr-shpeh-tûng*/delay

verstehen/*fêr-shtehn*/to understand

vielleicht/*fee-lyHt*/perhaps

Visum/n/*vee-zûm*/visa

Vogel/m/*foh-gl*/bird

Vollpension/f/*fôl-pâng-zîohn*/room with full board

vor/*fohr*/in front of

Vorname/m/*fohr-nah-me*/first name

vorstellen/*fohr-shtêln*/to introduce

Vorstellung/f/*fohr-shtê-lûng*/show

Wald/m/*vâlt*/forest

W

wann/*vân*/when

was/*vâs*/what

Wasserski laufen/*vâ-ser-shee low-fen*/to waterski

Wechselkurs/m/*vêk-sel-kûr-z*/exchange rate

Weg/m/*vehgk*/trail, path, way

Wein/m/*vyn*/wine

weit/*vyt*/far
werden/*vehr-den*/to become
Westen/m/*wês-ten*/West
wie/*vee*/how
wieder/*vee-der*/again
wiederholen/*vee-der-hoh-len*/to repeat
wirklich/*vîrk-līH*/really
wo/*voh*/where
Woche/f/*vô-He*/week
Wurst/f/*vûrst*/sausage

Z

Zeit/f/*tsyt*/time
Zentrum/n/*tsên-trûm*/center
ziehen/*tsee-hen*/to pull
Zimmer/n/*tsî-mer*/room
Zimmerservice/m/*tsî-mer-ser-vîs*/room service
Zoll/m/*tzôl*/customs
zu Hause/*tsû how-ze*/at home
Zug/m/*tsoogk*/train
Zugabe/f/*tsoo-gah-be*/encore
zusammen/*tsu-zamn*/together
zwischen/*tsvî-shen*/between

English-German Mini Dictionary

A

accident/**Unfall**/m/*ūn-fāl*

accommodation/**Übernachtung**/f/*uu-ber-nāH-tūng*

actor/**Schauspieler**/m/*show-shpee-ler*

actress/**Schauspielerin**/f/*show-spee-le-rīn*

afternoon/**Nachmittag**/m/*nāH-mī-tahgk*

again/**wieder**/*vee-der*

agreed/**einverstanden**/*ayn-fēr-shtān-den*

air conditioning/**Klimaanlage**/f/*klee-mah-ān-lah-ge*

air mail/**Luftpost**/f/*lūft-pôst*

airplane/**Flugzeug**/n/*floogk-tsoyg*

airplane ticket/**Flugticket**/n/*floogk-tīket*

airport/**Flughafen**/m/*floogk-hah-fen*

aisle/**Gang**/m/*gāng*

all/**ganz**/*gānts*

all/**alles**/*ā-les*

also/**auch**/*owH*

ambulance/**Krankenwagen**/m/*krānkn-vah-gn*

amount/**Betrag**/m/*be-trahgk*

and/**und**/*ūnt*

answering machine/**Anrufbeantworter**/m/*ān-roof-be-ānt-vôrtr*

antiques/**Antiquitäten**/*ān-tī-kvī-teh-ten*

appointment/**Termin**/m/*tēr-meen*

approximately/**ungefähr**/*ūn-ge-fair*

April/**April**/m/*ah-prīl*

area/**Gegend**/f/*geh-gent*

arrival/**Ankunft**/f/*ān-kūnft*

ask/**fragen**/*frah-gen*

at/**an**/*ān*

at home/**zu Hause**/*tsū how-ze*

ATM/**Geldautomat**/m/*gēlt-ow-tō-maht*

August/**August**/m/*ow-gūst*

B

bag/**Tasche**/f/*tā-she*

bank/**Bank**/f/*bānk*

bar/restaurant/**Kneipe**/f/*kny-pe*

basketball/**Basketball**/m/*bahs-ket-bāl*

bathtub/**Bad**/n/*baht*

be/**sein**/*zyn*

be called/**heißen**/*hy-sen*

be glad about/**sich freuen über**/*zīH froy-en uu-ber*

be happy/**sich freuen**/*zīH froy-en*

be interested in/**sich interessieren für**/*zīH īn-te-rê-see-ren fuur*

beard/**Bart**/m/*bahrt*

become/**werden**/*vehr-den*

become acquainted with/**kennenlernen**/*kēn-nen-lēr-nen*

beer/**Bier**/n/*beer*

beginning/**Anfang**/m/<u>ân</u>-fâng

behind/**hinter**/<u>hîn</u>-ter

between/**zwischen**/<u>tsvî</u>-shen

bicycle/**Fahrrad**/n/<u>fah</u>-rât

big/**groß**/grohs

bill/**Schein**/m/shyn

bird/**Vogel**/m/foh-gl

boarding pass/**Bordkarte**/f/<u>bôrd</u>-kâr-te

book/**buchen**/<u>boo</u>-Hen

boring/**langweilig**/<u>lâng</u>-vy-lîg

bread/**Brot**/n/Broht

breakfast/**Frühstück**/n/<u>fruuh</u>-shtuuck

bric-a-brac/**Trödel**/m/<u>truo</u>-dl

bring/**bringen**/<u>brîng</u>-en

bus/**Bus**/m/bûs

bus stop/**Bushaltestelle**/f/<u>bûs</u>-hâl-te-shtê-le

busy/**besetzt**/<u>be</u>-zêtst

but/**aber**/<u>ah</u>-ber

butter/**Butter**/f/<u>bû</u>-têr

buy/**kaufen**/<u>kow</u>-fen

by/**bei**/by

Bye (informal)/**Tschüs**/tshuus

C

cake/**Kuchen**/m/<u>koo</u>-Hen

calendar/**Kalender**/m/kâ-<u>lên</u>-der

call/**anrufen**/<u>ân</u>-roo-fen

car/**Auto**/n/<u>ow</u>-tô

cash/**bar**/bâr

cash register/**Kasse**/f/<u>kâ</u>-se

center/**Zentrum**/n/<u>tsên</u>-trûm

cereals/**Cerealien**/tseh-rê-<u>ah</u>-lî-en

check (bill)/**Rechnung**/f/<u>rêH</u>-nûng

check/**Scheck**/m/shêk

Cheers!/**Prost!**/prohst

church/**Kirche**/f/<u>kîr</u>-He

city/**Stadt**/f/shtât

clap/**klatschen**/<u>klât</u>-shen

close/**nah**/nah

closed/**geschlossen**/ge-<u>shlôsn</u>

coast/**Küste**/f/<u>kuus</u>-te

coffee/**Kaffee**/m/<u>kâ</u>-fê

cold/**Erkältung**/f/êr-<u>kêl</u>-tûng

come/**kommen**/<u>kô</u>-men

company/**Firma**/f/<u>fîr</u>-mâ

concert/**Konzert**/n/kôn-<u>tsert</u>

consulate/**Konsulat**/n/kôn-zû-<u>laht</u>

country(side)/**Land**/n/lânt

cow/**Kuh**/f/koo

cup/**Tasse**/f/<u>tâ</u>-se

customs/**Zoll**/m/tzôl

D

dance/**tanzen**/<u>tân</u>-tsen

date/**Datum**/n/<u>dah</u>-tûm

day/**Tag**/m/taghk

December/**Dezember**/m/deh-<u>tsêm</u>-ber

deer/**Reh**/n/reh

delay/**Verspätung**/f/fêr-<u>shpeh</u>-tûng

delayed/**verspätet**/fêr-<u>shpeh</u>-tet

depart/**abfliegen**/<u>âp</u>-flee-gen

departure/**Abflug**/m/<u>âp</u>-floogk

describe/**beschreiben**/be-<u>shrybn</u>

dessert/**Nachtisch**/m/<u>naH</u>-tîsh

dinner/**Abendessen**/n/<u>ah</u>-bnt- êsn

do/**machen**/<u>mâ</u>-Hen

doctor/**Arzt**/m/ârtst

doctor's office/**Arztpraxis**/f/<u>ârtst</u>-prâ-xîs

door/**Tür**/f/tuur

doorman/**Portier**/m/<u>pôr</u>-tjeh

double room/**Doppelzimmer**/n/<u>dôpl</u>-tsî-mer

drink/**trinken**/trînkn

drive/**fahren**/<u>fah</u>-ren

E

early/**früh**/*fruu*
east/**Osten**/m/*ô-sten*
easy/**einfach**/*ayn-fâH*
eat/**essen**/*êsn*
e-mail/**E-mail**/f/*ee-mail*
embassy/**Botschaft**/f/*boht-shâft*
emergency room/**Notaufnahme**/f/
   noht-owf-nah-me
encore/**Zugabe**/f/*tsoo-gah-be*
end/**Ende**/n/*ên-de*
evening/**Abend**/m/*ah-bnt*
excellent/**ausgezeichnet**/*ows-ge-tsyH-net*
exchange rate/**Wechselkurs**/m/
   vêk-sel-kûr-z
excuse me/**Entschuldigung**/
   ênt-shûl-dî-gûng
exhibition/**Ausstellung**/f/*ows-shtê-lûng*
exit/**Ausfahrt**/f/*ows-fahrt*

F

fantastic/**phantastisch**/*fân-tâs-tîsh*
far/**weit**/*vyt*
farm/**Bauernhof**/m/*bow-êrn-hohf*
fax/**faxen**/*fâ-ksen*
February/**Februar**/m/*feh-brû-ahr*
fee/**Gebühr**/f/*ge-buu-r*
fever/**Fieber**/n/*fee-ber*
fill out/**ausfüllen**/*ows-fuu-ln*
fire department/**Feuerwehr**/f/*foy-er-vehr*
first name/**Vorname**/m/*fohr-nah-me*
flight/**Flug**/m/*floogk*
fly/**fliegen**/*flee-gen*
for/**für**/*fuor*

forest/**Wald**/m/*vâlt*
fork/**Gabel**/f/*gah-bl*
form/**Formular**/n/*fôr-mû-lahr*
Friday/**Freitag**/m/*fry-tâgk*
friend/**Freund**/m/*froynt*
friend/**Freundin**/f/*froyn-dîn*

G

game/**Spiel**/n/*shpeel*
gate (airport)/**Flugsteig**/m/*floogk-shtyk*
German/**deutsch**/*doytsh*
glass/**Glas**/n/*glahs*
go/**gehen**/*geh-en*
golf/**Golf**/n/*gôlf*
good/**gut**/*gût*
good bye/**Auf Wiedersehen**/*owf*
   vee-der-zehn
Good day/**Guten Tag**/*gûtn tahk*
Good evening/**Guten Abend**/*gûtn ah-bnt*
Good morning/**Guten Morgen**/*gûtn*
   môr-gn
Good night/**Gute Nacht**/*gû-te nâHt*
Great!/**Prima/Klasse/Toll!**/*pree-mah/*
   klâ-se/tôl

H

hair/**Haar**/n/*hah-r*
handball/**Handball**/m/*hânt-bâl*
Have a good trip/**Gute Reise**/*gû-te ry-ze*
hear/**hören**/*huo-ren*
Hello/**Hallo**/*hâ-lo*
help/**helfen**/*hêl-fen*
help/**Hilfe**/f/*hîl-fe*
here/**hier**/*heer*
hill/**Hügel**/m/*huu-gel*

hobby/**Hobby**/n/_hô_-bee
horse/**Pferd**/n/_pfêrt_
hospital/**Krankenhaus**/n/_krânkn_-hows
hotel/**Hotel**/n/_hoh-têl_
hour/**Stunde**/f/_shtûn_-de
how/**wie**/vee
hungry/**hungrig**/_hûngrîg_
hurt/**verletzt**/_fêr-lêtst_

I

in front of/**vor**/fohr
interesting/**interessant**/_în-te-re-sânt_
Internet/**Internet**/n/_în_-ter-nêt
intersection/**Kreuzung**/f/_kroy_-tsûng
introduce/**vorstellen**/_fohr_-shtêln
introduce oneself/imagine/**sich
    vorstellen**/zîh _fohr_-shtê-len
invalid/**ungültig**/_ûn_-guul-tîg
invitation/**Einladung**/f/_ayn_-lah-dûng
invite/**einladen**/_ayn_-lah-den

J

January/**Januar**/m/_yâ_-nû-ahr
jog/**joggen**/_jô_-gen
juice/**Saft**/m/_Zâft_
July/**Juli**/m/_yoo-lee_
June/**Juni**/m/_yoo_-nee
just/**nur**/noor

K

key/**Schlüssel**/m/_shluu_-sêl
knife/**Messer**/n/_mê_-ser
know one's way around/**sich
    auskennen**/zîH ows-kê-nen

L

lake/**See**/f/_zeh_
last/**dauern**/_dow_-ern
laugh/**lachen**/_lâ_-Hen
lawyer/**Anwalt**/m/_ân_-vâlt
lay/**legen**/_leh_-gen
leave/**abreisen**/_âp_-ry-zên
left/**links**/_lînks_
letter/**Brief**/m/_breef_
line/**Leitung**/f/_ly_-tûng
liter/**Liter**/n/_lîtr_
little/**bisschen**/_bîs_-Hen
local train/**S-Bahn**/f/_ês-bahn_
look forward to/**sich freuen auf**/zîH
    froy-en owf
luggage/**Gepäck**/n/ge-_pêk_
lunch/**Mittagessen**/n/_mî_-tahgk-êsn

M

mailbox/**Briefkasten**/m/_breef-kâstn_
main dish/**Hauptspeise**/f/_howpt_-shpy-ze
make a call/**telefonieren**/tê-le-foh-_nee_-ren
make a turn/**abbiegen**/_âp_-beegn
map/**Karte**/f/_kâr_-te
March/**März**/m/_mêrts_
market/**Markt**/m/_mârkt_
May/**Mai**/m/my
meeting/**Besprechung**/f/be-_shprê_-Hûng
menu/**Speisekarte**/f/_shpy_-ze-kâr-tê
message/**Nachricht**/f/_nahH_-rîHt
middle/**Mitte**/f/_mî_-te
milk/**Milch**/f/mîlH
minute/**Minute**/f/mî-_noo_-te
Monday/**Montag**/m/_mohn_-tahgk

money/**Geld**/n/*gēlt*
month/**Monat**/m/*moh-nât*
morning/**Morgen**/m/*mōr-gn*
mountain/**Berg**/m/*bērg*
mountains/**Gebirge**/n/*ge-bīr-ge*
movie house/**Kino**/n/*kee-nō*
museum/**Museum**/n/*mū-zeh-ûm*
my/**mein**/*myn*

N

name/**Name**/m/*nah-me*
nationality/**Nationalität**/f/
nâ-tsjoh-nah-lī-tait
naturally/**natürlich**/*nâ-tuur-līH*
nature preserve/**Naturschutzgebiet**/n
nâ-toor-shûts-ge-beet
near/**beim**/*bym*
never/**nie**/*nee*
Never mind/**Macht nichts**/*mâHt nīHts*
next to/**neben**/*neh-bn*
no/**nein**/*nyn*
noon/**Mittag**/m/*mī-tahgk*
North/**Norden**/m/*nōr-den*
November/**November**/m/*nō-vêm-ber*
nurse/**Krankenschwester**/f/
krânkn-shvês-ter

O

occupation/**Beruf**/m/*bê-roof*
o'clock/**Uhr**/f/*oor*
October/**Oktober**/m/*ōk-toh-ber*
of course/**selbstverständlich**/
zêlpst-fêr-shtant-līH
on/**auf**/*owf*
on time/**pünktlich**/*puunkt-līH*
open/**geöffnet**/*ge-ūof-net*

open/**öffnen**/*uof-nen*
opera/**Oper**/f/*oh-per*
opposite/**gegenüber**/*geh-gen-uu-ber*

P

package/**Paket**/n/*pâ-keht*
pain/**Schmerz**/m/*shmêr-ts*
park/**Park**/m/*pârk*
parking lot/**Parkplatz**/m/*pârk-pläts*
participate/**teilnehmen an**/*tyl-neh-men ân*
passport/**Reisepass**/m/*ry-ze-pâs*
pay/**bezahlen**/*be-tsah-len*
per/**pro**/*proh*
perhaps/**vielleicht**/*fee-lyHt*
phone/**Telefon**/n/*tê-le-fohn*
phone book/**Telefonbuch**/n/
tê-le-fohn-booH
phone booth/**Telefonzelle**/f/
tê-le-fohn-tsê-le
phone cards/**Telefonkarte**/f/
tê-le-fohn-kâr-te
phone number/**Telefonnummer**/f/
tê-le-fohn-nû-mer
Personal Identification Number
(PIN)/**Geheimzahl**/f/*ge-hym-tsahl*
plate/**Teller**/m/*tê-ler*
play/**spielen**/*shpee-len*
please/**bitte**/*bî-te*
police/**Polizei**/f/*pô-lī-tsy*
post office/**Postamt**/n/*pôst-âmt*
post office/**Post**/f/*pôst*
postcard/**Postkarte**/f/*pôst-kâr-te*
pretty/**schön**/*shuon*
pull/**ziehen**/*tsee-hen*
purchase/buy/**Ankauf**/m/*ân-kowf*
push/**drücken**/*drū-kn*

R

read/**lesen**/_leh_-zen
really/**wirklich**/_vĩrk-lĩH_
receipt/**Quittung**/f/_kvĩ_-tũngk
reception desk/**Rezeption**/f/_rẽ_-tsêp-tsjohn
recommend/**empfehlen**/êm-_pfeh_-len
remember/**sich erinnern**/zĩH êr-_ĩn_-ern
repeat/**wiederholen**/_vee_-der-hoh-len
reserve/**reservieren**/_reh_-zêr-_vee_-ren
restaurant/**Restaurant**/n/rês-toh-_rong_
right/**rechts**/rêHts
river/**Fluss**/m/_flũs_
roll/**Brötchen**/n/_bruoht_-Hên
room/**Zimmer**/n/_tsĩ_-mer
room service/**Zimmerservice**/m/
    tsĩ-mer-ser-vĩs
room with full board/**Vollpension**/f/_fôl_-
    pâng-_zĩohn_
room with half board/**Halbpension**/
    f/_hâlp_-pâng-_zĩohn_
roundtrip ticket/**Rückflugticket**/n/
    ruuk-floogk-tĩ-ket

S

sailing/**segeln**/_zeh_-geln
sale/**Verkauf**/m/_fêr_-kowf
Saturday/**Samstag**/m/_zâms_-tahgk
Saturday/**Sonnabend**/m/_zôn_-ah-bênt
sausage/**Wurst**/f/_vũrst_
say/**sagen**/_zah_-gn
school/**Schule**/f/_shoo_-le
sea, ocean/**Meer**/n/_mehr_
second/**Sekunde**/f/sê-_kũn_-de
see/**sehen**/_zeh_-en
send/**schicken**/_shĩ_-ken
separate/**getrennt**/ge-_trênt_

September/**September**/m/zêp-_têm_-ber
sheep/**Schaf**/n/_shahf_
short/**klein**/_klyn_
show/**Vorstellung**/f/_fohr_-shtê-lũng
shower/**Dusche**/f/_doo_-she
sick/**krank**/_krânk_
signature/**Unterschrift**/f/_ũn_-ter-shrĩft
sing/**singen**/_zĩn_-gen
singer/**Sänger**/m/_zên_-ger
singer/**Sängerin**/f/_zên_-ge-rĩn
single room/**Einzelzimmer**/n/_ayn_-tsêl-
    tsĩ-mer
sit down/**sich setzen**/zĩH _zê_-tsen
small/**klein**/_klyn_
soccer/**Fußball**/m/_foos_-bâl
somebody/**jemand**/_yeh_-mânt
something/**etwas**/_êt_-vâs
soup/**Suppe**/f/_zũ_-pe
soup bowl/**Suppenteller**/m/_zũ_-pen-têl-ler
South/**Süden**/m/_zuu_-den
speak/**sprechen**/_shprê_-Hen
spoon/**Löffel**/m/_luofl_
stamp/**Briefmarke**/f/_breef_-_mâr_-ke
station, stop/**Haltestelle**/f/_hâl_-te-stê-le
stay/**bleiben**/_bly_-ben
stop/**halten**/_hâl_-ten
straight ahead/**geradeaus**/_grah_-de-ows
street/**Straße**/f/_shtrah_-se
streetcar/**Straßenbahn**/f/_shtrah_-sn-bahn
subway station/**U-Bahnhaltestelle**/f/
    _oo_-bahn-_hâl_-te-shtê-le
subway station/**U-Bahnstation**/f/
    _oo_-bahn-shtâts-yohn
suitcase/**Koffer**/m/_kô_-fer
Sunday/**Sonntag**/m/_zôn_-tahgk
suspenseful/**spannend**/_shpâ_-nênt
swimming/**schwimmen**/_shvĩ_-men
swimming pool/**Schwimmbad**/n/
    shvĩm-baht

T

take/**nehmen**/*neh-men*

take a walk/**spazieren gehen**/*shpâ-tsee-ren gehn*

talk/**reden**/*reh-den*

talk, to enjoy oneself/**sich unterhalten**/*zîH ûn-têr-hâl-ten*

tall/**groß**/*grohs*

taxi/**Taxi**/n/*tâxee*

taxi stand/**Taxistand**/m/*tâxee-shtânt*

tea/**Tee**/m/*the*

team/**Mannschaft**/f/*mân-shâft*

teller window/**Schalter**/m/*shâl-ter*

tennis/**Tennis**/n/*tê-nîs*

Thanks/**Danke**/*dâng-ke*

theater/**Theater**/n/*teh-ah-ter*

there/**dort**/*dôrt*

thirsty/**durstig**/*dûrstîg*

Thursday/**Donnerstag**/m/*dônrs-tahgk*

ticket/**Karte**/f/*kâr-te*

time/**Zeit**/f/*tsyt*

tip/**Trinkgeld**/n/*trîngk-gêlt*

to/**nach**/*nahH*

toast/**Toast**/m/*tohst*

today/**heute**/*hoy-te*

together/**zusammen**/*tsu-zamn*

tomorrow/**Morgen**/*môr-gn*

tonight/**Nacht**/f/*nâHt*

tourist information/**Fremdenverkehrsbüro**/n/*frêm-den-fêr-kehrs-buu-roh*

track/**Gleis**/n/*glys*

traffic light/**Ampel**/f/*âm-pel*

trail, path, way/**Weg**/m/*vehgk*

train/**Zug**/m/*tsoogk*

train station/**Bahnhof**/m/*bahn-hohf*

travel/**reisen**/*ry-zen*

travel/**verreisen**/*fêr-ry-zen*

travel agency/**Reisebüro**/n/*ry-ze-buu-roh*

traveler's check/**Reisescheck**/m/*ry-ze-shêk*

tree/**Baum**/m/*bowm*

Tuesday/**Dienstag**/m/*deens-tahgk*

U

understand/**verstehen**/*fêr-shtehn*

unfortunately/**leider**/*ly-der*

V

vacation/**Urlaub**/m/*oor-lowp*

valid/**gültig**/*guul-tîg*

valley/**Tal**/n/*tahl*

very/**sehr**/*zehr*

village/**Dorf**/n/*dôrf*

visa/**Visum**/n/*vee-zûm*

W

waiter/**Kellner**/m/*kêl-nêr*

wallet/**Brieftasche**/f/*breef-tâ-she*

waterski/**Wasserski laufen**/*vâ-ser-shee low-fen*

Wednesday/**Mittwoch**/m/*mît-vôH*

week/**Woche**/f/*vô-He*

West/**Westen**/m/*wês-ten*

what/**was**/*vâs*

when/**wann**/*vân*

where/**wo**/*voh*

win/**gewinnen**/*gê-vî-nen*

wind surfing/**Wind surfen**/*vînt surfen*

window/**Fenster**/n/*fêns-ter*

wine/**Wein**/m/*vyn*

with/**mit**/*mît*

Y

year/**Jahr**/n/*yahr*
yes/**ja**/*yah*
yesterday/**gestern**/*gês-tern*
youth hostel/**Jugendherberge**/f/*yoo-gênt-hêr-bêr-ge*

Z

zip code/**Postleitzahl**/f/*pôst-lyt-tsahl*

Appendix C

About the CD

∙ ∙

*F*ollowing is a list of the tracks that appear on this book's audio CD, which you can find inside the back cover. Note that this is an audio-only CD, so just pop it into your stereo (or whatever you use to listen to regular music CDs).

Track 1: Introduction and Pronunciation Guide: How to pronounce the sounds in the German alphabet

Track 2: Chapter 3: Greetings and Introductions: Formal greetings

Track 3: Chapter 3: Greetings and Introductions: Informal greetings

Track 4: Chapter 3: Greetings and Introductions: Meeting for the first time

Track 5: Chapter 3: Greetings and Introductions: Introducing someone formally

Track 6: Chapter 3: Greetings and Introductions: Very informal introduction

Track 7: Chapter 4: Making Small Talk: Talking about a job

Track 8: Chapter 4: Making Small Talk: Chatting about plans and the weather

Track 9: Chapter 5: Dining Out: Calling to make a reservation

Track 10: Chapter 5: Dining Out: Being seated at a restaurant

Track 11: Chapter 5: Dining Out: Taking your order

Track 12: Chapter 5: Dining Out: Getting the check and tipping

Track 13: Chapter 5: Dining Out: Buying food at an open air market

Track 14: Chapter 6: Shopping Made Easy: Getting help from a salesperson

Track 15: Chapter 6: Shopping Made Easy: Trying something on

Track 16: Chapter 7: Going Out on the Town: Making a date to go to the movies

Track 17: Chapter 7: Going Out on the Town: Talking about a theater performance

Track 18: Chapter 8: Recreation: Talking about vacation plans

Track 19: Chapter 8: Recreation: Getting information at the tourist office

Track 20: Chapter 8: Recreation: Discussing travel plans

Track 21: Chapter 9: Talking on the Phone: Leaving your name

Track 22: Chapter 9: Talking on the Phone: Making an appointment

Track 23: Chapter 10: At the Office and Around the House: Calling about apartments

Track 24: Chapter 10: Asking about an apartment

Track 25: Chapter 10: At the Office and Around the House: Office talk

Track 26: Chapter 11: Money, Money, Money: Exchanging money

Track 27: Chapter 12: Asking Directions: Finding the nearest taxi stand

Track 28: Chapter 12: Asking Directions: Asking for directions

Track 29: Chapter 13: Staying at a Hotel: Reserving a room

Track 30: Chapter 13: Staying at a Hotel: Checking into a hotel

Track 31: Chapter 14: Transportation: Picking up a ticket at the airport

Track 32: Chapter 14: Transportation: Asking which bus to take

Track 33: Chapter 15: Travel Abroad: Booking a flight with a travel agent

Track 34: Chapter 16: Handling Emergencies: Talking to the doctor

Appendix D

Answer Keys

On the following pages, we provide you with the answer keys to some of the puzzles in the book.

Chapter 8: Outdoors and Recreation

Chapter 9: Talking on the Phone and Sending Mail

	P	O	S	T						
	O				P	A	C	K	E	T
F	I	R	M	A			A			E
	T				D	A	N	N		L
P	R	O	B	L	E	M		N		E
			E				I			F
	S	C	H	I	C	K	E	N		O
			T		O					N
	F	R	A	U	L					
	R		N		N	A	M	E		
	E		G		I					
H	I	E	R		B	I	T	T	E	

Index

• H •

• P •

Notes

Notes

Notes

Notes

Notes

Notes

 *The world's most trusted name in foreign language learning.*

Get one
Free
lesson

Redeemable at any
Berlitz Language Center in
The United States and Canada

Take a language lesson on us!

Millions of people have learned to speak a new language with Berlitz. Why not you?

No matter where you're going or where you're from, odds are Berlitz is already there. We are the global leader in language services with over 70 locations in the United States and Canada. And right now, you can get a free trial language lesson at any one of them and in any language! Experience the unique Berlitz Method® and start speaking a new language confidently from your very first class. Berlitz has over 120 years of proven success, so no matter what your language needs, you can be sure you're getting the best value for your money.

To schedule your free lesson, call Berlitz toll free at 1-800-457-7958 (outside the U.S. call 609-514-9650) for the Language Center nearest you. Or check your telephone book or visit our Web site at www.berlitz.com.

To confirm availability of a teacher for the language of your choice, you must call 24 hours in advance. No purchase is necessary.

Learn German the Berlitz® Way!

There's no better way to understand more about other cultures and people than by trying to speak their language. Whether you want to speak a few essential phrases during your next business trip or vacation or you want to achieve real fluency, Berlitz can help you reach your goals. Here are some time-honored Berlitz tips to help get you on your way:

- Immerse yourself in the language. Read German on the Internet, in newspapers, and in fashion magazines — you'll be surprised at how much you can understand already. Watch German news programs on cable TV, rent German language films, or consider hosting a German-speaking exchange student for the summer. And check out your nearest Berlitz language center for information about special courses and cultural nights.
- Take home a self-study language course and set aside time to work with the material a couple of times a week. Berlitz courses are available in book, cassette, audio CD, and CD-ROM formats.
- Set your own pace, but try to put aside a regular block of time at least twice a week to work with your new language. It's more important to set a steady pace than an intensive one. Several 30-minute sessions during the week are better than one longer session a couple of times per month.
- Speak out loud. Don't just read to yourself or listen to a self-study program. Learning a language is as much a physical workout as it is an intellectual one. You have to train your vocal chords to do things they aren't used to doing. Remember: You only learn to speak by speaking!
- Talk to German people! And don't be afraid to make mistakes. You'll notice that most people appreciate an attempt to speak their language.
- Try speaking English with a German accent. Then, when you start speaking German, your brain will already be in the mood.
- Keep an open mind. Don't expect your new language to work the same as your own, and don't look for a neat set of rules. Accept the differences.
- Enjoy yourself! Learning a foreign language can help you see the world and yourself from an entirely different perspective.

About Berlitz®

The name "Berlitz" has meant excellence in language services for over 120 years. Today, at over 400 locations and in 50 countries worldwide, Berlitz offers a full range of language and language-related services, including instruction, cross-cultural training, document translation, software localization, and interpretation services. Berlitz also offers a wide array of publishing products such as self-study language courses, phrase books, travel guides, and dictionaries.

Berlitz has programs to meet everyone's needs: The world-famous **Berlitz Method®** is the core of all Berlitz language instruction. From the time of its introduction in 1878, millions have used this method to learn a new language. Join any one of the classes available throughout the world, and immerse yourself in a new language and culture with the help of a Berlitz trained native instructor.

For those who may not have time for live instruction, **self-study language courses** may be the answer. In addition to several outstanding courses, Berlitz publishes **Bilingual Dictionaries**, **Workbooks**, and **Handbooks**.

Put the world in your pocket . . . with **Berlitz Pocket Guides** and **Phrase Books**, the renowned series that together are the ideal travel companions that will make the most of every trip. These portable full-color pocket guides are packed with information on history, language, must-see sights, shopping, and restaurant information; the Phrase Books help you communicate with ease and confidence.

Berlitz Kids™ has a complete range of fun products such as the **Kids Language Packs**, **1,000 Words**, and **Picture Dictionaries**. Parents and teachers will find **Help Your Child with a Foreign Language** especially informative and enlightening.

Berlitz Cross-Cultural™ programs are designed to bridge cultural gaps for international travelers and business transferees and their families. From vital information about daily life to social and business do's and don'ts, these programs can prepare you for life in any part of the world.

For more information, please consult your local telephone directory for the Language Center nearest you. Or visit the Berlitz Web site at www.berlitz.com, where you can enroll or shop directly online.

IDG BOOKS WORLDWIDE BOOK REGISTRATION

We want to hear from you!

Visit **http://my2cents.dummies.com** to register this book and tell us how you liked it!

- ✔ Get entered in our monthly prize giveaway.

- ✔ Give us feedback about this book — tell us what you like best, what you like least, or maybe what you'd like to ask the author and us to change!

- ✔ Let us know any other *For Dummies*® topics that interest you.

Your feedback helps us determine what books to publish, tells us what coverage to add as we revise our books, and lets us know whether we're meeting your needs as a *For Dummies* reader. You're our most valuable resource, and what you have to say is important to us!

Not on the Web yet? It's easy to get started with *Dummies 101*®: *The Internet For Windows*® *98* or *The Internet For Dummies*® at local retailers everywhere.

Or let us know what you think by sending us a letter at the following address:

For Dummies Book Registration
Dummies Press
10475 Crosspoint Blvd.
Indianapolis, IN 46256

BESTSELLING BOOK SERIES

German For Dummies®

Cheat Sheet

The German Calendar

Days (die Tage)

Monday: Montag *(mohn-tahgk)*

Tuesday: Dienstag *(deens-tahgk)*

Wednesday: Mittwoch *(mît-vôH)*

Thursday: Donnerstag *(dônrs-tahgk)*

Friday: Freitag *(fry-tahgk)*

Saturday: Samstag / Sonnabend *(zâmss-tahgk / zôn-ah-bênt)*

Sunday: Sonntag *(zôn-tahgk)*

Months (die Monate)

January: Januar *(yâ-nû-ahr)*

February: Februar *(feh-brû-ahr)*

March: März *(mêrts)*

April: April *(ah-prîl)*

May: Mai *(my)*

June: Juni *(yoo-nee)*

July: Juli *(yoo-lee)*

August: August *(ow-gûst)*

September: September *(zêp-têm-ber)*

October: Oktober *(ôk-toh-ber)*

November: November *(nô-vêm-ber)*

December: Dezember *(deh-tsêm-ber)*

Numbers

0 null *(nûl)*	15 fünfzehn *(fuunf-tsehn)*	70 siebzig *(zeep-tsîgk)*
1 eins *(ayns)*	16 sechzehn *(zêH-tsehn)*	80 achtzig *(âH-tsîgk)*
2 zwei *(tsvy)*	17 siebzehn *(zeeb-tsehn)*	90 neunzig *(noyn-tsîgk)*
3 drei *(dry)*	18 achtzehn *(âH-tsehn)*	100 hundert *(hûn-dert)*
4 vier *(veer)*	19 neunzehn *(noyn-tsehn)*	200 zweihundert *(tsvy-hûn-dert)*
5 fünf *(fuunf)*	20 zwanzig *(tsvân-tsîgk)*	300 dreihundert *(dry-hûn-dert)*
6 sechs *(zêks)*	21 einundzwanzig *(ayn-ûnt-tsvân-tsîgk)*	400 vierhundert *(feer-hûn-dert)*
7 sieben *(zeebn)*	22 zweiundzwanzig *(tsvy-ûnt tzvân-tsîgk)*	500 fünfhundert *(fuunf-hûn-dert)*
8 acht *(âHt)*	23 dreiundzwanzig *(dry-ûnt-tsvân-tsîgk)*	1000 tausend *(tow-zent)*
9 neun *(noyn)*	24 vierundzwanzig *(feer-ûnt-tsvân-tsîgk)*	300 dreihundert *(dry-hûn-dert)*
10 zehn *(tsehn)*	25 fünfundzwanzig *(fuunf-ûnt-tsvân-tsîgk)*	400 vierhundert *(feer-hûn-dert)*
11 elf *(êlf)*	30 dreissig *(dry-sîgk)*	500 fünfhundert *(fuunf-hûn-dert)*
12 zwölf *(tsvuolf)*	40 vierzig *(fîr-tsîgk)*	1000 tausend *(tow-zent)*
13 dreizehn *(dry-tsehn)*	50 fünfzig *(fuunf-tsîgk)*	
14 vierzehn *(feer-tsehn)*	60 sechzig *(sêH-tsîgk)*	

For Dummies™: Bestselling Book Series for Beginners

German For Dummies®

Cheat Sheet

Useful Questions

Do you speak English? Sprechen Sie Englisch? *(shprê-Hen zee êng-lîsh)*

How are you? Wie geht es Ihnen? *(vee geht êss ee-nen)*

Would you help me please? Würden Sie mir bitte helfen? *(vuur-dn zee meer bî-te hêl-fn)*

What's your name? Wie heißen Sie? *(vee hyss-sen zee)*

What time is it? Wie viel Uhr ist es? *(vee feel oor îsst êss)*

What's the weather like? Wie ist das Wetter? *(vee îst dâs vê-ter)*

How much does . . . cost? Wie viel kostet . . .? *(vee feel kôs-tet)*

Where do I find . . .? Wo finde ich . . .? *(voh fîn-de îH)*

Where are the bathrooms? Wo sind die Toiletten? *(voh zînt dee tô-ah-lê-tn)*

When do you open? Wann öffnen Sie? *(vân uof-nen zee)*

When do you close? Wann schließen Sie? *(vân shlee-sn zee)*

Could you please talk more slowly? Können Sie bitte langsamer sprechen? *(kuon-nen zee bî-te lâng-zah-mer sprê-Hen)*

Could you repeat that, please? Können Sie das bitte wiederholen? *(kuon-nen zee dâs bî-te vee-der-hoh-len)*

Useful Expressions

Hello! Hallo! *(hâ-lo)*

Good day! Guten Tag! *(gûtn tahgk)*

Good evening! Guten Abend! *(gûtn ah-bnt)*

Good-bye! Auf Wiedersehen! *(owf vee-der-zehn)*

Please. Bitte. *(bî-te)*

Thank you. Danke. *(dâng-ke)*

Excuse me. Entschuldigung. *(ênt-shûl-dee-gûng)*

My name is . . . Ich heiße . . . *(îH hy-sse)*

Pleased to meet you. Freut mich. *(froyt mîH)*

Phrases for Emergencies

Help! Hilfe! *(hîl-fe)*

Police! Polizei! *(pô-lî-tsy)*

Fire! Feuer! *(foy-êr)*

Get a doctor! Holen Sie einen Arzt! *(hoh-ln zee ay-nen ârtst)*

I am sick. Ich bin krank. *(îH bîn krânk)*

Someone has stolen . . . Man hat . . . gestohlen. *(mân hât . . . ge-shtoh-len)*

I don't know my way around here. Ich kenne mich hier nicht aus. *(îH kê-ne mîH heer nîHt ows)*

For Dummies™: Bestselling Book Series for Beginners